Beyond Animal Rights
A Feminist Caring Ethic for the Treatment of Animals

Beyond Animal Rights

A Feminist Caring Ethic for the Treatment of Animals

∎

EDITED BY
Josephine Donovan
and Carol J. Adams

CONTINUUM | NEW YORK

1996
The Continuum Publishing Company
370 Lexington Avenue
New York, NY 10017

Copyright © 1996 by Josephine Donovan and Carol J. Adams

All rights reserved. No part of this book may be
reproduced, stored in a retrieval system, or
transmitted, in any form or by any means, electronic,
mechanical, photocopying, recording, or otherwise,
without the written permission of
The Continuum Publishing Company.

Printed in the United States of America

Library of Congress Cataloging-in-Publication Data

Beyond animal rights : a feminist caring ethic for the treatment
of animals / edited by Josephine Donovan and Carol J. Adams.
p.   cm.
Includes bibliographical references and index.
ISBN 0-8264-0836-2 (hc : alk. paper)
1. Animal welfare. 2. Animal rights. 3. Feminist theory.
I. Donovan, Josephine, 1941–   II. Adams, Carol J.
HV4708.B48 1996
179'.3'082—dc20   95-17448
                                                       CIP

FOR BATYA

... all animals be
my brothers and sisters
—Mary Webb
Gone to Earth (1917)

Contents

Preface 11

Introduction 13

The Liberation of Nature: A Circular Affair (1985)
MARTI KHEEL 17

Animal Rights and Feminist Theory (1990)
JOSEPHINE DONOVAN 34

Toward an Ecological Ethic of Care (1991)
DEANE CURTIN 60

Justice, Caring, and Animal Liberation (1992)
BRIAN LUKE 77

Caring for Animals (1992)
RITA C. MANNING 103

The Caring Sleuth: Portrait of
an Animal Rights Activist (1994)
KENNETH SHAPIRO 126

Attention to Suffering: Sympathy as a
Basis for Ethical Treatment of Animals (1994)
JOSEPHINE DONOVAN 147

Caring about Suffering:
A Feminist Exploration (1995)
CAROL J. ADAMS 170

10 | *Beyond Animal Rights*

Selected Bibliography and Suggestions
for Further Reading 197

Notes on Contributors 202

Index 205

Preface

This collection grew out of a suggestion made by Batya Bauman, president of Feminists for Animal Rights, that there was a need for a book that laid out the theoretical basis for a caring ethic for animals. She felt that many activists were uncomfortable with the abstractness and hyperrationalism of the "animal rights" position that has dominated contemporary animal advocacy theory, and that they sought an alternative that would valorize the emotional dimension of the human-animal relation.

Several articles, which are included here, had initiated this direction in animal defense theory, but they were not readily accessible to the general public. In addition, we editors agreed to write original articles for this collection.

This book takes its place within the "rights-care debate" that has occurred in feminist philosophy in recent years (as explained in the Introduction), a discussion that we believe may be fruitfully extended to the question of animal well-being. We hope that these articles will provide theoretical support to grassroots activists who seek an alternative to rights language, and at the same time enrich the philosophical discussion. Our overall concern, of course, is to extend peoples' ethical awareness concerning animals, and we believe that some people—especially women, who compose the majority of the animal defense movement—might respond more to a discourse rooted in care theory than to one based on rights.

We do not offer these articles as the last word, but rather hope that they open an exploration of ways in which care theory—which we feel is in many ways more appropriate to animals than rights theory—can be extended to animals. Nor do we believe that rights theory has to be jettisoned. We recognize that it has provided an important basis for theorizing about animal defense. We particularly respect the pioneering work of Tom Regan and Peter Singer. But we also believe that feminist care theory can provide important new ethical approaches to the treatment of animals, and we offer this book as a first step in that direction.

Finally, a note about terminology: instead of the more common phrase "animal rights," we editors have used the terms *animal defense* or *animal advocacy*, where possible, in the preface, introduction, and our own most recent articles (thus, "animal defense theory" or "animal advocacy movement"). We have restricted the term *animal rights* to that theory which is rooted in the liberal philosophical tradition of rights and interests. However, many of the earlier articles in this book use the term *animal rights* more generally to refer to all contemporary theorizing about and activism on behalf of animals.

Introduction

*F*or some time now a rich and extensive philosophical discussion has been going on among scholars and theorists about the so-called ethic of care, which many link to the nurturing practices traditionally and historically ascribed to women, such as mothering and nursing. The discussion has revolved primarily around Carol Gilligan's now celebrated book *In a Different Voice* (1982). In that work Gilligan contrasted a women's "conception of morality," which she saw as "concerned with the activity of care ... responsibility and relationships" with a men's "conception of morality as fairness" more concerned with "rights and rules."[1] Gilligan called the feminine conception "a morality of responsibility," in contrast to the masculine "morality of rights," which emphasizes "separation rather than connection" and focuses more upon the autonomy of the individual than on the context and the relationship (19). In analyzing one woman subject's response to a hypothetical, Gilligan extrapolates that it implies a morality that is concerned with "sustaining connection ... keeping the web of relationships intact" (59). Where the masculine concern with rights, rules, and an abstract idea of justice tends often to seem like "a math problem with humans" (28), the feminine approach offers a more flexible, situational, and particularized ethic.

Gilligan's book was soon followed by several others, notably Nel Noddings's *Caring* (1984) and Sara Ruddick's *Maternal Thinking* (1989), which further explored the idea of a women's caring ethic. And there have been numerous works that criticize and/or refine aspects of Gilligan's theory (see Kittay and Meyers, Cole and Coultrap-McQuin, Larabee, and Tong in the bibliography).

Meanwhile, in the area of animal advocacy the discourse of rights and interests has dominated, largely because of Tom Regan's *The Case for Animal Rights* (1983) and Peter Singer's *Animal Liberation* (1975; rev. ed. 1989).

Beginning, however, in 1985, with Marti Kheel's "Liberation of Nature" (included here) and continuing with articles by Josephine Donovan (1990), Deane Curtin (1991), and Brian Luke (1992)—all included here—theorists began to question whether rights theory was adequate as a basis for an animal defense ethic, and whether, instead, a feminist care-based theory might be more appropriate. Subsequent articles have further refined aspects of this idea. These are also included in this collection: Rita Manning explores the problematics of specific caring situations; Kenneth Shapiro considers how animal advocacy activists come to see things differently because of their awareness of animal suffering; Josephine Donovan explores the history of an alternative animal advocacy tradition—that of sympathy theory (presenting a variation of the ethic of care). Carol Adams concludes by considering how humans' responses to animal suffering may vary depending upon their gendered inscription in the "sex-species system."

It is apparent from these explorations that rights theory is in certain ways problematic when applied to animals. For one, rights theory was developed in the seventeenth and eighteenth centuries, the so-called Age of Reason, and it reflects its rationalist ideological roots, relying on a mechanistic ontology of territorial atomism. That is, it envisages a society of rational, autonomous, independent agents whose territory or property is entitled to protection from external agents (other people and the government). These rights-holders, or "persons," were presumed from the beginning to be white, male property-owners, and indeed the founding documents of the United States reflect this bias. Women, slaves, and the propertyless were excluded from the category of personhood and therefore had no rights. These injustices have, of course, since been addressed.

Animal rights theorists have argued, in effect, that animals are entitled to be considered "persons" and to have rights similar to those held by citizens—that is, the basic rights to have their territory (their selves, their bodies, their space) held inviolate from unwarranted human intrusions and/or abuse. To sustain this claim they have had to argue that animals are in many respects similar to humans, that they are autonomous individuals who have an intelligence that is similar to human reason (this is Regan's position; he confines right-holders to adult mammals. Singer argues that sentience rather than rationality be the basis upon which rights are distributed or interests are held).

Here the first difficulty in the concept of animal rights becomes apparent: it requires an assumption of similarity between humans and animals, eliding the differences. In reality, animals are only with considerable strain appropriable to Cartesian man.

The second difficulty in applying rights theory to animals also lies in the ontology that undergirds rights discourse. That ontology presumes a society of equal autonomous agents, who require little support from others, who need only that their space be protected from others' intrusions. Animals are not equal to humans; domestic animals, in particular, are dependent for survival upon humans. We therefore have a situation of unequals, and need to develop an ethic that recognizes this fact. Of course, rights theory has also been criticized by feminists when applied to humans because its vision of the independent, autonomous individual (male) ignores the network of supporting persons (usually female) who enable his autonomy—that is, who raise him, who feed him, who clothe him, and so forth.

A third problem with the rights approach is that it devalues, suppresses, or denies the emotions. This means that a major basis for the human-animal connection—love—is not encompassed. Since the exclusion of emotional response is a major reason why animal abuse and exploitation continue, it seems contradictory for animal defense advocates to also claim that feelings are inappropriate guides to ethical treatment.

Finally, the rights approach (as well as utilitarian interest theory) tends to be abstract and formalistic, favoring rules that are universalizable or judgments that are quantifiable. Many ethical situations, however, including those involving animals, require a particularized situational response, one that considers context and history—the relational web Gilligan described—a response that may not be universalizable or quantifiable.

In all these ways, caring theory may be more appropriate for animals than rights discourse.

First, caring theory is rooted in a relational ontology that does not privilege the rational individual nor require rationality as a "means test" for ethical treatment. Second, caring theory developed out of unequal relationships—where the carer has more power than the cared for. Consider the case of mother and child, or of healthy nurse and sick patient. The psychology of these relationships—where the cared-for is in some ways dependent upon the care-giver—seems more relevant to the human-animal situation than does one that assumes an inherent equality.

Caring theory also, of course, values the emotions and considers sympathy, empathy, love—feelings that often characterize humans' responses to animals—as central to any ethical theory. Indeed, it can be argued that rights or justice theories depend upon prior emotional intuition as to who is considered entitled to rights. Historically, rights have been granted by humans to those humans most like them—those to whom they can best relate (through identification, empathy, or similar responses). This seems also to be the case with animal rights theory; rights have been granted to those with whom one most readily sympathizes. Caring theory recognizes the emotional basis for many human judgments, and while an ethic of care may privilege the near and local over the distant—or at least the known over the less well known (as to whom it most cares for)—its bias is at least acknowledged—unlike rights theory, which likewise privileges the familiar and the similar.

Finally, an ethic of care is more flexible and more focused upon the particulars of a given situation. In this way too it would seem to be more useful to the development of an ethic for animals than the universalizing imperatives of the rights approach.

In a recent article, legal scholar Robin West pointed out that "a community and a judiciary that relies on nurturant, caring, loving, empathic values rather than exclusively on the rule of reason will not melt into a murky quagmire, or sharpen into the dreaded specter of totalitarianism.... Community, nurturance, responsibility, and the ethic of care are values at least as worthy ... as autonomy, self-reliance, and individualism."[2] Humans' relationships with animals should similarly be informed by an ethic of care, nurturance, sympathy, and love, and caring theory provides the basis for this realization.

Notes

1. Carol Gilligan, *In a Different Voice: Psychological Theory and Women's Development* (Cambridge: Harvard University Press, 1982), 19. Further references follow in the text.
2. Robin West, "Jurisprudence and Gender," *University of Chicago Law Review* 55, no. 1 (winter 1988): 65–66.

The Liberation of Nature: A Circular Affair (1985)

Marti Kheel

> The new understanding of life must be systemic and interconnected. It cannot be linear and hierarchical, for the reality of life on earth is a whole, a circle, an interconnected system in which everything has its part to play and can be respected and accorded dignity.
>
> *Elizabeth D. Gray*[1]

Introduction

Over the last twenty years feminist thought has shed a radically new light on many fields of inquiry. One of the most recent areas to receive the benefit of such illumination has been that of our society's attitudes toward nature. During this same time period, a voluminous body of literature has emerged in a new field of philosophy called "environmental ethics."[2] The writers in this field (predominantly men) have shown little or no interest in the feminist literature. In the following, I attempt to redress this neglect and to show that feminist thought can, indeed, shed significant light on this important new area of study.

Central to feminist thought has been a critique of Western dualistic

---

The author thanks Lene Sjerup, Steve Sapontzis, Marcia Keller, Darlaine Gardetto, and Peter Radcliffe for their encouragement and helpful comments.

[*Environmental Ethics* 1985, vol. 7, no. 2] © 1985 by Marti Kheel. Published by permission of author and *Environmental Ethics*.

thinking. Western dualistic thought sees the world in terms of static polarities—"us and them," "subject and object," "superior and inferior," "mind and body," "animate and inanimate," "reason and emotion," "culture and nature." All such dualities have two characteristics in common: (1) the first half of the duality is always valued more than the other, and (2) the more valued half is always seen as "male" and the less valued half as "female." The Western dualistic worldview can be traced back to early Greek philosophy and the Jewish and Christian religions, being reinforced in the 1600s by the increasingly mechanistic worldview of modern science.[3] The result of this long history of dualistic thinking has been the ruthless exploitation of women, animals, and all of nature. In place of dualistic thinking feminists have posited a holistic vision of reality in which everything is integrally interconnected and thus part of a larger "whole." Thus, whereas dualistic thought has perceived the world through a "spatial metaphor (up-and-down),"[4] these feminists have seen diversity within a larger whole. The recent findings of quantum physics have reaffirmed this feminist vision. They have verified in the world of matter what many people have experienced in the world of spirit—namely, the oneness of the universe.

Thus, we learn from quantum physics that atoms instead of being hard and indestructible consist, instead, of vast regions of space in which extremely small particles move. At the subatomic level, we are told, matter consists of very abstract entities that have a dual aspect: "Depending on which way the experiments are performed, they appear sometimes as particles, sometimes as waves."[5] The Taoist notion that everything is in flux, and that the only constant is change, turns out to have a solid grounding in the world of matter. Thus, we learn that "subatomic particles do not exist with certainty at definite places, but rather show 'tendencies to exist,' and atomic events do not occur with certainty at definite times and in definite ways, but rather show 'tendencies to occur.'"[6] Consequently, we can never predict an atomic event with certainty; we can only say how likely it is to happen. As Fritjof Capra puts it, "Quantum theory forces us to see the universe not as a collection of physical objects, but rather as a complicated web of relations between the various parts of a unified whole."[7]

Hierarchical Thought within Environmental Ethics

The Dualistic Heritage

By contrast with the holistic vision set forth by both feminists and quantum physicists, the goal of much of the literature in environmental ethics has been the establishment of hierarchies of value for the different parts of nature. It is assumed that hierarchy is necessary to aid us in making moral choices in our interactions with nature. Conflict is taken for granted; it is assumed that one part of nature must always win, while another must always lose. Thus, in a real sense, the field of environmental ethics perpetuates the tradition of dualistic thought.[8]

Holism

The concept of hierarchy finds two major forms of expression in the literature. One form is expressed through the ongoing debate over whether individual beings or the larger concept of "the whole" (or the "biotic community") should be given moral preference. Some "animal liberationists"[9] argue that it is the individual who must be considered over the whole, whereas many "holists" argue that it is the good of the whole that must take precedence. Many holists will protest that theirs is a nonhierarchical paradigm in that everything is viewed as an integral part of an interconnected web. However, holists such as Aldo Leopold and J. Baird Callicott clearly indicate that the interconnected web does, indeed, contain its own system of ranking.[10] Such writers have dispensed with the system of classification that assigns value to a being on the basis of its possession of certain innate characteristics, only to erect a *new* form of hierarchy in which individuals are valued on the basis of their relative contribution to the good of the whole (that is, the biotic community).

According to Callicott, the "good of the community as a whole, serves as a standard for the assessment of the relative value and relative ordering of its constitutive parts and therefore provides a means of adjudicating the often mutually contradictory demands of the parts considered separately for *equal* consideration."[11] At the top of Callicott's scale are rare and endangered species: "*Specimens* of rare and endangered species, for example, have a *prima facie* claim to preferential consideration from the perspective of the land ethic."[12] At the bottom of Callicott's hierarchy of value are domestic animals: "Environmental ethics sets a very low priority on domestic animals as they very frequently contribute to the erosion of the integrity, stability, and beauty of the biotic communities into which they have been insinuated."[13] Callicott goes so far as to posit a mathematical equation by which the value of an individual being may be gauged: "The preciousness of individual deer, as of any other specimen, is inversely proportional to the population of the species."[14] To eliminate any doubt concerning his views on equality, he adds that "the land ethic manifestly does not accord equal moral worth to each and every member of the biotic community."[15]

There is a sense in which the three different camps to which Callicott refers in the field of environmental ethics may be seen to reflect three different political positions: monarchists, liberals, and totalitarians.[16] The "ethical humanists," as Callicott has labeled them, may be viewed as the monarchists, with their insistence on ranking certain individuals (namely, humans) as being the most worthy individuals (that is, the aristocrats). As in a true monarchy, status is conferred by one's birth into a particular "class" or in this case "species." The "animal liberationists," on the other hand, may be seen as the free enterprise liberals arguing for extension of rights to individual beings within a competitive framework. Status is conferred on the basis of merit and does not necessarily follow rigid division by species. No concern for the whole (as in the "state" or the "biotic community") is manifested, since it is felt that a respect for the rights of the individual being is all that is necessary to achieve a just society. Finally, the "holists," such as Callicott and Leopold, may be compared to totalitarians, with their insistence on the subordination of the individual to the greater good of the collective whole.

Callicott perceives an analogy between the holist concept of the good of the biotic community and Plato's totalitarian conception of the good of the society as a whole. In an attempt to differentiate his own views, however, he goes on to reprimand Plato for the "temerity to insist that the good of the whole transcends individual claims," asserting that "moral problems involving individual human beings in a political context are very different from moral problems pertaining to a different whole."[17] This assertion, however, does not explain why one set of moral rules should apply to nature, while another applies to society. To dichotomize reality in such a manner is simply to accept the existing divisions of our society which views itself as separate from (and, in fact, opposed to) nature, rather than simply an extension of it. Callicott thus fails to show how his ideas differ in their implications from those of Plato.

Ironically, Callicott's "holism" may be seen to have much in common with utilitarianism. In both systems, the individual is treated as a means for the attainment of a greater end. In the former case, that which is good is judged by the standard of the biotic community, whereas in the latter case, it is gauged by the happiness of the greatest number. Although the content of the hierarchy varies, the structure remains the same. Both systems of thought also share the problem inherent in any scheme that claims the ability to compare the rela-

tive value of such abstractions as "happiness" or the "biotic good"—
that is, who should establish such values and how?

Individual Rights

The other form of hierarchical thought within environmental ethics is reflected in the attempt by both "ethical humanists" and "animal liberationists" to establish the relative values of the individual parts of nature. In this endeavor various criteria are proposed such as "sentience," "consciousness," "rationality," "self-determination," "interests." A being that possesses one of these characteristics is said to have "intrinsic value" or the right to "moral consideration," whereas a being without them is said to lack these. A large part of this literature consists of debating which beings possess these characteristics—that is, arguing whether divisions should occur along the lines of species or whether some overlap may exist. Ironically, although many of these writers feel that they are arguing against notions of hierarchy, the vast majority simply remove one set of hierarchies only to establish another. Thus, many writers on the subject of animal liberation may raise the status of animals to a level that warrants our moral concern only to exclude other parts of nature, such as plants and trees. Thus, Bernard Rollin, who clearly feels that animals merit our ethical consideration, emphatically states that "in and of itself, the physical environment has no interests in life and is, therefore, not a direct object of moral concern."[18]

Some animal liberationists have attempted to expand the notion of rights arguing for the concept of the inherent value of individual beings. Even these writers, however, often fail to overcome the concept of hierarchy. Thus, according to Tom Regan, beings are deserving of rights if they can have a life that is "better or worse for them, independently of whether they are valued by anyone else."[19] But if we were, as Regan suggests, to accord rights or value only to those beings that can have a life that is better or worse for them, our current understanding of the word *life* would exclude from direct moral consideration such parts of nature as streams, mountains, and air.

Regan seems to show some concern over this limitation. In his words:

> But limiting the class of beings that have inherent value to the class of living beings seems to be an arbitrary decision and one that does not serve well as a basis for an environmental ethic.... If I am right, the development of what can properly be called an

environmental ethic requires that we postulate inherent value in nature.[20]

Outside of this important reference, however, Regan has failed to argue for the inherent value of all of nature. What has, perhaps, hindered him from so doing is the belief that this notion necessarily precludes a valuing of the individual parts of nature. The holist camp, by contrast, is convinced that a valuing of the individual for itself will somehow detract from a valuing of the whole. Both schools of thought are trapped within the dualistic mindset. Neither can see that moral worth can exist *both* in the individual parts of nature *and* in the whole of which they are a part. It is reliance on reason as the sole arbiter in our dealings with nature that makes the two schools of thought appear distinct. But these positions are not polar opposites, nor even part of a "triangular affair" (each position representing one extreme of a triangle, as Callicott argues). If we allow for an element of feeling in our interactions with nature, the positions represented by these camps dissolve into different points on a circle. No point may, thus, be said to be more important than any other. The liberation of nature is, in fact, a circular affair.

A vision of nature that perceives value both in the individual and in the whole of which it is a part is a vision that entails a reclaiming of the term *holism* from those for whom it signifies a new form of hierarchy (namely, a valuing of the whole over the individual). Such a vision asks us to abandon the dualistic way of thinking that sees value as inherently exclusive (that is, the belief that the value of the whole cannot also be the value of the individual). It invites us to see value not as a commodity to be assigned by isolated rational analysis, but rather as a living dynamic that is constantly in flux. If we can believe the findings of quantum physics, ecology, and the spiritual experiences of many individuals, we can agree with the holists that the nature of reality is, indeed, a web of interconnections, a circle or a "whole." What most holists seem to forget, however, is that the whole consists of individual beings—beings with emotions, feelings, and inclinations—and that these, too, are part of the whole. To rely on rational analysis alone to determine what the good of the whole might be is to ignore the reality of such feelings as well as their expression in particular circumstances.

The concept of holism I am advocating here does not view the "whole" as composed of discrete individual beings connected by static relationships that rational analysis can comprehend and control. Rather, I am proposing a concept of holism that perceives nature (much like the new physics perceives subatomic particles) as comprising individual beings that are part of a *dynamic* web of interconnections in which feelings, emotions, and inclinations (or energy) play an integral role. Just as quantum physics cannot predict atomic events with certainty at exact times and specific places, so too we cannot postulate that one species or one individual is of greater or lesser value than another. The attempt to formulate universal, rational rules of conduct ignores the constantly changing nature of reality. It also neglects the emotional-instinctive or spontaneous component in each particular situation, for in the end, emotion cannot be contained by boundaries and rules; in a single leap it can cross over the boundaries of space, time, and species. It is, I feel, the failure of most writers within environmental ethics to recognize the role of emotion that has perpetuated within the environmental ethics literature the dualistic thinking so characteristic of Western society.

Reason versus Emotion in Environmental Ethics

The Rule of Reason

Most of the literature within the field of environmental ethics may be seen as an attempt to establish rationally both hierarchies of value and universal rules of conduct based on such values. Most such literature presumes that reason alone will tell us which beings are of greatest value and, thus, what rules of conduct should govern our interactions with them. Singer refers to this idea when he states, "Ethics requires us to go beyond 'I' and 'you' to the universal law, the universalizable judgment, the standpoint of the impartial spectator or ideal observer or whatever we choose to call it."[21]

Interestingly, the field of environmental ethics is an outgrowth of two movements that were (and are) highly charged emotionally—that is, the animal rights and environmental movements. Significantly, the members (mostly women)[22] of the early animal rights movement were often labeled "animal lovers" or "sentimentalists" in an attempt to belittle their concerns. But, as James Turner points out, "animal lovers were not ashamed to admit that their campaign to protect brutes from abuse was more the result of sentiment than of reason."[23]

With the publication of Peter Singer's *Animal Liberation*, the animal liberation movement took a new direction. It was assumed that one of the reasons for the failure of the earlier movement was its appeal to emotion, rather than hard, logical, well-reasoned arguments. The new movement for animal rights (as well as environmental ethics) proudly grounds itself in rationality. As Peter Singer states, "Nowhere in this book, however, do I appeal to the reader's emotions where they cannot be *supported by reason.*"[24] Elsewhere Singer elaborates, "Ethics does not demand that we eliminate personal relationships and partial affections, but it does demand that when we act we assess the moral claims of those affected by our actions *independently of our feelings for them.*"[25] Dieter Birnbacher echoes this same idea when he states, "To be classed as moral, a norm must not express the contingent preferences of a certain individual or of a certain group, but must be issued from an interpersonal, *impartial* point of view and claim to be *rationally justifiable* to everyone."[26] In a similar vein, Paul W. Taylor states, "I hold that a set of moral norms (both standards of character and rules of conduct) governing human treatment of the natural world is a *rationally grounded* set if and only if, first, commitment to those norms is a practical entailment of adopting the attitude of respect for nature as an ultimate moral attitude, and second, the adopting of that attitude on the part of all *rational agents* can itself be *justified.*"[27]

The appeal to reason in ethics has a long philosophical tradition. One of its most notable proponents was Kant, who felt that an action was moral only if it was derived from a rationally grounded conception of the universally right or morally correct course of action. Kant went so far as to maintain that no action that springs from a natural inclination can have moral worth. Although most modern-day philosophers do not elevate reason to quite such heights, most still feel that any appeal to emotion is tantamount to having no argument at all.

The Limits of Reason

Although the literature in environmental ethics relies predominantly on the use of rational arguments, references to the limitations of rationality still manage to insinuate themselves. The frequent reference to an idea being "intuitive," "counterintuitive," or "reasonable" is, at least, a partial recognition of the significance of intuition or nonrational thought in moral decisions. Less frequent are direct references to the limitations of reason, as in the statement by Alistair S. Gunn: "It may be that an environmental ethic involves a return to intuitionism, perhaps even a quasi-religious philosophical idealism."[28] In a similar vein, Tom Regan states, "How then, are we to settle these matters. I wish I knew. I am not even certain that they can be settled in a rationally coherent way, and hence the tentativeness of my closing remarks."[29]

Although often not explicitly stated, a significant portion of the literature does, in fact, rely on appeals to intuition or emotion. The argument from "marginal cases"[30] (that is, "defective humans") is, perhaps, the most notable example of this occurrence. The argument from "marginal cases" concludes that if we do not wish to treat a marginal human being in a particular manner, there is no ethically defensible reason for treating at least some animals in a similar fashion. The proponents of this argument rely on our "intuition" or "feeling" that such behavior toward humans is wrong. Thus, Regan states, "Let us agree that there are certain immoral ways of treating (say) marginal beings; for example, suppose we agree that it is morally wrong to cause them gratuitous pain or arbitrarily to restrict them in their ability to move about as they will."[31] Why we should accord "marginal human beings," or even "nonmarginal human beings," such rights is never established. The limitations of rational argument may, in fact, make it impossible to prove rationally why *anyone* or *anything* should have rights. Again, we fall back on the need to recognize and affirm the significance of feeling in our moral choices.

Rational arguments are also often used in the literature in emotionally selective ways. Thus, many writers fail to follow their arguments to their "rational" conclusion when this appears to be counterintuitive. It could be argued, for example, that the rational or logical extension of the arguments of the two major camps within environmental ethics would be to advocate the ultimate extinction of the human species. Callicott, for example, maintains that value distinctions should be established by ascertaining the importance of an organism to the stability of the biotic community. However, it is not at all clear that human beings contribute in any positive way to such stability, and a great deal of evidence suggests the reverse. In the words of James D. Heffernan, "If the integrity, stability, and beauty of the biotic community is the *summum bonum*, the best thing we can do is to find some ecologically sound way of disposing of the human race or at least drastically reducing the human population."[32] Similarly, it could be argued that the utilitarian goal of the minimization of suffering and pain could be most successfully implemented if human beings were thoughtful enough to become extinct.

The call to reason is also used by other writers as a means of learning our "natural place" within nature. Such writers argue that by understanding our "natural place" within nature we can learn what our moral actions should be. But, one might ask, why should *is* imply *ought*? Why should our natural place within nature dictate what it *should* be? To my knowledge, no philosopher to date has answered this question with a convincing "rational" argument, and I suspect that none will. Pragmatic arguments about how we will destroy all life on Earth unless we find our natural place within nature cannot persuade those who have no regard for life to begin with. Only those who *feel* their connection to all of nature to begin with will take an interest in its continuation. In more ways than one, the liberation of nature is a circular affair.

Dissolving the Dichotomies

What seems to be lacking in much of the literature in environmental ethics (and in ethics in general) is the open admission that we cannot even begin to talk about the issue of ethics unless we admit that we care (or feel something). And it is here that the emphasis of many feminists on personal experience and emotion has much to offer in the way of reformulating our traditional notion of ethics. Although this may appear at first to support the stereotypical divisions of our society that associate men with rationality and women with emotion, the emphasis on feeling and emotion does not imply the exclusion of reason. Rather, a kind of unity of reason and emotion is envisioned by many feminists.[33] As Carol McMillan puts it, "to contrast thought and emotion by assuming that the latter is devoid of all cognition is to miss one of its crucial features."[34] Similarly, Mary Midgley states that "feeling and action are essential elements in morality, which concentration on thought has often made philosophers overlook.... In general, feelings, to be effective must take shape as thought, and thoughts, to be effective must be powered by suitable feelings."[35] In the words of Sara Ruddick, "intellectual activities are distinguishable but not separable from disciplines of feeling. There is a unity of reflection, judgment and emotion."[36] Robin Morgan has used the term *unified sensibility* to describe this fusion of feeling and thought. In her words:

> How often have feminists called ... for the "peculiar blend of feeling and ratiocination" in our battles against the patriarchal dichotomization of intellect and emotion! It is the insistence on the connections, the demand for synthesis, the refusal to be narrowed

into desiring less than everything—that is so much the form of metaphysical poetry and of metaphysical feminism. The unified sensibility.[37]

How, then, are we to attain such a "unified sensibility"? The difficulty lies in conceiving of something as alien to our usual conception of hierarchy and rules as what is proposed. The problem of unifying our own nature is compounded further when we, ourselves, are removed from the rest of nature. Emotion easily divides from reason when we are divorced from the immediate impact of our moral decisions. A possible step, therefore, in striving to fuse these divisions is to experience directly the full impact of our moral decisions. If we *think*, for example, that there is nothing morally wrong with eating meat, we ought, perhaps, to visit a factory farm or slaughterhouse to see if we still *feel* the same way. If we, ourselves, do not want to witness, let alone participate in, the slaughter of the animals we eat, we ought, perhaps, to question the morality of indirectly paying someone else to do this on our behalf. When we are physically removed from the direct impact of our moral decisions—that is, when we cannot see, smell, or hear their results—we deprive ourselves of important sensory stimuli, which may be important in guiding us in our ethical choices.

Feminists have often emphasized the importance of personal experience in political and other seemingly impersonal matters. Its importance for ethical decisions is equally vital. This is, perhaps, the most practical implication of a feminist ethic: that we must involve ourselves as directly as possible in the *whole* process of our moral decisions. We must make our moral choices a circular affair.

Elizabeth Dodson Gray also highlights the importance of direct experience in moral decision-making through an analogy with the situation faced by parents in making decisions about their children. In her words:

> The point is that we parents continually find some ground for making our decisions, grounds other than ranking our children in some hierarchy of their worth. What we perceive instead is that our children have differing needs, differing strengths, differing weaknesses. And occasions differ too. It is upon the basis of some convergence of all these factors that we make our decisions. And our decisions are always made within the overriding imperative that we seek to preserve the welfare of each of them as well as the welfare of the entire family.[38]

Carol McMillan adds weight to this notion by her statement:

> The whole search in philosophy for universals, substances, essences, is a symptom of this preoccupation with the methods of science, of the craving for generality and the contemptuous attitude toward the particular case.... A refusal to grant that action based on natural inclination may sometimes be a legitimate way of responding to a moral difficulty obscures not only the nature of a moral difficulty but also the nature of goodness.[39]

In her book *In a Different Voice*, Carol Gilligan argues that the emphasis on particularity and feeling is a predominantly female mode of ethical thought. As she puts it:

> The moral imperative that emerges repeatedly in interviews with women is an injunction to care, a responsibility to discern and alleviate the real and recognizable trouble of this world.... The reconstruction of the dilemma in its contextual particularity allows the understanding of cause and consequence which engages the compassion and tolerance repeatedly noted to distinguish the moral judgments of women.[40]

Men, on the other hand, she states, develop a sense of morality in which "relationships are subordinated to rules (stage four) and rules to universal principles of justice (stages five and six)."[41] According to Gilligan, "the rights conception of morality that informs [Lawrence] Kohlberg's principled level (stages five and six) is geared to arriving at an objectively fair or just resolution to moral dilemmas upon which all rational persons could agree."[42]

The problems entailed in implementing a female mode of ethical thought within a patriarchal society are obvious. With men building bigger and better bombs, rapidly depleting our natural resources, and torturing millions of animals in laboratories, one rightly worries what a particular individual's natural inclination might be. As Sara Ebenreck puts it, "If the answer to how to treat a tree or a field is dependent on what the person 'hears intuitively' from the field or tree, then—as John Kultgen points out—we must be open to the possibility that some people will hear a message which is 'rape us, despoil us, enslave us.'"[43]

It needs to be said in this context that men may respond in different ways to the call to ground our ethics in practical experience. Clearly, men do have a greater propensity toward violence as can be seen by their greater involvement in such violent activities as wars, violent crime, hunting, trapping, and the like. Whether this propensity is biological or environmental or a combination of both is still an unanswered question. Whatever else we may conclude from this difference, however, it is difficult to escape the conclusion that in our dealings with nature, men have much to learn from women. Indeed, many men, including Buckminster Fuller, Lionel Tiger, Lyall Watson, have concluded that "the only hope may be to turn the world over to women."[44]

Most nonhumans seem instinctively to take only what they need from the environment to survive. If humans ever had such an ability, we seem to have lost it.[45] The further divorced human beings are from this instinct or sensibility that nonhuman animals have, the more we seem to require rationality to act as its substitute. Interestingly, Aldo Leopold suggests that "ethics are possibly a kind of community instinct in-the-making."[46] Perhaps, then, we are fortunate in that the human capacity to destroy life, to ravage the Earth, and to otherwise wreak havoc on the world around us coexists with yet another capacity—namely, the capacity to question our right to do so.

It is only when our instincts have failed us that we turn to such concepts as rights. Thus, it is not surprising that the idea of individual rights and natural law emerged during the civil war in England, a time of great social upheaval.[47] The notion of *rights* can, in fact, be conceived of only within an antagonistic or competitive environment. The concept of competition is inherent in the very definition of rights. As Joel Feinberg states, "To have a right is to have a claim to something *against* someone."[48] The concept of rights is, thus, inherently dualistic. Unfortunately, however, we do live in a dualistic society where competition is a fact of life. The concept of rights in an expanded form to include all of nature thus sometimes may be a necessary tactical device within our current society.

Conclusion

Feminist spirituality has shown us how the concept of a patriarchal religion, which views God as a male figure of authority in the sky telling us how we should think or feel, does not speak to the needs of those who feel that their spirituality flows from within. In a similar vein, it may be argued, the concept of ethics as a hierarchical set of rules to be superimposed upon the individual does not address the needs of those people (perhaps, mostly women) who feel that their morality or inclinations toward nature reside within themselves.

For such people, an environmental ethic might be described in the words of Elizabeth Dodson Gray:

> Some day, perhaps, we shall have an identity that can enjoy the earth as friend, provider and home. When that happens, we will know that when the earth hurts, it will hurt us. Then, the environmental ethic will not just be in our heads but in our hearts—in the nerve endings of our sensitivity.[49]

With such a sensitivity we could perhaps then dispense with the rigid, hierarchical rules of the past. If guidelines were to exist at all, they might simply flow from the desire to minimize human interference with the rest of nature.

In its highest form this sensitivity is, perhaps, simply love, for it is love that unifies our sensibilities and connects us with all of life. As Starhawk puts it:

> Love connects; love transforms. Loving the world, for what it is and our vision of what it could be, loving the world's creatures (including ourselves), caring for the stream, picking up the garbage at our feet, we can transform. We can reclaim our power to shape ourselves and our world around us.[50]

This sensitivity—the "unified sensibility"—cannot, however, be developed on only an abstract, rational plane any more than I can learn to love someone that I have never seen. It is a sensitivity that must flow from our direct involvement with the natural world, and the actions and reactions that we bring about in it. If such direct involvement is often not a possibility for many of us, this does not mean that we should abandon the attempt to achieve the sensitivity described. Although in our complex, modern society we may never be able to fully experience the impact of our moral decisions (we cannot, for example, directly experience the impact that eating meat has on world hunger),[51] we can, nonetheless, attempt as far as possible to experience emotionally the knowledge of this fact.

What does all of this mean for environmental ethics as a field of study? How might the field of environmental ethics be changed by a recognition of the importance of feeling and emotion and personal experience in moral decision-making? For one thing, writers in environmental ethics might spend less time formulating universal laws and dividing lines, and spend more time using reason to show the limitations of its own thought. They might, for instance, show how seemingly "rational" rules and ideas are, in fact, based on distinct feelings. Few of us, for example, would relinquish the idea that we, as humans, are more important than a stone. Yet, by showing that such a thought is based, in fact, on a feeling and that it cannot be justified by rational thought alone, we may be able to detach from our egos long enough to see that we are, indeed, all part of a whole of which no part may rationally be said to be more important than another. Currently, those with power in our society use rationality as a means of enforcing their own morality. If it could also be shown that such rationality is, in fact, derived from particular feelings, we could then begin to genuinely assess those feelings and the morality that flows from them.

Environmental theorists also might begin to talk more openly about their experiences and feelings, and their relevance to their ideas and actions. Rather than spending time trying to find a moral dividing line within nature, they might, instead, examine their own internal divisions (such as that between reason and emotion). In order to unite these dualities within themselves they might then attempt as far as possible to experience in practice the full implications of their own moral theories. In a similar vein, an appeal to their readers' emotions and sympathies might be considered more relevant in an argument for moral vegetarianism than an appeal to reason.

Finally, environmental ethics might become more willing to recognize that the most fundamental questions about nature and the universe cannot, in the end, be answered rationally. Such an admission may not leave us with the sense of resolution and control that so many of us seem to hunger for, but it may, on the other hand, bring us closer to a feeling of the wonder of the universe and, perhaps, as a consequence, a greater appreciation of all of life.

Notes

1. Elizabeth Dodson Gray, *Green Paradise Lost* (Wellesley, Mass.: Roundtable, 1979), 58.
2. Throughout this chapter I have used the generally accepted term *environmental ethics* to refer to the literature on the ethics of our treatment of animals as well as nature more generally. My own preference is for the term *nature ethics*, since it more clearly implies the inclusion of human beings within its parameters.
3. According to Carolyn Merchant, *The Death of Nature* (San Francisco: Harper, 1980), the worldview that saw nature as a living organism composed of interdepen-

dent parts was replaced in the 1600s by a mechanistic worldview that saw nature as an inanimate object operating much like a machine.
4. Gray, *Green Paradise Lost*, 58.
5. Fritjof Capra, *The Tao of Physics* (New York: Bantam Books, 1983), 55.
6. Ibid., 120.
7. Ibid., 124.
8. Although hierarchical thought is not dualistic in the sense of referring necessarily to only two values on a given scale, it may be seen as dualistic in the sense of always judging the value of a given being as more or less than that of another, rather than simply perceiving diversity. Hierarchical thought is also dualistic in its design, its major purpose being to assign rights to some and exclude them to others. In these ways hierarchical thought may be seen as a major expression of dualistic thinking.
9. I prefer the term *animal liberationist* to Callicott's *humane moralist*. My definition of this camp, however, is broader than Callicott's, which refers only to the utilitarian school.
10. Callicott has subsequently softened his earlier position in an attempt to achieve a reconciliation between liberation and environmental ethics. See "Animal Liberation and Environmental Ethics: Back Together Again" in *In Defense of the Land Ethic: Essays in Environmental Philosophy* (Albany, N.Y.: SUNY Press, 1989), 49–59.
11. J. Baird Callicott, "Animal Liberation: A Triangular Affair," *Environmental Ethics* 2 (1980): 324–25.
12. Ibid., 325.
13. Ibid., 337.
14. Ibid., 326.
15. Ibid., 327.
16. According to Callicott there are three major camps within the environmental ethics literature. These are the "humane moralists," the "ethical humanists," and the "ethical holists." The three camps are said to represent three separate poles of a triangle. See Callicott, "Animal Liberation: A Triangular Affair," 315–16, 324–25.
17. Ibid., 329.
18. Bernard Rollin, *Animal Rights and Human Morality* (Buffalo, N.Y.: Prometheus, 1981), 63.
19. Tom Regan, *All That Dwell Therein* (Berkeley: University of California Press, 1982), 71.
20. Ibid., 202–3.
21. Peter Singer, *Practical Ethics* (New York: Cambridge University Press, 1979), 11.
22. The animal rights movement emerged from the humane movements of both England and the United States. According to Sydney Coleman, women made up such a large part of the humane movement that "were the support of the women of America suddenly withdrawn, the large majority of societies for the prevention of cruelty to children and animals would cease to exist." Sydney Coleman, *Humane Society Leaders in America* (Albany, N.Y.: American Humane Association, 1924), 178.
23. James Turner, *Reckoning with the Beast* (Baltimore: Johns Hopkins University Press, 1980), 33.
24. Peter Singer, *Animal Liberation* (New York: Avon Books, 1975), xi. Italics added.
25. Singer, *Practical Ethics*, 11.
26. Dieter Birnbacher, "A Priority Rule for Environmental Ethics," *Environmental Ethics* 4 (1980): 14.
27. Paul W. Taylor, "The Ethics of Respect for Nature," *Environmental Ethics* 3 (1981): 197.
28. Alistair S. Gunn, "Why Should We Care about Rare Species?" *Environmental Ethics* 2 (1980): 203.

29. Regan, *All That Dwell Therein*, 202–3.
30. See, for example, Singer, *Practical Ethics*, and Regan, *All That Dwell Therein*.
31. Regan, *All That Dwell Therein*, 119.
32. James D. Heffernan, "The Land Ethic: A Critical Appraisal," *Environmental Ethics* 4 (1982): 243.
33. Some of the ideas of Eastern religions also address the false division between reason and emotion. As Capra points out (*The Tao of Physics*), the notion of "enlightenment" (the awareness of the "unity and mutual interrelation of all things") is "not only an intellectual act, but is an experience which involves the whole person and is religious in its ultimate nature." The feminist notion of a "unified sensibility" may differ primarily from this notion of enlightenment in that feminists place less emphasis on withdrawal from the world (as in the inward activity of meditation) and more on a full participation in it.
34. Carol McMillan, *Women, Reason and Nature* (Princeton, N.J.: Princeton University Press, 1982), 28.
35. Mary Midgley, *Heart and Mind* (New York: St. Martin's, 1981), 12, 4.
36. Sara Ruddick, "Maternal Thinking," *Feminist Studies* 6, no. 2 (1980): 348.
37. Robin Morgan, "Metaphysical Feminism," in *The Politics of Women's Spirituality*, ed. Charlene Spretnak (Garden City, N.Y.: Anchor, 1982), 387.
38. Gray, *Green Paradise Lost*, 148.
39. McMillan, *Women, Reason and Nature*, 28.
40. Carol Gilligan, *In A Different Voice* (Cambridge: Harvard University Press, 1982), 100.
41. Ibid., 18. According to Lawrence Kohlberg, children undergo six stages of moral development, the sixth stage representing a fully mature moral being. Unfortunately, Kohlberg's study was based on interviews with boys only and ignores the significance and value of the different way in which women develop morally.
42. Ibid., 21–22.
43. Sara Ebenreck, "A Partnership Farmland Ethic," *Environmental Ethics* 5 (1983): 40.
44. Laurel Holliday, *The Violent Sex* (Guerneville, Calif.: Blue Stocking, 1978), 171.
45. Exceptions to this generalization may, perhaps, be found among certain tribal peoples.
46. Aldo Leopold, *A Sand County Almanac* (Oxford: Oxford University Press, 1966), 36.
47. See Raymond Polin, "The Rights of Man in Hobbes and Locke," in *Political Theory and the Rights of Man*, ed. D. D. Raphael (Bloomington: Indiana University Press, 1967) and S. F. Sapontzis, "The Value of Human Rights," *Journal of Value Inquiry* 12 (1978): 210–24.
48. Joel Feinberg, "The Rights of Animals and Unborn Generations," in *Responsibilities to Future Generations*, ed. Ernest Partridge (Buffalo, N.Y.: Prometheus, 1980), 139.
49. Gray, *Green Paradise Lost*, 85.
50. Starhawk, *Dreaming the Dark* (Boston: Beacon, 1982), 44.
51. Meat eating has been implicated by a number of writers as a major contributor to world hunger. It is estimated that eighty to ninety percent of all grain grown in America is used to feed animals, that seventeen times as much land is used as the amount needed to plant grains such as soybeans, and that "if we ate half as much meat, we could release enough food to feed the entire 'developing world'." See Barbara Parham, *What's Wrong with Eating Meat?* (Denver, Colo.: Ananda Marga, 1979), 38, and John Robbins, *Diet for a New America* (Walpole, N.H.: Stillpoint, 1987).

Animal Rights and Feminist Theory (1990)

JOSEPHINE DONOVAN

*P*eter Singer prefaces his ground-breaking treatise *Animal Liberation* (1975) with an anecdote about a visit he and his wife made to the home of a woman who claimed to love animals, had heard he was writing a book on the subject, and so invited him to tea. Singer's attitude toward the woman is contemptuous: she had invited a friend who also loved animals and was "keen to meet us. When we arrived our hostess's friend was already there, and ... certainly was keen to talk about animals. 'I do love animals,' she began ... and she was off. She paused while refreshments were served, took a ham sandwich, and then asked us what pets we had."[1] Singer's point is not only to condemn the woman's hypocrisy in claiming to love animals while she was eating meat but also to dissociate himself from a sentimentalist approach to animal welfare. Speaking for his wife as well, he explains:

> We were not especially "interested in" animals. Neither of us had ever been inordinately fond of dogs, cats, or horses.... We didn't "love" animals.... The portrayal of those who protest against cruelty to animals as sentimental, emotional "animal lovers" [has meant] excluding the entire issue ... from serious political and moral discussion.

In other words, he fears that to associate the animal rights cause with "womanish" sentiment is to trivialize it.[2]

This article is dedicated to my great dog Rooney (1974–87), who died as it was being completed but whose life led me to appreciate the nobility and dignity of animals.

[Signs: *Journal of Women in Culture and Society* 1990, vol. 15, no 2] © 1990 by The University of Chicago. All rights reserved. Published by permission of the author and *Signs*.

Singer's concerns about the image and strategies of animal rights activists are shared by another major contemporary theorist of animal rights, Tom Regan. In his preface to *The Case for Animal Rights* (1983) Regan stresses that "since all who work on behalf of the interests of animals are . . . familiar with the tired charge of being 'irrational,' 'sentimental,' 'emotional,' or worse, we can give the lie to these accusations only by making a concerted effort not to indulge our emotions or parade our sentiments. And that requires making a sustained commitment to rational inquiry."[3] In a later article Regan defends himself against charges of being hyperrational by maintaining that "reason—not sentiment, not emotion—reason compels us to recognize the equal inherent value of . . . animals and . . . their equal right to be treated with respect."[4] Regan's and Singer's rejection of emotion and their concern about being branded sentimentalist are not accidental; rather, they expose the inherent bias in contemporary animal rights theory toward rationalism, which, paradoxically, in the form of Cartesian objectivism, established a major theoretical justification for animal abuse.

Women animal rights theorists seem, indeed, to have developed more of a sense of emotional bonding with animals as the basis for their theory than is evident in the male literature. Mary Midgley, for example, another contemporary animal rights theorist, urges, "What makes our fellow beings entitled to basic consideration is surely not intellectual capacity but emotional fellowship." Animals, she notes, exhibit "social and emotional complexity of the kind which is expressed by the formation of deep, subtle, and lasting relationship."[5] Constantia Salamone, a leading feminist animal rights activist, roundly condemns the rationalist, masculinist bias of current animal rights theory.[6] In the nineteenth century, women activists in the antivivisection movement, such as Frances Power Cobbe, viewed as their enemy the "coldly rational materialism" of science, which they saw as threatening "to freeze human emotion and sensibility. . . . Antivivisection . . . shielded the heart, the human spirit, from degradation at the hands of heartless science."[7]

Yet Singer's anecdote points up that one cannot simply turn uncritically to women as a group or to a female value system as a source for a humane relationship ethic with animals. While women have undoubtedly been less guilty of active abuse and destruction of animals than men (Virginia Woolf observes in *Three Guineas*: "The vast majority of birds and beasts have been killed by you; not by us"),[8] they nevertheless have been complicit in that abuse, largely in their use of luxury items that entail animal pain and destruction (such as furs) and in their consumption of meat. Charlotte Perkins Gilman, an animal welfare crusader as well as a feminist, criticized such hypocrisy decades before Singer in her "A Study in Ethics" (1933). Condemning women's habit of wearing "as decoration the carcass of the animal," Gilman remarks the shocking inconsistency that

> Civilized Christian women, sensitive to cruelty, fond of pets, should willingly maintain the greatest possible cruelty to millions of harmless little animals.... Furs are obtained by trapping. Trapping means every agony known to an animal, imprisonment, starvation, freezing, frantic fear, and pain. If one woman hung up or fastened down hundreds of kittens each by one paw in her backyard in winter weather, to struggle and dangle and freeze, to cry in anguish and terror that she might "trim" something with their collected skins ... she would be considered a monster.[9]

Recognizing that such problems are involved in women's historical relationship with animals, I believe that cultural feminism, informed by an awareness of animal rights theory, can provide a more viable theoretical basis for an ethic of animal treatment than is currently available.

Contemporary animal rights theory includes two major theoretical approaches, one based on natural rights theory and the other on utilitarianism. The major theoretician for the natural rights position is Tom Regan, whose primary statement appears in *The Case for Animal Rights*. In this lengthy, impressive, but sometimes casuistical document Regan argues that animals—in particular, adult mammals—are moral entities who have certain inalienable rights, just as humans do, according to the natural rights doctrine enunciated in the eighteenth century (particularly by Locke).[10]

Regan builds his case primarily by refuting Kant, who had stipulated in his second formulation of the Categorical Imperative that "man and generally any rational being *exists* as an end in himself, *not merely as a means*," that rational beings possess "*absolute worth*," and that therefore they are entitled to treatment as ends.[11] It is on the basis of their rationality that humans are identified by Kant and other Enlightenment thinkers as moral agents who are therefore entitled to such natural rights as to be treated as ends.

In the articulation of Locke and the framers of the U.S. Declaration of Independence and Constitution not all humans were in fact considered sufficiently rational as to be considered "persons" entitled to rights: only white, male property holders were deemed adequately endowed to be included in the category of personhood. Indeed, much of the nineteenth-century women's rights movement was devoted to urging that women be considered persons under the Constitution.[12] Here as elsewhere in Western political theory women and animals are cast together. Aristotle, for example, linked women and animals in the *Nicomachean Ethics* by excluding them from participation in the moral life. As Keith Thomas points out, the centuries-long debate over whether women have souls paralleled similar discussions about the moral status of animals.[13]

In building his case for animal rights, Regan extends the category of those having absolute worth or inherent value to include nonrational but still intelligent nonhuman creatures. He does this by elaborating the distinction between moral agents (those who are capable of making rational, moral judgments) and moral patients (those who cannot make such formulations but who are nevertheless entitled to be treated as ends). This is contrary to Kant, who maintains that "animals ... are there merely as a means to an end. That end is man."[14]

Regan makes his case by countering Kant's theory that human moral patients (that is, those who are severely retarded, infants, or others unable to reason) need not be treated as ends. This to Regan is unacceptable. Therefore, if one accepts both moral agents and moral patients as entitled to the basic respect implied in the notion of rights, Regan argues, it follows that nonhuman moral patients (animals) must be included in the category of those entitled to be treated as ends. To argue otherwise is speciesist; that is, it arbitrarily assumes that humans are worth more than other life-forms. Speciesism is a concept borrowed from feminist and minority group theory. It is analogous to sexism and racism in that it privileges one group (humans, males, whites, or Aryans) over another.[15] Regan, therefore, maintains an absolutist deontological nonconsequentialist position; treating animals as ends is, he insists, a moral duty. It is a matter of justice, not kindness.[16]

Although Regan rejects Kant's determination of rationality as the basis for entry into the "kingdom of ends," he specifies that those who have "inherent value" must have a subjective consciousness (be "subject of a life") and/or have the kind of complex awareness found in adult mammals.[17] This criterion leaves open the question of severely retarded humans, humans in irreversible comas, fetuses, even human infants. Regan's criterion in fact privileges those with complex awareness over those without.[18] Therefore, though it rejects Kantian rationalism, Regan's theory depends on a notion of complex consciousness that is not far removed from rational thought, thus, in effect, reinvoking the rationality criterion. I do not quarrel with the idea that adult mammals have a highly developed intelligence that may be appropriated to human reason; rather I question the validity of the rationality criterion. Regan's difficulty here stems in part, it seems, from natural rights theory, which privileges rationalism and individualism, but it may also reflect his own determined exclusion of sentiment from "serious" intellectual inquiry.

From a cultural feminist point of view, the position developed by utilitarian animal rights theorists is more tenable in this regard because it dispenses with the higher-intelligence criterion, insisting instead on the capacity to feel—or the capacity to suffer—as the criterion by which to determine those who are entitled to be treated as ends.

The utilitarian position in animal rights theory has been developed principally by Peter Singer. Indeed, it is his admirable and courageous book *Animal Liberation* that largely galvanized the current animal rights movement. Singer's central premise derives from a key passage in Jeremy Bentham's *Introduction to the Principles of Morals and Legislation* (1789). During a high tide of the natural rights doctrine, the French Revolution, Bentham wrote:

> The day *may* come when the rest of the animal creation may acquire those rights which never could have been withholden from them but by the hand of tyranny. . . . It may one day come to be recognized that the number of the legs, the villosity of the skin, or the termination of the *os sacrum* are reasons . . . insufficient for abandoning a sensitive being to the same fate. What else is it that should trace the insuperable line? Is it the faculty of reason, or perhaps the faculty of discourse? But a full-grown horse or dog is beyond comparison a more rational, as well as a more conversable animal than an infant of a day, or a week, or even a month, old. But suppose the case were otherwise, what would it avail? The question is not, Can they *reason*? nor, Can they *talk*? but, *Can they suffer*?[19]

A similar passage occurs in Rousseau's *Discourse on the Origin of Inequality* (1755). It seems in part to be a rejoinder to the Cartesian view of animals as machines (discussed below):

> We may put an end to the ancient disputes concerning the participation of other animals in the law of nature; for it is plain that, as

they want both reason and free will, they cannot be acquainted with that law; however, as they partake in some measure of our nature in virtue of that sensibility with which they are endowed, we may well imagine they ought likewise to partake of the benefit of natural law, and that man owes them a certain kind of duty. In fact, it seems that, if I am obliged not to injure any being like myself, it is not so much because he is a reasonable being, as because he is a sensible being.[20]

Thus, both Bentham and Rousseau advocate that natural rights, or entrance into Kant's kingdom of ends, be accorded to creatures who can feel. Their assumption is that the common condition that unites humans with animals is sensibility, the capacity to feel pain and experience pleasure.

The utilitarian position proceeds from this premise to establish that if a creature is sentient, it has interests that are as equally worthy of consideration as any other sentient creature's interests when humans make decisions about their well-being. In Singer's words, "The capacity for suffering and enjoyment is *a prerequisite for having interests.*"[21] A stone, for example, does not have interests in the question of being kicked because it cannot suffer, whereas a mouse does have such interests because she can experience pain as a result. "If a being suffers," Singer maintains, "there can be no moral justification for refusing to take that suffering into consideration.... The principle of equality requires that its suffering be counted equally with the like suffering ... of any other being." In short, "pain and suffering are bad and should be prevented or minimized, irrespective of the race, sex, or species of the being that suffers."[22] This is the essence of the utilitarian animal rights position.

Utilitarian animal rights theory has the virtue of allowing some flexibility in decision-making, as opposed to Regan's absolutist stance that no animal's suffering is justifiable under any circumstances. As a utilitarian, Singer insists, for example, that an awareness of consequences can and should influence the evaluation of an individual's fate in any given situation. This leads him to admit that "there could conceivably be circumstances in which an experiment on an animal stands to reduce suffering so much that it would be permissible to carry it out even if it involved harm to the animal ... [even if] the animal were a human being."[23] Elsewhere he says that if the suffering of one animal would have the result of curing all forms of cancer, that suffering would be justifiable.[24] Singer's basic position is that "similar interests must count equally, regardless of the species of the being involved. Thus, if some experimental procedure would hurt a human being and a pig to the same extent, and there were no other relevant consequences . . . it would be wrong to say that we should use the pig because the suffering of the pig counts less than the suffering of a human being."[25]

Therefore, although Singer also uses the term "animal rights," his modifications take it even farther from traditional natural rights doctrine than do Regan's reconceptions. It is not a matter of political rights of a rational citizen, such as the right to free speech or to vote, nor is it the right of an intelligent creature to be treated as an end (in Kantian terms). Rather it is the right of a sentient creature to have its interests in remaining unharmed considered equally when weighed against the interests of another sentient creature.[26]

Singer's insistence that animals have interests equal to humans makes his argument as morally compelling as Regan's contention that animals have rights. Nevertheless, there are some weaknesses in the utilitarian position. One is that a precise value standard for decision-making or weighing of interests is not provided, which allows unacknowledged prejudices to intrude. Second, it requires a quantification of suffering, a "mathematization" of moral beings, that falls back into the scientific modality that legitimates animal sacrifice. Thus, while it recognizes sensibility or feeling as the basis for treatment as a moral entity, the utilitarian position remains locked in a rationalist, calculative mode of moral reasoning that distances the moral entities from the decision-making subject, reifying them in terms of quantified suffering. Just as the natural rights theory proposed by Regan inherently privileges rationality, Singer's utilitarianism relapses into a mode of manipulative mastery that is not unlike that used by scientific and medical experimenters to legitimate such animal abuses as vivisection. It is for this reason that we must turn to cultural feminism for alternative theory.

Cultural feminism has a long history. Even during feminism's "first wave," thinkers otherwise as diverse as Margaret Fuller, Emma Goldman, and Charlotte Perkins Gilman articulated a critique of the atomistic individualism and rationalism of the liberal tradition.[27] They did so by proposing a vision that emphasized collectivity, emotional bonding, and an organic (or holistic) concept of life. In *Woman in the Nineteenth Century* (1845), for example, Fuller argued that the "liberation" of women and their integration into public life would effect a feminization of culture, which would mean a reign of "plantlike gentleness," a harmonic, peaceful rule, an end to violence of all kinds (including, she specifies, the slaughter of animals for food) and the institution of vegetarianism (substituting, she urges, "pulse [beans] for animal food").[28] Gilman put forth a similar vision in her utopian novel *Herland* (1915). Indeed, in addition to Fuller and Gilman there is a long list of first-wave feminists who advocated either vegetarianism or animal welfare reform, including Mary Wollstonecraft, Harriet Beecher Stowe, Lydia Maria Child, Elizabeth Blackwell, Elizabeth Stuart Phelps Ward, Victoria Woodhull, Elizabeth Cady Stanton, the Grimké sisters, Lucy Stone, Frances Willard, Frances Power Cobbe, Anna Kingsford, Caroline Earle White, and Agnes Ryan.[29]

In the second wave of feminist theory there were a few articles specifically linking feminism with animal rights: for example, Carol Adams's articles on vegetarianism and Constantia Salamone's piece in *Reweaving the Web of Life* (1982).[30] A number of other works linked feminism more generally with ecology, such as those by Susan Griffin, Carolyn Merchant, Rosemary Radford Ruether, Marilyn French, Paula Gunn Allen, Chrystos, and Ynestra King.[31]

From the cultural feminist viewpoint, the domination of nature, rooted in postmedieval, Western, male psychology, is the underlying cause of the mistreatment of animals as well as of the exploitation of women and the environment. In her pathbreaking study, *The Death of Nature: Women, Ecology, and the Scientific Revolution*, Carolyn Merchant recognizes that "we must reexamine the formation of a world view and a science that, by reconceptualizing reality as a machine rather than a living organism, sanctioned the domination of both nature and women."[32]

Critiques of the logical fallacies inherent in the epistemology of science are not new. Wittgenstein demonstrated the tautological nature of the analytic judgment in his *Tractatus* in 1911, indeed, a point Hume made in the *Enquiry Concerning Human Understanding* in 1748; but it was the critique offered by Max Horkheimer and Theodor Adorno in their *Dialectic of Enlightenment* (1944) that first made the connection between what Husserl called the "mathematization of the world,"[33] and the derogation of women and animals.[34]

The scientific or experimental method converts reality into mathematical entities modeled on the physical universe, which, as seen in Newton's laws, is cast in the image of a mechanism that operates according to fixed repetitions. No distinction is made between lifeforms such as human and animal bodies, which are seen as machines in the Cartesian view, and nonlife forms such as rocks.

Horkheimer and Adorno argue that the imposition of the mathematical model upon reality reflects a psychology of domination. "In [scientific] thought, men distance themselves from nature in order thus imaginatively to present it to themselves—but only in order to determine how it is to be dominated." Using the term *enlightenment* to refer to the scientific viewpoint, they note that "enlightenment is as totalitarian as any system"; it operates "as a dictator toward men. He knows them in so far as he can manipulate them."[35]

The pretensions of universality of scientific knowledge and the generalizing character of the machine metaphor mean that differences and particularities are erased, subdued, dominated: "In the impartiality of scientific language, that which is powerless has wholly lost any means of expression."[36] As Max Scheler noted, "Those aspects which cannot be represented in the chosen symbolic language of mathematics . . . are assigned a fundamentally different status: they belong to the realm of the 'subjective' and 'unscientific.'"[37] Thus, all that is anomalous—that is, alive and nonpredictable—is erased or subdued in the Newtonian/Cartesian epistemological paradigm. The anomalous and the powerless include women and animals, both of whose subjectivities and realities are erased or converted into manipulable objects—"the material of subjugation"[38]—at the mercy of the rationalist manipulator, whose self-worth is established by the fact that he thus subdues his environment. "Everything—even the human individual, not to speak of the animal—is converted into the repeatable, replaceable process, into a mere example for the conceptual models of the system."[39]

Horkheimer and Adorno conclude that this scientific epistemology is an ideological form that is rooted in the material conditions of social domination—particularly that of men over women. In "their nauseating physiological laboratories" scientists "force [information] from defenseless [animals]. . . . The conclusion they draw from mutilated bodies [is that] . . . because he does injury to animals, he and he alone in all creation voluntarily functions. . . . Reason . . . belongs to man. The animal . . . knows only irrational terror."[40] But the scientist feels no compassion for or empathy with his victims because "for rational beings . . . to feel concern about an irrational creature is a futile occupation. Western civilization has left this to women . . . [through] the division of labor imposed on her by man."[41]

The association of the postmedieval split between reason and the emotions with the division of labor and in particular with the rise of industrial capitalism is a well-developed thesis, particularly among Marxist theorists. Eli Zaretsky, in *Capitalism, the Family and Personal Life* (1976), suggests that the reification of public life occasioned by alienated industrial labor meant personal relationships were relegated to the private sphere: "The split in society between 'personal feelings' and 'economic production' was integrated with the sexual division of labour. Women were identified with emotional life, men with the struggle for existence."⁴²

Women's connection with economic life has been nearly universally "production for use" rather than "production for exchange"—that is, their labor has prepared material for immediate use by the household rather than for use as a commodity for exchange or for monetary payment. Such a practice, theorists have argued, tends to create a psychology that values the objects of production emotionally in a way that alienated production for exchange cannot. Since in the capitalist era it is largely women who engage in use-value production, it may be a basis for the relational, contextually oriented epistemology that contemporary theorists ascribe to Western women.⁴³ The relegation of women, emotions, and values to the private sphere, to the margins, allowed, as Horkheimer, Adorno, and others have noted, masculine practices in the public political and scientific sphere to proceed amorally, "objectively," without the restraint of "subjective" relational considerations, which are in any event elided or repressed by the dominant disciplines.

Like Carolyn Merchant, Horkheimer and Adorno recognize that the witchhunts of the early modern period were symptomatic of the new need to erase and subdue anomalous, disorderly (and thus feminine) nature. Horkheimer and Adorno consider that the eradication of witches registered "the triumph of male society over prehistoric matriarchal and mimetic stages of development" and "of self-preserving reason . . . [in] the mastery of nature."⁴⁴ Merchant suggests witches represent that aspect of nature that did not fit into the orderly pattern of the mathematical paradigm; they therefore were seen as dangerously rebellious: "Disorderly woman, like chaotic nature, needed to be controlled."⁴⁵

Merchant notes that Bacon, one of the formulators of the experimental method, used the analogy of a witch inquisition to explain how the scientist manipulates nature in order to extract information from it. He wrote: "For you have but to follow it and as it were hound nature in her wanderings, and you will be able when you like to lead and drive her afterward to the same place again."⁴⁶ The image of nature as a female to be dominated could not be more explicit.

The mathematical paradigm imposed the image of the machine on all reality. It was Descartes who most fully developed the idea that nonmental life-forms function as machines, which some of his followers (La Mettrie, e.g., in *L'homme machine*) carried to its extreme. Tom Regan critiques the Cartesian view at length in *The Case for*

Animal Rights;[47] it is clear that the notion of animals as feelingless, unconscious robots (which Rousseau, among others—see above—rejected) legitimated (and continues to legitimate) atrocious scientific experimentation. One early anonymous critic of Descartes noted:

> The [Cartesian] scientists administered beatings to dogs with perfect indifference and made fun of those who pitied the creatures as if they felt pain. They said the animals were clocks; that the cries they emitted when stuck were only the sound of a little spring that had been touched, but that the whole body was without feeling. They nailed the poor animals up on boards by their four paws to vivisect them to see the circulation of the blood which was a great subject of controversy.[48]

In "The Cartesian Masculinization of Thought" Susan Bordo describes Cartesian objectivism as an "aggressive intellectual 'flight from the feminine.'"[49] "The 'great Cartesian anxiety' [seen especially in the *Meditations*] is over separation from the organic female universe of the Middle Ages and the Renaissance. Cartesian objectivism [is] a defensive response to that separation anxiety."[50] In the process "the formerly female earth becomes inert *res extensa*: dead, mechanically interacting nature.... 'She' becomes 'it'—and 'it' can be understood. Not through sympathy, of course, but by virtue of the very *object*-ivity of 'it.'"[51]

Natural rights theory, likewise an expression of Enlightenment rationalism, similarly imposes a machine grid upon political and moral reality. Recent feminist theorists have criticized the neutral and objective pretenses of the liberal theoretical tradition for leaving out the anomalous context in which events occur, inscribing them instead in an abstract grid that distorts or ignores the historical environment. For example, Catharine A. MacKinnon has criticized the traditional liberal interpretation of U.S. constitutional law for its neutral approach to justice. She urges that we "change one dimension of liberalism as it is embodied in law: the definition of justice as neutrality between abstract categories," for this approach ignores the "substantive systems"—that is, the real conditions in which the abstractions operate. MacKinnon therefore rejects, to use her example, the idea that "strengthening the free speech of the Klan strengthens the free speech of Blacks."[52] This thesis is invalid, she maintains, because it equates "substantive powerlessness with substantive power"[53] through the use of a mechanistic conceptual model. Thus, MacKinnon, like the cultural feminists discussed below, rejects the "mathematizing" elisions of Enlightenment rationalism in favor of a view that "sees" the environmental context. Had the vivisectionists described above allowed this epistemological shift, they presumably would have "seen" the pain—the suffering and emotions—of the animals, which the machine abstraction through which they were viewing them ignored.

Unfortunately, contemporary animal rights theorists, in their reliance on theory that derives from the mechanistic premises of Enlightenment epistemology (natural rights in the case of Regan and utilitarian calculation in the case of Singer) and in their suppression/denial of emotional knowledge, continue to employ Cartesian, or objectivist, modes even while they condemn the scientific practices enabled by them.

Two of the earliest critics of Cartesian mechanism were women: Margaret Cavendish, the Duchess of Newcastle (1623–73), and Anne Finch, Lady Conway (1631–79). Finch emphatically rejected the Cartesian view; she felt that animals were not "composed of 'mere fabric' or 'dead matter,' but had spirits within them 'having knowledge, sense, and love, and divers other faculties and properties of a spirit.'"[54] Cavendish, an untutored genius, challenged Descartes directly. She met him while she and her husband were in exile in France in the 1640s, and she later exchanged letters with him about his *Treatise on Animals*. In one of his letters, dated November 23, 1646, he is prompted by her to defend his notion of animals as machines: "I cannot share the opinion of Montaigne and others who attribute understanding or thought to animals."[55]

As Keith Thomas (in *Man and the Natural World*) recognizes, Cavendish was one of the first to articulate the idea of animal rights.[56] Her biographer, Douglas Grant, notes: "Her writings ... constantly illustrate her sensibility to nature [and] its creatures: how she felt for 'poor Wat,' the hunted hare ... the stag; her pity for their unnecessary sufferings making her speak out in a century when cruelty to animals was all too common."[57] "As for man, who hunts all animals to death on the plea of sport, exercise, and health," she asked, "is he not more cruel and wild than any bird of prey?"[58]

The resistance of Finch and Cavendish to the impositions of early modern science were not isolated accidents, I propose. Indeed, if we accept Michel Foucault's contention that the ascendancy of the scientific disciplines and their attendant institutions was a historical process of colonization that intensified through the postmedieval period, reaching a height in the late nineteenth century, we must read Finch and Cavendish's critiques as an early feminist resistance to a process that inevitably meant the destruction of women's anomalous worlds. The suppression of women's social realities effected by the pseudoscientific medical theories (especially those of the sexologists) of the late nineteenth century was the final stage in what Foucault has labeled the *médicalisation de l'insolite*—the medicalization of the anomalous.[59] This process itself involved the social imposition of sexologist paradigms analogous to the scientific imposition of the mathematical machine paradigm on all living forms.

Perhaps this is why many women of the period seem to have felt a kinship to animals. Both were erased (at best) or manipulated (at worst) to behave in accordance with paradigms imposed by the rationalist lords—whether vivisectors or sexologists. Women in fact became the primary activists and energizers of the nineteenth-century antivivisection movement, which should be seen, I propose, as one manifestation of a counterhegemonic resistance undertaken by women against the encroachments of the new disciplines. Just as sexologists anatomized women's world "of love and ritual," "entomologizing" it (to use Foucault's term) into various species and subspecies of deviance, so vivisectors turned animal bodies into machines for dissection.

In her study of the nineteenth-century English antivivisection movement, *The Old Brown Dog*, Coral Lansbury argues that women activists thus identified with the vivisected dog: "Every dog or cat strapped down for the vivisector's knife reminded them of their own condition." It was an image of dominance. Indeed, pioneer woman doctor Elizabeth Blackwell saw ovarectomies and other gynecological surgery as an "extension of vivisection." For the suffragists, "the image of the vivisected dog blurred and became one with the militant suffragette being force fed in Brixton Prison."[60]

The dominance over nature, women, and animals inherent in this scientific epistemology, which requires that the anomalous other be forced into ordered forms, may be rooted in the Western male maturation process that requires men to establish their autonomous identity against the maternal/feminine. Hanna Fenichel Pitkin's recent analysis of the psychological development of Machiavelli, a prototypical formulator of postmedieval secularism, is most instructive in this regard. She reveals that "Machiavelli's writings show a persistent preoccupation with manhood."[61] "If *virtù* [manliness] is Machiavelli's favorite quality, *effeminato* . . . is one of his most frequent and scathing epithets."[62] In *The Prince* Machiavelli asserts that a leader rules "either by fortune or by ability (*virtù*)."[63] *Virtù* implies manipulative rationality and a certain macho willingness to exert military control. *Funtuna*, on the other hand, represents the nonrational, that which is unpredictable, all that is other to the exertion of rational control and masculine domination. In another celebrated passage in *The Prince* Machiavelli asserts: "Fortune is a woman and in order to be mastered she must be jogged and beaten."⁶⁴

In an unfinished poem that treats the Circe legend, Machiavelli opposes the world of women, nature, and animals to the civilized world of public order, the world of men. Pitkin notes that Circe is seen as a witch who has the power to turn men into beasts; much is made by Machiavelli of the "contrast between her feminine, natural world, and the world of men which is political and the product of human artifice.... Juxtaposed to the masculine world of law and liberty [is] the forest world where men are turned into animals and held captive in permanent dependence."⁶⁵ "Male culture," therefore, "symbolizes control over nature."⁶⁶

Pitkin concludes, "Civilization . . . history, culture, the whole *vivere civile* that constitute the world of adult human autonomy are . . . male enterprises won from and sustained against female power—the engulfing mother . . . women as the 'other'. . . . The struggle to sustain civilization . . . thus reflects the struggle of boys to become men."⁶⁷ In "Gender and Science" (1978) Evelyn Fox Keller similarly argues that the autonomy and objectivity of the male scientist reflect the basic dissociation from the feminine affective world required in the male maturation process.⁶⁸

Beyond this ontogenetic theory is the phylogenetic thesis developed by Rosemary Radford Ruether that patriarchal civilization is built upon the historical emergence of a masculine ego consciousness that arose in opposition to nature, which was seen as feminine. Sexism, she notes, is rooted in this "'war against the mother,' the struggle of the transcendent ego to free itself from bondage to nature."⁶⁹ Developing the existentialist notion of the transcendent masculine *pour soi*, and the immanent feminine *en soi*, Ruether urges (thereby rejecting Simone de Beauvoir's thesis in *The Second Sex*) that the continual cultural attempt to transcend the feminine is what has led to our present ecological and moral crisis.

The fundamental defect in the "male ideology of transcendent dualism" is that its only mode is conquest. "Its view of what is over against itself is not that of the conversation of two subjects, but the conquest of an alien object. The intractability of the other side of the dualism to its demands does not suggest that the 'other' has a 'nature' of her own that needs to be respected and with which one must enter into conversation. Rather, this intractability is seen as that of disobedient rebellion." Thus, "patriarchal religion ends ... with a perception of the finite cosmos itself as evil in its intractability" to technological, scientific progress.[70]

In *Beyond Power* (1985) Marilyn French argues that "patriarchy is an ideology founded on the assumption that man is distinct from the animal and superior to it. The basis for this superiority is man's contact with a higher power/knowledge called god, reason, or control. The reason for man's existence is to shed all animal residue and realize fully his 'divine' nature, the part that *seems* unlike any part owned by animals—mind, spirit, or control."[71] French sees a sadomasochism inherent in this cultural impulse to mutilate or kill off the animal/feminine in the self. According to French, patriarchal society has reached a frightening impasse: "Our culture, which worships above all else the power to kill, has reached the point of wishing to annihilate all that is 'feminine' in our world."[72]

Recent cultural feminist theorists have identified alternative epistemological and ontological modes that must, I believe, replace the mode of sadomasochistic control/dominance characteristic of patriarchal scientific epistemology. Ruether, for example, urges the development of new ways of relating to nature and to nonhuman lifeforms. "The project of human life," she says, "must cease to be seen as one of 'domination of nature'.... Rather, we have to find a new language of ecological responsiveness, a reciprocity between consciousness and the world systems in which we live and move and have our being."[73] In *Sexism and God-Talk* (1983) Ruether suggests that human consciousness be seen not as different from other lifeforms but as continuous with the "biomorphic" spirit inherent in other living beings:

> Our intelligence is a special, intense form of ... radial energy, but it is not without continuity with other forms; it is the self-conscious or "thinking dimension" of the radial energy of matter. We must respond to a "thou-ness" in all beings. This is not romanticism or an anthropomorphic animism that sees "dryads in trees," although there is truth in the animist view.... We respond not just as "I to it," but as "I to thou," to the spirit, the life energy that lies in every being in its own form of existence. The "brotherhood of man" needs to be widened to embrace not only women but also the whole community of life.[74]

Ruether calls for "a new form of human intelligence," one based on a relational, affective mode popularly called "right-brain thinking," which moves beyond the linear, dichotomized, alienated consciousness characteristic of the "left-brain" mode seen in masculinist scientific epistemology. Linear, rationalist modes are, Ruether enjoins, "ecologically dysfunctional."[75] What is needed is a more "disordered" (my term—if order means hierarchical dominance) relational mode that does not rearrange the context to fit a master paradigm but sees, accepts, and respects the environment.

In *The Sacred Hoop: Recovering the Feminine in American Indian Traditions* (1986), Paula Gunn Allen finds in those traditions attitudes toward nature that are quite different from the alienation and dominance that characterize Western epistemology and theology. God and the spiritual dimension do not transcend life but rather are immanent in all life-forms. All creatures are seen as sacred and entitled to fundamental respect. Allen, herself a Laguna Pueblo–Sioux, recalls that "when I was small, my mother often told me that animals, insects, and plants are to be treated with the kind of respect one customarily accords to high-status adults." Nature, in her culture, is seen "not as blind and mechanical, but as aware and organic." There is "a seamless web" between "human and nonhuman life."[76]

Rather than linear, hierarchical, mechanistic modes, Allen proposes a return to the achronological relational sensibility characteristic of her people. Recognizing that "there is some sort of connection between colonization and chronological time," Allen observes:

> Indian time rests on a perception of individuals as part of an entire gestalt in which fittingness is not a matter of how gear teeth mesh with each other but rather how the person meshes with the revolving of the seasons, the land, and the mythic reality that shapes all life into significance.... Women's traditional occupations, their arts and crafts, and their literatures and philosophies are more often accretive than linear, more achronological than chronological, and more dependent on harmonious relationships of all elements within a field of perception than western culture in general.... Traditional peoples perceive their world in a unified-field fashion.[77]

In her study of contemporary women's art, *Women as Mythmakers* (1984), Estella Lauter identified the contours of a new myth that involves women and nature. "Many of these artists accept the affinity between woman and nature as a starting point—in fact, creating hybrid images of woman/animal/earth until the old distinctions among the levels in the Great Chain of Being seem unimportant."[78]

Recognizing Susan Griffin's *Woman and Nature* (1978) as prototypical, Lauter detects in contemporary women's literature and art "an image of relationships among orders of being that is extremely fluid without being disintegrative."[79]

In these works, boundaries between the human world and the vegetable and animal realm are blurred. Hybrid forms appear: women transform into natural entities, such as plants, or merge with animal life. Lauter finds "surprising numbers of women" poets have a "high degree of identification with nature, without fear and without loss of consciousness." Many of these artists have revalidated ancient mythic figures that emblematize aspects of women's relationship with nature: Demeter/Kore, Artemis/Diana, Daphne, Circe. The earth is seen not as "dead matter to be plundered, but wounded matter from which renewal flows. The two bodies, women's and earth's, are sympathetic."[80]

The women artists and the feminist theorists cited here point to a new mode of relationship; unlike the subject-object mode inherent in the scientific epistemology and the rationalist distancing practiced by the male animal rights theorists, it recognizes the varieties and differences among the species but does not quantify or rank them hierarchically in a Great Chain of Being. It respects the aliveness and spirit (the "thou") of other creatures and understands that they and we exist in the same unified field continuum. It appreciates that what we share—life—is more important than our differences. Such a relationship sometimes involves affection, sometimes awe, but always respect.

In "Maternal Thinking" Sara Ruddick urges that a maternal epistemology, derived from the historical practice of mothering—that is, caring for an other who demands preservation and growth—can be identified. She calls it a "holding" attitude, one that "is governed by the priority of keeping over acquiring, of conserving the fragile, or maintaining whatever is at hand and necessary to the child's life." Ruddick contrasts the "holding" attitude to "scientific thought, as well as . . . to the instrumentalism of technocratic capitalism." Maternal practice recognizes "excessive control as a liability," in sharp distinction to scientific modes of manipulation.[81]

The maternal ethic involves a kind of reverential respect for the process of life and a realization that much is beyond one's control. Citing Iris Murdoch and Simone Weil as her philosophical predecessors, Ruddick calls this an ethic of humility. It is an attitude that "accepts not only the facts of damage and death, but also the facts of the independent and uncontrollable, developing and increasingly separate existences of the lives it seeks to preserve." Ruddick calls such an attitude "attentive love," the training to ask, "What are you going through?"[82] Were vivisectionists to ask such a question, we would not have vivisection.

In a recent article Evelyn Keller draws similar distinctions to Ruddick's in her observations of Nobel prize winner Barbara McClintock's "feminine" scientific practice (which contrasts so markedly to the aggressive manipulation of nature proposed by Bacon, seen at its worst in laboratory animal experimentation). McClintock believes in "letting the material speak to you," allowing it to "tell you what to do next." She does not believe that scientists should "impose an answer" upon their material, as required in the mathematical paradigm of traditional scientific epistemology; rather, they should respond to it and retain an empathetic respect for it.[83] It is interesting that numerous women scientists and naturalists who have worked with and observed animal life for years—such as Jane Goodall, Dian Fossey, Sally Carrighar, Francine Patterson, Janis Carter—exhibit this ethic implicitly: a caring, respecting attitude toward their "subjects."[84]

Finally, Carol Gilligan's *In a Different Voice* (1982) suggests that a feminine ethic is one rooted in a "mode of thinking that is contextual and narrative rather than formal and abstract."[85] What she names a "morality of responsibility" is in direct contrast to the "morality of rights" seen in Regan's animal rights theory. In the former, a feminine mode, "morality and the preservation of life are contingent upon sustaining connection . . . [and] keeping the web of relationships intact." She contrasts this with the "rights" approach (which is seen in her study as more characteristically masculine) that relies upon "separation rather than connection," and on a "formal logic" of hierarchically ranged quantitative evaluations.[86]

Gilligan, Ruddick, Lauter, Allen, Ruether, and French all propose an ethic that requires a fundamental respect for nonhuman lifeforms, an ethic that listens to and accepts the diversity of environmental voices and the validity of their realities. It is an ethic that resists wrenching and manipulating the context so as to subdue it to one's categories; it is nonimperialistic and life affirming.

It may be objected that this ethic is too vague to be practicable in decisions concerning animals. My purpose here, however, is not to lay out a specific practical ethic but, rather, to indicate ways in which our thinking about animal/human relationships may be reoriented. Some may persist: suppose one had to choose between a gnat and a human being. It is, in fact, precisely this kind of either/or thinking that is rejected in the epistemology identified by cultural feminism. In most cases, either/or dilemmas in real life can be turned into both/ands. In most cases, dead-end situations such as those posed in lifeboat hypotheticals can be prevented. More specifically, however, it is clear that the ethic sketched here would mean feminists must reject carnivorism; the killing of live animals for clothing; hunting; the trapping of wildlife for fur (largely for women's luxury consumption); rodeos; circuses; and factory farming; and that they must support the drastic redesigning of zoos (if zoos are to exist at all) to allow animals full exercise space in natural habitats; that they should reject the use of lab animals for testing of beauty and cleaning products (such as the infamous "LD-50" and Draize tests) and military equipment, as well as psychological experimentation such as that carried out in the Harlow primate lab at the University of Wisconsin; that they should support efforts to replace medical experiments by computer models and tissue culture; that they should condemn and work to prevent further destruction of wetlands, forests, and other natural habitats. All of these changes must be part of a feminist reconstruction of the world.

Natural rights and utilitarianism present impressive and useful philosophical arguments for the ethical treatment of animals. Yet, it is also possible—indeed, necessary—to ground that ethic in an emotional and spiritual conversation with nonhuman life-forms. Out of a women's relational culture of caring and attentive love, therefore, emerges the basis for a feminist ethic for the treatment of animals. We should not kill, eat, torture, and exploit animals because they do not want to be so treated, and we know that. If we listen, we can hear them.

Notes

1. Peter Singer, *Animal Liberation* (New York: Avon, 1975), ix–x. Throughout this chapter I use the shorthand term *animal rights theory* to refer to any theorizing about humane treatment of animals, regardless of its philosophical roots. I would like to acknowledge the contribution of Gloria Stevenson, who introduced me to the concept of animal rights years ago, and my dog Jessie.
2. In the *Ethics* Spinoza remarked that opposition to animal slaughter was based on "superstition and womanish pity" rather than on reason (as cited in Mary Midgley, *Animals and Why They Matter* [Athens: University of Georgia Press, 1983], 10). This is the kind of charge that disconcerts Singer.
3. Tom Regan, *The Case for Animal Rights* (Berkeley: University of California Press, 1983), xii.
4. Tom Regan, "The Case for Animal Rights," in *In Defense of Animals*, ed. Peter Singer (New York: Basil Blackwell, 1985), 24.

5. Mary Midgley, "Persons and Non-Persons," in *In Defense*, ed., Singer, 60.
6. Constantia Salamone, xeroxed form letter, July 1986.
7. James Turner, *Reckoning with the Beast: Animals, Pain and Humanity in the Victorian Mind* (Baltimore: Johns Hopkins University Press, 1980), 101, 103. Roswell C. McCrea, *The Humane Movement: A Descriptive Survey* (1910; reprint, College Park, Md.: McGrath, 1969), 117, notes that sentimentalism versus rationalism as a basis for animal rights theory was an issue in the nineteenth-century animal rights campaign: "As a rule humane writings [and] work, are based on a 'faith' rather than any rationalistic scheme of fundamentals. The emotional basis is a common one, and the kind treatment of animals is assumed to be a thing desirable in itself." The exception was the Humanitarian League under Henry Salt, which tried to place "humane principles on a consistent and rational basis." It was based "not merely on a kindly sentiment, a product of the heart rather than of the head." However, Frances Power Cobbe and other women theorists of the time were not afraid to privilege the heart. For an introduction to their ideas, see Coral Lansbury, *The Old Brown Dog: Women, Workers, and Vivisection in Edwardian England* (Madison: University of Wisconsin Press, 1985).
8. Virginia Woolf, *Three Guineas* (1938; reprint, New York: Harcourt, Brace, 1963), 6. Woolf's note to this passage indicates she had done some research on the issue.
9. Charlotte Perkins Gilman, "A Study in Ethics" (Schlesinger Library, Radcliffe College, Cambridge, Mass., 1933, typescript). Published by permission of the Schlesinger Library. It must be noted that the women criticized by Singer and Gilman are guilty of sins of omission rather than commission; they are not actively conducting atrocities against animals. Their failure is due to ignorance and habit, traits that are presumably correctable through moral education. In this article I focus mainly on the rationalist ideology of modern science because it is the principal contemporary legitimization of animal sacrifice and because its objectifying epistemology, which turns animals into "its," has become the pervasive popular view of animals, thus legitimizing other forms of animal abuse such as factory farming.
10. Despite his accent on rigorously rational inquiry, Regan throughout uses the term *counterintuitive* as a kind of escape clause whenever deductive reason per se proves inadequate. An example of where Regan's argument becomes (to me at least) illogical is his lifeboat hypothetical where he maintains that with four normal adult humans and one dog, it is the dog who must be sacrificed. His reasoning here suggests an unacknowledged hierarchy with humans still at the top. See Regan, *The Case for Animal Rights*, 324–25. See also Peter Singer's critique in "Ten Years of Animal Rights Liberation," *New York Review of Books* (January 17, 1985), 46–52, esp. 49–50, and "The Dog in the Lifeboat," *New York Review of Books* (April 25, 1985), 57.
11. Kant, "Theory of Ethics," in *Kant Selections*, ed. Theodore M. Greene (New York: Scribner's, 1927), 308–9.
12. See further discussion in Josephine Donovan, *Feminist Theory: The Intellectual Traditions of American Feminism*, rev. ed. (New York: Continuum, 1992), 5–7.
13. Keith Thomas, *Man and the Natural World: A History of the Modern Sensibility* (New York: Pantheon, 1983), 43. For further thoughts on the "cultural symbolism" that links women and animals, see Midgley, *Animals and Why They Matter* (n. 2, above), 78–79.
14. Kant, "Duties to Animals and Spirits," as cited in Regan, *The Case for Animal Rights*, 177.
15. Ibid., 155; the term *speciesist* was coined, according to Regan, by Richard D. Ryder in *Victims of Science* (London: Davis-Poynter, 1975). See also Singer, *Animal Liberation* (n. 1, above), 7, 9.
16. Regan, *The Case for Animal Rights*, 280.
17. Ibid., 243.
18. Ibid., 77, 247, 319.

19. Jeremy Bentham, *Introduction to the Principles of Morals and Legislation* (1789), in *The English Philosophers from Bacon to Mill*, ed. Edwin A. Burtt (New York: Modern, 1939), 847, n. 21.
20. Jean-Jacques Rousseau, *The Social Contract and Discourse on the Origin and Foundation of Inequality among Mankind*, ed. Lester G. Crocker (New York: Washington Square, 1967), 172. See also Midgley, *Animals and Why They Matter*, 62.
21. Singer, *Animal Liberation*, 8.
22. Ibid., 8, 18.
23. Peter Singer and Tom Regan, "The Dog in the Lifeboat: An Exchange," *New York Review of Books* (April 25, 1985), 57. It should be noted that however much Regan and Singer disagree in theory, in practice their positions are similar: each opposes animal experimentation, exploitation of animals for food and clothing, factory farming, trapping, hunting, rodeos, and circuses.
24. Singer, "Ten Years of Animal Rights Liberation" (n. 10, above), 48.
25. Ibid.
26. Peter Singer, "Ethics and Animal Liberation," in Singer, ed. (n. 4, above), 1–10. Historically, utilitarianism developed as part of the wave of sentimentalism that emerged in late eighteenth-century Europe, which paved the way intellectually for the animal protection movement of the nineteenth century. See Turner (n. 7, above), 31–33; and Thomas (n. 13 above), 173–80. Of course, women's increasing participation in cultural life in the eighteenth century undoubtedly contributed to the emergence of sentimentalism and to the growing empathy for animals seen in Bentham's and Rousseau's statements.
27. For a full discussion, see Donovan, *Feminist Theory* (n. 12, above), 31–63. The other major theoretical tradition that one might wish to turn to for alternative ideas about human relationship with the natural world is Marxism; however, as Isaac D. Balbus perceptively points out in *Marxism and Domination: A Neo-Hegelian, Feminist, Psychoanalytic Theory of Sexual, Political, and Technological Liberation* (Princeton, N.J.: Princeton University Press, 1982), Marxism is rooted in a philosophy of domination. Marx indeed saw human identity as formed through labor that manipulates an objectified physical world. Balbus turns instead to Hegel, who urged that "all substance is subject," that is, motivated by a specific teleology, but all subjects are not identical (285). "Neither instrumental reason nor mere intuition or feeling but rather a new form of instrumental, empathic reason will guide the interactions between humans and the world on which they depend" (286). Such a "postobjectifying consciousness" (285) will emerge, Balbus believes, when new child-rearing practices are developed that intervene in the present male maturation process, which requires the development of enmity for the mother. Thus, Balbus turns in the latter part of his book to neo-Freudian cultural feminist theory—specifically that developed by Dorothy Dinnerstein—to substantiate his position.
28. Margaret Fuller, *Woman in the Nineteenth Century* (1845; reprint, New York: Norton, 1971), 113.
29. Mary Wollstonecraft, *A Vindication of the Rights of Woman* (1792; reprint, Baltimore: Penguin, 1975), 291–92, and *Original Stories from Real Life* (London: J. Johnson, 1788); Harriet Beecher Stowe, "Rights of Dumb Animals," *Hearth and Home* 1, no. 2 (January 2, 1869): 24; Elizabeth Blackwell, *Essays in Medical Sociology* (London: Longmans Green, 1909); Elizabeth Stuart Phelps Ward, "Loveliness: A Story," *Atlantic Monthly* 84 (August 1899): 216–29; "'Tammyshanty,'" *Woman's Home Companion* 35 (October 1908): 7–9, *Trixy* (Boston: Houghton Mifflin, 1904), *Though Life Do Us Part* (Boston: Houghton Mifflin, 1908), and various articles on vivisection; Frances Power Cobbe, *The Modern Rack* (London: Swann, Sonnenshein, 1899), *The Moral Aspects of Vivisection* (London: Williams & Margater, 1875); Anna Bonus Kingsford, *The Perfect Way in Diet*, 2d ed. (London: Kegan, Paul, Trench, 1885), *Addresses and Essays on Vegetarianism* (London:

Watkins, 1912). Woodhull, the Grimké sisters, Stone, and Willard are mentioned by various sources as being vegetarian, and Child as being concerned with animal protectionism. See Singer, *Animal Liberation*, 234. Elizabeth Griffith, in her biography *In Her Own Right* (New York: Oxford University Press, 1984), notes that Elizabeth Cady Stanton followed the Grahamite (largely vegetarian) regime in her youth, following the practices of the Grimkés (34–35). Ruth Bordin, in *Frances Willard: A Biography* (Chapel Hill: University of North Carolina Press, 1986), 122, says Frances Willard believed flesh-eating was "savagery" and that the "enlightened mortals of the twentieth century [would] surely be vegetarians." Indeed, there is an interesting connection between the nineteenth-century temperance and humane movements. In 1891 the WCTU in Philadelphia (probably under the aegis of Mary F. Lovell) developed a "Department of Mercy" dedicated to antivivisectionism. According to Turner, 94, it was virulently antiscience. In *Letters of Lydia Maria Child* (1883; reprint, New York: Negro Universities Press, 1969), Child says she is a member of the SPCA and supports the humane movement. She stresses the close kinship between animals and humans as her rationale (letter of 1872, 213–14). Caroline Earle White was a leading animal protectionist in nineteenth-century Philadelphia; she wrote numerous articles on the subject. Much of Agnes Ryan's material is unpublished in the Schlesinger Library in Cambridge. It includes an "animal rights" novel, *Who Can Fear Too Many Stars?* Charlotte Perkins Gilman wrote numerous articles on animal issues, including "The Beast Prison," *Forerunner* 31 (November 1912): 128–30, and "Birds, Bugs and Women," *Forerunner* 4 (May 1913): 131–32. A further useful reference on women in the U.S. nineteenth-century animal welfare movement is Sydney H. Coleman, *Humane Society Leaders in America* (Albany, N.Y.: American Humane Association, 1924).

30. Carol Adams, "The Oedible Complex: Feminism and Vegetarianism," in *The Lesbian Reader*, ed. Gina Covina and Laurel Galana (Oakland, Calif.: Amazon, 1975), 145–52, and "Vegetarianism: The Inedible Complex," *Second Wave* 4, no. 4 (1976): 36–42; Constantia Salamone, "The Prevalence of the Natural Law: Women and Animal Rights," in *Reweaving the Web of Life: Feminism and Nonviolence*, ed. Pam McAllister (Philadelphia: New Society, 1982), 364–75. See also the articles by Janet Culbertson, Cynthia Branigan, and Shirley Fuerst in "Special Issue: Feminism and Ecology," *Heresies*, no. 13 (1981); Joan Beth Clair (Newman), "Interview with Connie Salamone," *Woman of Power*, no. 3 (winter/spring 1986), 18–21; Andrée Collard, "Freeing the Animals," *Trivia*, no. 10 (Spring 1987), 6–23; Karen Davis, "Farm Animals and the Feminine Connection," *Animals' Agenda* 8, no. 1 (January/February 1988): 38–39, which provides an important feminist critique of the macho vein in the ecology movement; and Andrée Collard with Joyce Contrucci, *Rape of the Wild: Man's Violence against Animals and the Earth* (Bloomington: Indiana University Press, 1989). Alice Walker also embraced the animal rights cause in the eighties. See her "Am I Blue?" *Ms.* (July 1986), reprinted in *Through Other Eyes: Animal Stories by Women*, ed. Irene Zahava (Freedom, Calif.: Crossing, 1988), 1–6; and Ellen Bring, "Moving toward Coexistence: An Interview with Alice Walker," *Animals' Agenda* 8, no. 3 (April 1988): 6–9.

More recent works include Deborah Slicer, "Your Daughter or Your Dog?: A Feminist Assessment of the Animal Research Issue," *Hypatia* 6, no. 1 (1991): 108–24; Carol Adams, *The Sexual Politics of Meat: A Feminist-Vegetarian Critical Theory* (New York: Continuum, 1990) and *Neither Man nor Beast: Feminism and the Defense of Animals* (New York: Continuum, 1994); and *Ecofeminism: Women, Animals, Nature*, ed. Greta Gaard (Philadelphia: Temple University Press, 1993).

31. Susan Griffin, *Woman and Nature: The Roaring Inside Her* (New York: Harper, 1978); Carolyn Merchant, *The Death of Nature: Women, Ecology, and the Scientific Revolution* (New York: Harper, 1980); Rosemary Radford Ruether, *New*

Woman/New Earth: Sexist Ideologies and Human Liberation (New York: Seabury, 1975), and *Sexism and God-Talk: Toward a Feminist Theology* (Boston: Beacon, 1983); Marilyn French, *Beyond Power: On Women, Men, and Morals* (New York: Summit, 1985); Paula Gunn Allen, *The Sacred Hoop: Recovering the Feminine in American Indian Traditions* (Boston: Beacon, 1986); Chrystos, "No Rock Scorns Me as Whore," in *This Bridge Called My Back: Writings by Radical Women of Color*, ed. Cherríe Moraga and Gloria Anzaldúa (Watertown, Mass.: Persephone, 1981); Ynestra King, "Feminism and the Revolt of Nature," *Heresies*, no. 13 (1981): 812–16.
32. Merchant, xviii.
33. As cited in Colin Gordon's afterword to *Power/Knowledge: Selected Interviews and Other Writings, 1972–1977*, by Michel Foucault (New York: Pantheon, 1980), 238.
34. Max Horkheimer and Theodor F. Adorno, *Dialectic of Enlightenment* (1944; reprint, New York: Herder & Herder, 1972).
35. Ibid., 39, 24, 9.
36. Ibid., 23.
37. As cited in William Leiss, *The Domination of Nature* (New York: Braziller, 1972), 111. Sandra Harding similarly observes that "it is the scientific subject's voice that speaks with general and abstract authority; the objects of inquiry 'speak' only in response to what scientists ask them, and they speak in the particular voice of their historically specific conditions and locations" (*The Science Question in Feminism* [Ithaca, N.Y.: Cornell University Press, 1986], 124).
38. Horkheimer and Adorno, *Dialectic*, 84.
39. Ibid.
40. Ibid., 245.
41. Ibid., 248; see also 14, 21.
42. Eli Zaretsky, *Capitalism, the Family and Personal Life* (New York: Harper, 1976), 64.
43. Nancy C. M. Hartsock, *Money, Sex and Power: Toward A Feminist Historical Materialism* (New York: Longman, 1983), 152, 246. On use-value production, see Karl Marx, *Capital*, in *Karl Marx: Selected Writings*, ed. David McLellan (Oxford: Oxford University Press, 1977), 422–23. See Harding (n. 37, above), 142–61, for a useful summary of what she calls "feminist standpoint epistemologies." They are rooted, she notes, in the assumption derived from Hegel's notion of the master/slave consciousness that "women's subjugated position provides the possibility of a more complete and less perverse understanding" (26). Women's historical experience of silence, of being in the "slave" position vis-à-vis the "master" may provide a basis for empathy with other silenced voices, such as those of animals.
44. Horkheimer and Adorno, *Dialectic*, 249.
45. Merchant (n. 31, above), 127.
46. Ibid., 168.
47. Regan, *The Case for Animal Rights* (n. 3, above), 3–33.
48. Ibid., 5.
49. Susan Bordo, "The Cartesian Masculinization of Thought," *Signs: Journal of Women in Culture and Society* 11, no. 3 (spring 1986): 439–56, esp. 441.
50. Ibid.
51. Ibid., 451.
52. Catharine A. MacKinnon, "Pornography, Civil Rights, and Speech," *Harvard Civil Rights/Civil Liberties Law Review* 20, no. 1 (winter 1985): 4.
53. Ibid., 15. See also Donovan (n. 12, above), 2–3, 28–30.
54. [Anne Finch], *The Principles of the Most Ancient and Modern Philosophy* (1690), as cited in Merchant (n. 31, above), 260.
55. Descartes, *Philosophical Letters*, trans. and ed. Anthony Kenny (Oxford: Oxford University Press, 1957), 44.

56. Thomas (n. 13, above), 128, 170, 173–74, 280, 293–94.
57. Douglas Grant, *Margaret the First* (Toronto: Toronto University Press, 1957), 44.
58. Ibid., 124. The principal sources of Margaret Cavendish's writings on animal rights are her *Poems and Fancies* (1653; 2d ed., 1664), *Philosophical Letters* (1664), and *The World's Olio* (1655). Her empathetic imagination extends to plant life, to which she also imputes a form of consciousness (see esp. "Dialogue *between* an Oake, *and a* Man *cutting him downe*," in *Poems and Fancies*).
59. Michel Foucault, *La Volonté de savoir*, vol. 1 of *Histoire de la sexualité* (Paris: Gallimard, 1976), 61 (my translation). For studies of female sexual deviance as defined by nineteenth-century sexologists, see George Chauncey, Jr., "From Sexual Inversion to Homosexuality: Medicine and the Changing Conceptualization of Female Deviance," *Salmagundi* 58/59 (fall 1982/winter 1983): 114–45; and Lillian Faderman, "The Morbidification of Love between Women by Nineteenth-Century Sexologists," *Journal of Homosexuality* 4, no. 1 (fall 1978): 73–90.
60. Lansbury (n. 7 above), 82, 89, 24.
61. Hanna Fenichel Pitkin, *Fortune Is a Woman: Gender and Politics in the Thought of Niccolò Machiavelli* (Berkeley: University of California Press, 1984), 125. Pitkin's analysis relies on the work of "object-relations" neo-Freudian feminists such as Nancy Chodorow, Dorothy Dinnerstein, and Jane Flax.
62. Ibid., 25.
63. Machiavelli, *The Prince and Selected Discourses*, ed. Daniel Donno (New York: Bantam, 1966), 13.
64. Ibid., 86–87.
65. Pitkin, *Fortune*, 124, 128.
66. Ruether, *Sexism and God-Talk* (n. 31, above), 76.
67. Pitkin, *Fortune*, 230.
68. Evelyn Fox Keller, "Gender and Science" (1978), in *Discovering Reality: Feminist Perspectives on Epistemology, Metaphysics, Methodology, and the Philosophy of Science*, ed. Sandra Harding and Merrill B. Hintikka (Dordrecht, Neth.: Reidel, 1983), 187–205, esp. 197. Hunting is, of course, the quintessential rite of passage in the male maturation process. As Barbara A. White notes in *The Female Novel of Adolescence* (Westport, Conn.: Greenwood, 1985), 126–27, "many initiation stories [involve] a hunt [where] the protagonist destroys a 'feminine principle.'" Numerous feminist theorists have connected hunting with male dominance. See Charlotte Perkins Gilman, *His Religion and Hers* (1923; reprint, Westport, Conn.: Hyperion, 1976), 37–38. A more recent scholarly study is Peggy Reeves Sanday, *Female Power and Male Dominance: On the Origins of Sexual Inequality* (Cambridge: Cambridge University Press, 1981), 66–69, 128–30.
69. Ruether, *New Woman/New Earth* (n. 31, above), 25.
70. Ibid., 195–96.
71. French (n. 31, above), 341. Coral Lansbury recognizes the inherent connection between vivisection and sadomasochistic pornography and, indeed, analyzes a number of late nineteenth-century works of pornography that include scenes of vivisection (n. 7, above), chap. 7.
72. French, *Beyond Power*, 523.
73. Ruether, *New Woman/New Earth*, 83.
74. Ruether, *Sexism and God-Talk*, 87.
75. Ibid., 89–90. See also Gina Covina, "Rosy Rightbrain's Exorcism/Invocation," in Covina and Galana, eds. (n. 30, above), 90–102.
76. Allen (n. 31, above), 1, 80, 100; see also 224.
77. Ibid., 154, 243, 244.
78. Estella Lauter, *Women as Mythmakers: Poetry and Visual Art by Twentieth-Century Women* (Bloomington: Indiana University Press, 1984), 18. A separate study could be written on animals in women's fiction. In a number of works animals are used to avenge injuries done to women; for example, Edith Wharton's

"Kerfol" (1916), in *The Collected Short Stories of Edith Wharton*, ed. R. W. B. Lewis (New York: Scribner's, 1968), 282–300; or Sylvia Plath's "The Fifty-ninth Bear" (1959), in *Johnny Panic and the Bible of Dreams* (New York: Harper, 1979), 105–14. In others the woman/animal identification is explicit. See Mary Webb, *Gone to Earth* (fox) (1917; reprint, New York: Dalton, 1974); Radclyffe Hall, *The Well of Loneliness* (fox) (New York: Covice, Freed, 1929); Ellen Glasgow, *The Sheltered Life* (ducks) (Garden City, N.Y.: Doubleday Doran, 1932); Zora Neale Hurston, *Their Eyes Were Watching God* (mule) (1937; reprint, Urbana: University of Illinois Press, 1978); Willa Cather, *A Lost Lady* (woodpecker) (New York: Knopf, 1923); Hariette Arnow, *Hunter's Horn* (fox) (New York: Macmillan, 1949). In many of Glasgow's novels the animal/woman connection is a central issue. See Josephine Donovan, *The Demeter-Persephone Myth in Wharton, Cather, and Glasgow* (University Park: Pennsylvania State University Press, 1989), esp. chap. 5. In many works by women, animals are women's closest companions and often there is a kind of psychic communication between them (especially when the women are witches). See Annie Trumbull Slosson, "Anna Malann," in *Dumb Foxglove and Other Stories* (New York: Harper, 1898), 85–117; Mary E. Wilkins (Freeman), "Christmas Jenny," in *A New England Nun and Other Stories* (New York: Harper, 1891), 160–77; Sarah Orne Jewett, "A White Heron," in *The Country of the Pointed Firs*, ed. Willa Cather (1925; reprint, Garden City, N.Y.: Anchor, 1956), 161–71; Virginia Woolf, "The Widow and the Parrot: A True Story," in *The Complete Shorter Fiction of Virginia Woolf*, ed. Susan Dick (San Diego: Harcourt Brace Jovanovich, 1985), 156–63; Rose Terry (Cooke), "Dely's Cow," in *"How Celia Changed Her Mind" and Selected Stories*, ed., Elizabeth Ammons (New Brunswick, N.J.: Rutgers University Press, 1986), 182–95; Susan Glaspell, "A Jury of Her Peers," in *American Voices/American Women*, ed. Lee R. Edwards and Arlyn Diamond (New York: Avon, 1973), 359–81. Sarah Grand's *The Beth Book* (1897; reprint, New York: Dial, 1980) and various works by Elizabeth Stuart Phelps Ward (n. 29, above) are explicitly antivivisectionist. See Lansbury for further works in this area. Flannery O'Connor exposed the male hubris involved in hunting; see "The Turkeys," in *Complete Stories* (New York: Farrar Straus & Giroux, 1971), 42–53. Other significant works include Colette's *Creatures Great and Small*, trans. Enid McLeod (London: Secker & Warburg, 1951); Virginia Woolf's *Flush: A Biography* (London: Hogarth, 1923); and May Sarton's *The Fur Person* (1957; reprint, New York: New American Library, 1970). See also Zahava, ed. (n. 30, above). Ellen Moers in *Literary Women* (Garden City, N.Y.: Doubleday, 1977) notes "a rich untapped field remains to yield a fortune in scholarly dissertations, and that is the animals in the lives of literary women. George Sand had a horse . . . named Colette; Christina Rossetti had the wombat; Colette had all those cats; Virginia Woolf was positively dotty about all sorts of animals. But it is their dogs who will serve the purpose best—Elizabeth Barrett's spaniel named Flush; Emily Dickinson's 'dog as large as myself'" (260). The most promising recent theoretical approach to the issue of women's connection with animals is that proposed by Margaret Homans in *Bearing the Word: Language and Female Experience in Nineteenth-Century Women's Writing* (Chicago: University of Chicago Press, 1986). Using Lacanian theory, Homans urges that women and nature are linked as "the absent referent" in patriarchal discourse. Her discussion of Heathcliff's sadistic treatment of birds in *Wuthering Heights* is especially suggestive. She observes that Cathy's aim is "to protect nature from figurative and literal killing at the hand of androcentric law" (78).

I further elaborate on Homans's analysis in "Ecofeminist Literary Criticism: Reading the Orange" (forthcoming). See also Marian Scholtmeijer, "The Power of Otherness: Animals in Women's Fiction," in *Animals and Women: Feminist Theoretical Explorations*, ed. Carol J. Adams and Josephine Donovan (Durham: N.C.: Duke University Press, 1995).

79. Lauter, *Women*, 19.
80. Ibid., 177, 174.
81. Sara Ruddick, "Maternal Thinking," *Feminist Studies* 6, no. 2 (summer 1980): 350–51. See also her *Maternal Thinking: Toward a Politics of Peace* (Boston: Beacon, 1989).
82. Ruddick, "Maternal Thinking," 351, 359.
83. Evelyn Fox Keller, "Feminism and Science," *Signs* 7, no. 3 (spring 1982): 599.
84. See Jane Goodall, *In the Shadow of Man* (Boston: Houghton Mifflin, 1971), *The Chimpanzees of Gombe: Patterns of Behavior* (Cambridge: Harvard University Press, 1986); Dian Fossey, *Gorillas in the Mist* (Boston: Houghton Mifflin, 1983); and Sally Carrighar, *Home to the Wilderness* (Boston: Houghton Mifflin, 1973). See Eugene Linden, *Silent Partners* (New York: Times, 1986), on Patterson and Carter. Janis Carter spent eight years trying to reintroduce Lucy, a chimpanzee who had learned sign language, to the wild in West Africa. She tells her moving story in "Survival Training for Chimps," *Smithsonian* 19, no. 5 (June 1988): 36–49. Goodall has sharply condemned the treatment of chimpanzees in American laboratories. See her "A Plea for the Chimps," *New York Times Magazine* (May 17, 1987). Also of interest is Cynthia Moss, *Elephant Memories: Thirteen Years in the Life of an Elephant Family* (New York: Morrow, 1988); and Sue Hubbell's relationship with her bees, seen in *A Country Year: Living the Questions* (New York: Random House, 1986).
85. Carol Gilligan, *In a Different Voice: Psychological Theory and Women's Development* (Cambridge: Harvard University Press, 1982), 19. For a further discussion of the ethic proposed in cultural feminist theory, see Donovan, "The New Feminist Moral Vision," in Donovan, *Feminist Theory* (n. 12, above), 171–86.
86. Gilligan, 59, 19, 73. Another important work that develops a cultural feminist ethic is Nel Noddings, *Caring: A Feminine Approach to Ethics and Moral Education* (Berkeley: University of California Press, 1984). Unfortunately, however, while Noddings believes the caring ethic she endorses is enhanced by a celebratory attitude toward the female domestic world, which includes, she notes, "feeding the cat," she nevertheless specifically rejects the main tenets of animal rights theory, including not eating meat. It is clear that her "caring" ethic extends only to humans; the arbitrariness of her position can only be attributed to an unexamined speciesism. Nodding's book, while admirable in other ways, is weakened by this bias, thereby illustrating how feminist theory must be informed by animal rights theory if we are to avoid the hypocrisies and inconsistencies of the tea-ladies condemned by Singer (for Noddings evinces affection for her pets even while endorsing carnivorism [154]).

For a further discussion see the dialogue between Noddings and Donovan in *Signs* 16, no. 2 (winter 1991): 418–25.

Toward an Ecological Ethic of Care (1991)

Deane Curtin

Introduction

Suddenly the animal rights movement is gaining the attention of the popular press as it never has before. Its hold on the public's attention may be due to the fact that, while its proposals are viewed as radical, it responds to what have become core intuitions in our culture about the basic project of moral theory: the establishment of human or natural rights. But as rights are expanded to new domains, particularly as this expansion has begun to interact with feminist conceptions of morality, the question arises whether the language of rights is the best conceptual tool for exploring distinctively feminist insights about ecological ethics.

Ecofeminism is the position that "there are important connections—historical, experiential, symbolic, theoretical—between the domination of women and the domination of nature."[1] It argues that the patriarchal conceptual framework that has maintained, perpetuated, and justified the oppression of women in Western culture has also, and in similar ways, maintained, perpetuated, and justified the oppression of nonhuman animals and the environment. This chapter affirms that perspective, but it raises questions about the best way to express from an ecofeminist position the moral connection between human and nonhuman animals.

Karen Warren has raised the issue of how to express ecofeminist

---

[*Hypatia* 1991, vol. 6, no. 1]

© 1991 by Deane Curtin. Published by permission of author.

moral insights in beginning to develop "ecofeminism as a feminist and environmental ethic."² She notes that a feminist ethic is pluralist and it may use rights language "in certain contexts and for certain purposes." But she says, and I agree, that ecofeminism "involves a shift *from* a conception of ethics as primarily a matter of rights, rules, or principles predetermined and applied in specific cases to entities viewed as competitors in the contest of moral standing" to an ethic that "makes a central place for values of care, love, friendship, trust, and appropriate reciprocity—values that presuppose that our relationships to others are central to our understanding of who we are."³

I think Warren raises the critical issue. If ecofeminism is going to make good on its claim that there are important conceptual connections between the domination of nature and the domination of women, and furthermore, that since there are these connections, an environmental ethic is incomplete if it does not take into account feminist ethical perspectives, the rights model must be examined for whether it is conceptually the best way of expressing ecofeminist insights.

I believe that the language of rights is not the best way to express ecofeminist insights, and that a better approach can be found in a politicized ethic of care. I shall consider the animal rights project and its conceptual limitations for feminists (and for ecofeminists in particular), I then briefly rehearse some of the feminist arguments concerning an alternative ethic of care. Finally, I extend a politicized version of that ethic to an ecologically based feminist ethic for the treatment of animals. Here I will be particularly interested in the ways feminism and ecology are connected through our relations to what we are willing to count as food.⁴

Feminism and Animal Rights

There are two quite different views that have gone under the label of a rights-based ethics. I focus on these because they have dominated discussions of animal rights. I make no claim within the context of this chapter, however, that these two alternatives exhaust the possibilities for a rights-based ethics. My more limited point is to choose the two approaches that have played the most central role in the animal rights literature and argue that they cannot be understood as expressing distinctively feminist insights. The first, which has not proven very sympathetic to the interests of animals, I call the exchange-value alternative. The second, which has been regarded as more promising, I call the cross-species identity alternative.

A version of the exchange-value alternative has been defended by Alan White. A right, he says, "is something which can be said to be exercised, earned, enjoyed, or given, which can be claimed, demanded, asserted, insisted on, secured, waived, or surrendered. . . . A right is related to and contrasted with a duty, an obligation, a privilege, a power, a liability."[5] To be capable of having a right, he argues, is to be a subject capable of being spoken about in "the full language of rights." It follows, according to White, that only persons can have rights because only persons can be spoken about in the full language of rights. Infants, the unborn, the comatose are still persons, or potential persons, so "they are logically possible subjects of rights to whom the full language of rights can significantly, however falsely, be used."[6] By contrast, White contends, nonhuman animals cannot exercise a right, nor can they recognize a correlative obligation.[7]

Jan Narveson has put the case against extending rights to animals bluntly. He insists that we recognize the rights of other beings only in contexts where we stand to gain from such recognition in the long run, and we observe rights relationships only with those who are capable of entering into and keeping an agreement. "Humans," he says, "have nothing generally to gain by voluntarily refraining from (for instance) killing animals or 'treating them as mere means,'"[8] nor are animals capable of making and sustaining agreements.

If we judge whether rights should be extended to new conceptual domains on the basis of considerations suggested by Narveson, nonhuman animals are excluded. Animals, in this view, are to be used according to the self-interest of human beings. If there are any moral strictures on the treatment of animals, they are based on whether certain practices offend the moral sensibilities of those who do possess rights. Nonhuman animals possess no rights themselves.

The second approach to rights depends not on exchange value but on the cross-species identity of certain rights-making characteristics. James Rachels's procedure depends on selecting clear cases in which humans can be said to have rights. He then asks whether there are relevant differences between humans and other animals that would justify refusing to ascribe the right possessed by the human to the nonhuman. If no difference is found, the right is said to be possessed by all animals that are identical in that respect, not just humans.

In some cases, Rachels finds that there are relevant differences. A right to exercise freedom of religion cannot be extended to other animals; the right to liberty can be. He asserts, "The central sense of Freedom is that in which a being is free when he or she is able to do as he or she pleases without being subject to external constraints on his or her actions."[9] This definition of liberty based on doing whatever one wishes without external constraints applies across species. The caged tiger in the zoo is not free; the tiger in the "wild" is.

In a similar vein, Tom Regan has argued that "inherent value . . . belongs equally to those who are the experiencing subjects of a life."[10] He emphasizes that this is a theory about the inherent value of "individuals" and that "reason—not sentiment, not emotion—reason compels us to recognize the equal inherent value of these animals and, with this, their equal right to be treated with respect."[11] According to this second approach to animal rights, then, nonhuman animals may have some, but not all, rights enjoyed by human animals.

Both of these approaches to animal ethics (particularly the cross-species identity approach since that has been regarded as the more likely alternative) make a number of assumptions that can be challenged if one's goal is to provide an ecofeminist ethic. My intention is not so much to make these arguments here as to rehearse positions that have been argued for elsewhere as a means of placing the present discussion in context.

First, it can be argued that views such as Rachels's and Regan's are too narrow to express feminist insights[12] because they allow us to recognize only those rights-making characteristics that nonhuman animals have in virtue of being in some way *identical* to humans. Rachels has granted, for example, that by his procedure of establishing animal rights on the basis of whether nonhuman animals are like humans, we are theoretically denied access to rights that other animals may possess uniquely.[13] (In fact, I am not sure what one could do to elucidate what this claim *means*, given that we cannot, in principle, know what the criteria for such rights would be.) Rachels's procedure recognizes only identity of interests, not diversity. Similarly, Regan's criterion for possession of inherent value picks out a common denominator in virtue of which humans and nonhumans are identical. But many of the interests an ecological ethic may have rest precisely on the differences between humans and other animals.

The assumption that moral status depends on identity of interests has been challenged by some feminists.[14] A feminist ethic tends to be pluralistic in its intention to recognize heterogeneous moral interests. It sees the attempt to reduce moral claims to identity of interests as one strand in a moral fabric that has tended to exclude women's voices. If ecofeminism is to make the claim that there are important conceptual connections between ecology and feminism, it should question whether a feminist ecological ethic is best expressed through the extension of rights to nonhuman animals on the basis of their partial identity to human beings.

The second concern about the compatibility of ecofeminism with the rights approach is that the rights approach to treatment of animals is formalistic. It is committed to the idea that equal treatment based on a criterion of cross-species identity is the central concept of morality where this is defined as treatment that is neutral with respect to context. It recommends a decision procedure by which those beings that have rights can be separated from those that do not. Its aspirations are universalistic. Feminist approaches to ethics, however, tend to be not only pluralistic but contextual.[15] They tend to be based on actual interests in the narrative context of lived experiences.[16]

Third, the rights approach does not express feminist moral insights because it is inherently adversarial. As Joel Feinberg has said, "To have a right is to have a claim *to* something *against* someone."[17] Though conflict certainly may arise over a feminist understanding of morality, it does not begin from a theoretical assumption of conflict. Rather, a feminist understanding is more likely to be based in a pluralistic context that is dialogical and seeks mutual accommodation of interests.[18]

Fourth, connected to a dialogical understanding of ethics, feminist moral thought tends to reconceptualize personhood as relational rather than autonomous.[19] Whereas the rights approach requires a concept of personhood that is individualistic enough to defend the sphere in which the moral agent is autonomous, feminist approaches to ethics tend to see moral inquiry as an ongoing process through which persons are defined contextually and relationally.

Fifth, whereas the rights approach has tended to argue that ethical judgments are objective and rational, and do not depend on affective aspects of experience, this has been questioned by feminist critics partly on the grounds that the conception of the purely rational is a myth, and partly on the grounds that this myth has tended to marginalize the experiences of women by portraying them as personal rather than moral.[20] Following the work of Carol Gilligan, many feminists suggest that an ethic of care is better able to express the connection between reason and feeling found in women's moral discourse.

Finally, as a result of the emphasis on the rational in traditional moral theory, feminist insights concerning the body as moral agent have been missed. But as some feminist philosophers have argued, the identification of woman with body has been one pretext on which women's lives have been marginalized.[21]

These six considerations suggest, then, that the rights approach as applied to the treatment of animals is not a very promising route for establishing a feminist ecological ethic. In a world where the language of rights is the common moral currency, there may be contexts in which it would be helpful for feminists to present the case for moral treatment of animals in terms of rights. However, I would argue that there is nothing distinctively feminist about this approach. If one accepts that there is a deep ideological connection between the oppression of nature and the oppression of women in Western culture, one must look to a distinctively feminist understanding of oppression.

A Politicized Ethic of Caring For

A source for much of the feminist literature on women's psychological and moral development is Carol Gilligan's *In a Different Voice*.[22] Whereas the rights approach tends to emphasize identity of moral interests, formalistic decision procedures, an adversarial understanding of moral discourse, personhood as autonomous, and a valorization of the nonbodily aspects of personhood, Gilligan's research indicates that women's moral experiences are better understood in terms of recognition of a plurality of moral interests, contextual decision-making, nonadversarial accommodation of diverse interests, personhood as relational, and the body as moral agent. Furthermore, an ethic of care has an intuitive appeal from the standpoint of ecological ethics. Whether or not nonhuman animals have rights, we certainly can and do care for them. This includes cases where we regularly experience care in return, as in a relationship with a pet, as well as cases where there is no reciprocity, as in the case of working to preserve natural habitats. It even seems possible to say we can care for nonsentient beings. Karen Warren has written about two attitudes one can bring to mountain climbing. One seeks to dominate and conquer the mountain; the other seeks to "climb respectfully with the rock." One can care for the rock partly *because* it is "independent and seemingly indifferent to my presence."[23]

Whereas an ethic of care does have an intuitive appeal, without further development into a political dimension Gilligan's research may be turned against feminist and ecofeminist objectives. First, if not politicized, an ethic of care can be used to privatize the moral interests of women. In contrast to the rights model, which seeks to cordon off "my" territory over which I have control, the caring-for model may often suggest that the interests of others should, in certain contexts, come before one's own, and that knowing what to do in a particular situation requires empathetic projection into another's life. Putting the other in front of oneself can easily be abused. The wife who selflessly cares for her husband, who cares only about himself, is only too well known.

In a society that oppresses women, it does no good to suggest that women should go on selflessly providing care if social structures make it all too easy to abuse that care. The injunction to care must be understood as part of a radical political agenda that allows for development of contexts in which caring for can be nonabusive. It claims that the relational sense of self, the willingness to empathetically enter into the world of others and care for them, can be expanded and developed as part of a political agenda so that it may include those outside the already established circle of caring for. Its goal is not just to make a "private" ethic public but to help undercut the public/private distinction.

An ethic of care that is not politicized can be localized in scope, thereby blunting its political impact. Caring for resists the claim that morality depends on a criterion of universalizability, and insists that it depends on special, contextual relationships. This might be taken to mean that we should care for the homeless only if our daughter or son happens to be homeless. Or it might mean that persons in dominant countries should feel no need to care for persons in dominated countries. Or it might mean that we should care only for those of the same species.

As part of a feminist political agenda, however, caring for can remain contextualized while being expanded on the basis of feminist political insights. To take a political example, one of the sources of the oppression of women in countries like India is that deforestation has a disproportionate effect on women whose responsibilities usually include food preparation. A common sight in these countries is village women walking farther every year in search of safe water and fuel for food. In such contexts, the destruction of the environment *is* a source of women's oppression.[24] The point here is not that there is a single cause of women's oppression, or that in countries like India women's oppression is always ecologically based. There are problems like the euphemistically termed "kitchen accident" in which women are burned to death by husbands who are disappointed with the dowry. I am arguing that, in the mosaic of problems that constitute women's oppression in a particular context, no complete account can be given that does not make reference to the connection between women and the environment. Caring for women in such a context includes caring for their environment. A distinctively feminist understanding of community development in countries like India may, then, provide a common context of related (though not identical!) interests that would connect women in the United States with women and the environment in India.

A distinction can be drawn between caring *about* and caring *for* that helps clarify how caring can be expanded. Caring about is a generalized form of care that may have specifiable recipients, but it occurs in a context where direct relatedness to specific others is missing. For example, feminist perspectives may lead one to a sense of connection between oneself and the plight of women in distant locations. But if one has not experienced the condition of women in India, for example, and more than that, if one has not experienced the particular conditions of women in a specific village in a specific region of India, caring remains a generalized caring about. As an element in a feminist political agenda, such caring about may lead to the kinds of actions that bring one into the kind of deep relatedness that can be described as caring for: caring for particular persons in the context of their histories.

Similar comments may be made about classic environmental issues. By reading about the controversy surrounding logging of old-growth forests, one might come to care about them. But caring for is marked by an understanding of and appreciation for a particular context in which one participates. One may, for example, come to understand the issue partly in terms of particular trees one has become accustomed to looking for on a favorite hike, trees that one would miss given changes in logging regulations. With these political and ecological considerations in mind, I conclude that an ethic of care can be expanded as part of a feminist political agenda without losing its distinctive contextual character. It can resist privatization and localization, retaining the contextualized character that is distinctive of caring for.

Another possible problem with a politicized ethic of care is the contention, argued for notably by Nel Noddings, that caring for can only be elucidated conceptually through the idea of reciprocity. If this is correct, it would be difficult to extend a politicized version of caring for to contexts of community development or to nonhuman animals where reciprocity is either inappropriate or impossible. It would also constitute an important similarity to the exchange-value theory of rights.

Noddings argues that "the caring relation ... requires ... a form of *responsiveness* or *reciprocity* on the part of the cared-for" to be a complete act of caring for.[25] Though she notes some cases where this may occur with nonhuman animals, she doubts in general whether our relations with animals do reach such a stage of completion in reciprocity. She doubts, therefore, whether we can really be said to care for nonhuman animals.

I find Noddings's requirement of reciprocity unconvincing. Reciprocity is important in certain contexts of caring for—those Noddings takes as her principal examples, such as caring education—because in those contexts we are looking for a response that indicates that caring has had the desired effect. But I regard these as special cases that become dangerous to feminist moral interests if generalized. Many of the contexts of caring for that an ecofeminist might be especially interested in are precisely those in which reciprocity cannot be expected. It seems quite possible that a feminist political consciousness may lead one to care for women in a Dalit village in India. But it would be dangerous to suggest that such caring for requires reciprocity. Is it really caring for if something is expected in return? We ought to distinguish the *contextualization* of caring for (the requirement that all caring for has a determinant recipient) from the *localization* of caring for, which resists the expansion of caring for to the oppressed who are geographically remote from us, or to nonhuman nature.

In summary, ecofeminist philosophy seeks not only to understand the condition of women but also to use that understanding to liberate women and nature from the structures of oppression. In achieving a new sense of relatedness of the kind that feminist and ecofeminist political philosophy can provide, one is enabled to enter into caring for relationships that were not available earlier. One may come to see, for example, that the white, middle-class American woman's typical situation is connected with—though not identical to—the condition of women in oppressed countries. Caring for can also be generated by coming to see that one's life (unknowingly) has been a cause of the oppression of others. The caring-for model does not require that those recipients of our care must be "equal" to us. Neither does it assume they are not equal. It is based on developing the capacity to care, not the criterion of equality. The resultant caring for may lead to a new sense of empowerment based on cultivating the willingness to act to empower ourselves and others.

Contextual Moral Vegetarianism[26]

In this section I provide an example of a distinctively ecofeminist moral concern: our relations to what we are willing to count as food. Vegetarianism has been defended as a moral obligation that results from rights that nonhuman animals have in virtue of being sentient beings.[27] However, a distinctively ecofeminist defense of moral vegetarianism is better expressed as a core concept in an ecofeminist ethic of care. One clear way of distinguishing the two approaches is that whereas the rights approach is not inherently contextual[28] (it is the response to the rights of all sentient beings), the caring-for approach responds to particular contexts and histories. It recognizes that the reasons for moral vegetarianism may differ by locale, by gender, as well as by class.

Moral vegetarianism is a fruitful issue for ecofeminists to explore in developing an ecological ethic because in judging the adequacy of an ethic by reference to its understanding of food one draws attention to precisely those aspects of daily experience that have often been regarded as beneath the interest of philosophy. Plato's remark in the *Gorgias* is typical of the dismissive attitude philosophers have usually had toward food. Pastry cooking, he says, is like rhetoric: both are mere "knacks" or "routines" designed to appeal to our bodily instincts rather than our intellects.[29]

Plato's dismissive remark also points to something that feminists need to take very seriously—namely, that a distinctively feminist ethic, as Susan Bordo and others argue, should include the body as moral agent. Here too the experience of women in patriarchal cultures is especially valuable because women, more than men, experience the effects of culturally sanctioned oppressive attitudes toward the appropriate shape of the body. Bordo has argued that anorexia nervosa is a psychopathology made possible by Cartesian attitudes toward the body at a popular level. Anorexics typically feel alienation from their bodies and the hunger "it" feels. Bordo quotes one woman as saying she ate because "my stomach wanted it"; another dreamed of being "without a body." Anorexics want to achieve "absolute purity, hyperintellectuality and transcendence of the flesh."[30]

Kim Chernin's account of her eating disorder in *The Obsession* brings out her discovery that her disorder was not caused by food but by a dysfunctional sense of herself as a person. To overcome her obsession "requires, in whatever form is appropriate, the evolution and expression of self."[31] She is returned to a healthy understanding of her *self* when she overcomes her estrangement from her *body*, when she accepts her body as her self: "My body, my hunger, and the food I give to myself, which have seemed like enemies to me, now have begun to look like friends" (8). Health returns when she is able to move from a Cartesian alienation from her body to a reconception as unified sensibility, a body/mind acting in unison.

Chernin's experience is extremely important philosophically. Her eating disorder is not so much a dysfunctional relation to food as it is a dysfunctional sense of personhood that shows itself through food. Specifically, it shows itself through her inability to accept herself as body, which prevents her from having a healthful relationship to food. Once she accepts herself as body, however, she is able, for the first time, to enter into a direct and healthful relationship to food.

Much can be learned from Chernin's acceptance of herself as body and of the food that becomes her body. Though experiences like Chernin's do not imply vegetarianism,[32] they do imply an openness to the reality of the way our relations to what we will count as food shape one's sense of personhood, and how one understands one's relations to others. Through accepting the possibility that our relations to food can define who we are, one comes to see the choice of what will count as food as a moral choice that reflects who one is and as an ontological commitment to the way the world will be ordered by that choice.

Taking these experiences of women seriously as expressive of what it means to be healthy, it is possible to see that our relations to food provide a philosophically interesting context that highlights the fact that personhood is bodily and relational. It develops in a social context. Just as men have typically been socialized in the agora, women have typically been socialized in the kitchen, and not just any kitchen, but a particular context with particular oral traditions including certain kinds of foods and certain methods of food preparation and presentation.[33] The kitchen has been an oppressive context for women, but it has also been a context of sociability and solidarity among women.

Another reason moral vegetarianism is an issue of particular interest to ecofeminists is that, as Carol Adams has vividly demonstrated in *The Sexual Politics of Meat*, there are important connections through food between the oppression of women and the oppression of nonhuman animals.[34] Typical of the wealth of evidence she presents are the following: the connection of women and animals through pornographic representations of women as "meat" ready to be carved up, for example, in "snuff" films; the fact that language masks our true relationship with animals, making them "absent referents" by giving meat words positive connotations ("That's a meaty question"; "Where's the beef?"), while disparaging nonflesh foods ("Don't watch so much TV! You'll turn into a vegetable"); men, athletes and soldiers in particular, are associated with red meat and activity ("To have muscle you need to eat muscle"), whereas women are associated with vegetables and passivity ("ladies' luncheons" typically offer dainty sandwiches with no red meat).

As a "contextual moral vegetarian," I cannot refer to an absolute moral rule that prohibits meat eating under all circumstances. There may be some contexts in which another response is appropriate. Though I am committed to moral vegetarianism, I cannot say that I would never kill an animal for food. Would I not kill an animal to provide food for my son if he were starving? Would I not generally prefer the death of a bear to the death of a loved one? I am sure I would. The point of a contextualist ethic is that one need not treat all interests equally as if one had no relationship to any of the parties.

Beyond personal contextual relations, geographical contexts may sometimes be relevant. The Ihalmiut, for example, whose frigid domain makes the growing of food impossible, do not have the option of vegetarian cuisine. The economy of their food practices, however, and their tradition of "thanking" the caribou for giving its life are reflective of a serious, focused, compassionate attitude toward the "gift" of a meal.

In some cultures violence against nonhuman life is ritualized in such a way that one is present to the reality of one's food. The Japanese have a Shinto ceremony that pays respect to the insects that are killed during rice planting. Tibetans, who as Buddhists have not generally been drawn to vegetarianism, nevertheless give their own bodies back to the animals in an ultimate act of thanks by having their corpses hacked into pieces as food for the birds.[35] Cultures such as these have ways of expressing spiritually the idea "we are what we eat," even if they are not vegetarian.

If there is any context, on the other hand, in which moral vegetarianism is completely compelling as an expression of an ethic of care, it is for economically well-off persons in technologically advanced countries. First, these are persons who have a *choice* of what food they want to eat; they have a choice of what they will *count* as food. Morality and ontology are closely connected here. It is one thing to inflict pain on animals when climate offers no other choice. But in the case of killing animals for human consumption where there is a choice, this practice inflicts pain that is completely unnecessary and avoidable. The injunction to care, considered as an issue of moral and political development, should be understood to include the injunction to eliminate needless suffering wherever possible, and particularly the suffering of those whose suffering is conceptually connected to one's own. It should be understood as an injunction that includes the imperative to rethink what it means to be a person, connected with the imperative to rethink the status of nonhuman animals. An ecofeminist perspective emphasizes that one's body is oneself, and that by inflicting violence needlessly, one's bodily self becomes a context for violence. One becomes violent by taking part in violent food practices. The ontological implication of a feminist ethic of care is that nonhuman animals should no longer count as food.

Second, most of the meat and dairy products in these countries do not come from mom-and-pop farms with little red barns. Factory farms are responsible for most of the six billion animals killed for food every year in the United States.[36] It is curious that steroids are considered dangerous for athletes, but animals that have been genetically engineered and chemically induced to grow faster, and come to market sooner, are considered to be an entirely different issue. One would have to be hardened to know the conditions factory-farm animals live in and not feel disgust concerning their treatment.[37]

Third, much of the effect of the eating practices of persons in industrialized countries is felt in oppressed countries. Land owned by the wealthy that was once used to grow inexpensive crops for local people has been converted to the production of expensive products (beef) for export. Increased trade of food products with these countries is consistently the cause of increased starvation. In cultures where food preparation is primarily understood as women's work, starvation is primarily a women's issue. Food expresses who we are politically just as much as bodily. One need not be aware of the fact that one's food practices oppress others in order to be an oppressor.

From a woman's perspective, in particular, it makes sense to ask whether one should become a vegan, a vegetarian who, in addition to refraining from meat and fish, also refrains from eating eggs and dairy products. Since the consumption of eggs and milk has in common that it exploits the reproductive capacities of the female, vegetarianism is not a gender-neutral issue.[38]

To *choose one's diet* in a patriarchal culture is one way of politicizing an ethic of care. It marks a daily, bodily commitment to resist ideological pressures to conform to patriarchal standards, and to establishing contexts in which caring for can be nonabusive.

Just as there are gender-specific reasons for women's commitment to vegetarianism, for men in a patriarchal society moral vegetarianism can mark the decision to stand in solidarity with women. It also indicates a determination to resist ideological pressures to become a "real man." Real people do not need to eat "real food," as the American Beef Council would have us believe.

Conclusion

Research on an ethic of care provides a very important beginning for an ecofeminist ethic, but it runs the risk of having its own aims turned against it unless it is regarded as part of a political agenda that consciously attempts to expand the circle of caring for. Ecofeminism is in a position to accomplish this expansion by insisting that the oppression of women, the oppression of the environment, and the oppressive treatment of nonhuman animals are deeply linked. As one kind of feminism it can emphasize that personhood is embodied, and that through the food which becomes our bodies, we are engaged in food practices that reflect who we are. Ecofeminism is also in a position to offer a politicized ethic that promises liberation from the forms of oppression that link women and the environment.

Notes

1. Karen Warren, "The Promise and Power of Ecofeminism," *Environmental Ethics* 12, no. 2 (1990): 126.
2. Ibid., 138.
3. Ibid., 141 and 143.
4. In attempting to work out a conception of morality that is consistent with ecofeminism, I am conscious of speaking as a man about the experiences of women. I do not intend to speak *for* women, but as a man who believes men as well as women can learn from the testimony of women's experiences, I believe, for example, that men can learn something important about what it means to be a person by listening to women speak about anorexia nervosa. This is not meant to deny that there are important gender differences in the ways women and men experience food.
5. Alan White, "Why Animals Cannot Have Rights," in *Animal Rights and Human Obligations*, 2d ed., ed. Tom Regan and Peter Singer (Englewood Cliffs, N.J.: Prentice-Hall, 1984). As excerpted from Alan White, *Rights* (Oxford: Oxford University Press, 1989), 120.
6. White, "Why Animals Cannot Have Rights," 120.
7. Ibid., 121.
8. Jan Narveson, "A Defense of Meat Eating," in *Animal Rights and Human Obligations*, 2d ed., ed. Regan and Singer, 193. Originally published as "Animal Rights

Revisited" in *Ethics and Animals*, ed. H. Miller and W. Williams (Clifton, N.J.: Humana, 1983).
9. James Rachels, "Why Animals Have a Right to Liberty," in *Animal Rights and Human Obligations*, 2d ed., Regan and Singer, 125.
10. Tom Regan, "The Case for Animal Rights," in *Animal Rights and Human Obligations*. Regan and Singer, 112.
11. Ibid., 113.
12. Feminist insights into ethics are those that can be seen as arising from and expressing the conditions of women's moral lives. While there is a broad range of views that have been advanced by feminist ethicists, there are also patterns of agreement. In what follows I am suggesting that these patterns of agreement are sufficiently well developed to call into question the conceptual link between ecofeminist ethics and the language of rights.
13. Rachels, "Why Animals Have a Right to Liberty," 124.
14. See Marilyn Frye, "In and Out of Harm's Way: Arrogance and Love" (*The Politics of Reality* [Trumansburg, N.Y.: Crossing, 1983], 66–72), for the distinction between arrogant and loving perception; María Lugones, "Playfulness, 'World'-Travelling, and Loving Perception" (*Hypatia* 2, no. 2 [1987]: 3–19) on the distinction between unity, which erases difference, and solidarity, which recognizes difference; and Seyla Benhabib, "The Generalized and the Concrete Other: The Kohlberg-Gilligan Controversy and Feminist Theory" (in *Feminism as Critique: On the Politics of Gender*, ed. Seyla Benhabib and Drucilla Cornell [Minneapolis: University of Minnesota Press, 1987] where she describes the rights approach as "monological" (91) in its inability to recognize the moral "other."
15. See Iris Marion Young, "Impartiality and the Civic Public: Some Implications of Feminist Critiques of Moral and Political Theory" (in *Feminism as Critique* ed. Benhabib and Cornell) where she connects deontological theories with what Adorno called the logic of identity which "eliminate(s) otherness" by denying "the irreducible specificity of situations and the difference among moral subjects" (61).
16. Not all feminists would agree that a feminist ethics should be inherently contextual. Susan Moller Okin has argued that the rights perspective can include both the requirement of universalizability and empathetic concern for others. She proposes that the rights approach can be contextualized; thus she doubts whether there is a "different voice" in morality. I question whether she has succeeded in showing this, however, since her suggestion that the rights perspective requires us "to think from the point of view of everybody, of every 'concrete other' whom one might turn out to be" still entails *"equal* concern for others" (Susan Moller Okin, "Reason and Feeling in Thinking about Justice," in *Feminism and Political Theory*, ed. Cass R. Sunstein [Chicago: University of Chicago Press, 1990], 32, 34, italics added], reprinted from *Ethics* 99 (Jan. 1989). This is still not fully compatible with the care perspective, which allows that a particular context of caring may include caring that is *un*equal. Even if contextualized, a rule-based ethic still proceeds by finding cross-situational identity. There is a difference between contextualizing a rule-governed theory, and a theory that is inherently contextualized. I therefore tend to side with those who argue that there is a distinctively feminist ethic of care that cannot be reduced to the justice perspective. In fact, I would be sympathetic to a position that is even more pluralistic than the alternatives of rights or care. Charles Taylor argues that there are moral perspectives based on personal integrity, perfection, and liberation (Charles Taylor, "The Diversity of Goods," in *Utilitarianism and Beyond*, ed. Amartya Sen and Bernard Williams [Cambridge: Harvard University Press, 1982], 133). These may not be reducible either to rights or care. I would suggest that an ecofeminist ethics of care is most appropriately developed in dialogue with what Taylor calls the liberation orientation rather than the rights orientation. I intend to do this by arguing in the next section that the care perspective needs to be politicized.

17. Joel Feinberg, "The Rights of Animals and Unborn Generations," in *Responsibilities to Other Generations*, ed. Ernest Partridge (Buffalo: Prometheus, 1980), 139.
18. See *Feminism as Critique*, Benhabib and Cornell, sec. 4.
19. See Ann Ferguson, "A Feminist Aspect Theory of the Self," in *Women, Knowledge, and Reality: Explorations in Feminist Philosophy* (Winchester, Mass.: Unwin Hyman, 1989) [reprinted from *Science, Morality, and Feminist Theory*, Hanen and Nielsen]; Lugones, "Playfulness, 'World'-Travelling, and Loving Perception"; and Deane Curtin, "Dogen, Deep Ecology and the Ecological Self," *Environmental Ethics* 16, no. 2 (1994): 195–213.
20. Alison Jaggar, "Love and Knowledge: Emotion in Feminist Epistemology," in *Gender/Body/Knowledge: Feminist Reconstructions of Being and Knowing*, ed. Alison M. Jaggar and Susan R. Bordo (New Brunswick, N.J.: Rutgers University Press, 1989), 139–43.
21. See Susan Bordo, "The Body and the Reproduction of Femininity: A Feminist Appropriation of Foucault," in *Gender/Body/Knowledge*, ed. Jaggar and Bordo (n. 20, above).
22. See *Women and Moral Theory*, ed. Eva Feder Kittay and Diana T. Meyers (Totowa, N.J.: Rowman & Littlefield, 1987), and *Feminism and Political Theory*, ed. Sunstein, for useful collections of papers illustrating the influence of Gilligan's research. Owen Flanagan and Kathryn Jackson ("Justice, Care, and Gender: The Kohlberg-Gilligan Debate Revisited" in *Feminism and Political Theory*) give a helpful overview of the large body of literature on this subject. They point out several changes that might be helpful to Gilligan's theory. For example, whereas she depicts the alternative between a rights perspective and a care perspective in terms of a gestalt shift, Flanagan and Jackson argue that this does not accurately represent the shift that occurs between the two perspectives. A gestalt shift, such as the duck-rabbit, only allows the image to be seen as either a duck or a rabbit. But research suggests that most people can see a particular moral situation from the perspective of either rights or care, but that one of these perspectives is regarded as more important, and the distinction in importance tends to be gender-based, women emphasizing care, men emphasizing rights (Flanagan and Jackson, "Justice," 38–40). This suggests the two perspectives are psychologically, not inherently, mutually exclusive, although one may find contexts in which the perspectives do conflict.
23. Warren, "The Promise and Power of Ecofeminism," 135.
24. An excellent source is Vandana Shiva's *Staying Alive: Women, Ecology, and Development* (London: Zed, 1988). See particularly her account of the Chipko movement (67–77), which began when women in the Himalayan foothills literally hugged trees that were sacred to them to spare them from deforestation. The movement has grown into a full-scale human development project.
25. Nel Noddings, *Caring: A Feminine Approach to Ethics and Moral Education* (Berkeley: University of California Press, 1984), 150.
26. By this term, I intend to indicate a distinction between vegetarianism based on considerations of health and vegetarianism based on moral considerations.
27. Tom Regan, *The Case for Animal Rights* (Berkeley: University of California Press, 1983), 330–53.
28. Regan calls the animal's right not to be killed a prima facie right that may be overridden. Nevertheless, his theory is not *inherently* contextualized.
29. Plato, *Gorgias*, in *Plato: The Collected Dialogues*, ed. Edith Hamilton and Huntington Cairns (Princeton, N.J.: Princeton University Press), 245.
30. Susan R. Bordo, "Anorexia Nervosa as the Psychopathology of Popular Culture," in *Feminism and Foucault: Reflections on Resistance*, ed. Irene Diamond and Lee Quinby (Boston: Northeastern University Press, 1988), 94–95. Reprinted from *The Philosophical Forum* 17, no. 2 (winter 1985–86).

31. Kim Chernin, *The Obsession: Reflections on the Tyranny of Slenderness* (New York: Harper, 1981), 12. A further reference follows in the text.
32. Vegetarianism, which can be understood as an expression of health, is also commonly tried by anorexics in their attempt to "transcend the flesh."
33. See Lisa Heldke's "Recipes for Theory Making" for a detailed account of the oral traditions of the kitchen, including recipe swapping (*Hypatia* 3, no. 2 [1988]: 15–30).
34. Carol J. Adams, *The Sexual Politics of Meat: A Feminist-Vegetarian Critical Theory* (New York: Continuum, 1990), 1.
35. This practice is also ecologically sound since it saves the enormous expense of firewood for cremation.
36. Adams, *Sexual Politics*, 6.
37. See John Robbins's *Diet for a New America* (Walpole, N.H.: Stillpoint, 1987). It should be noted that in response to such knowledge, some reflective nonvegetarians commit to eating range-grown chickens but not those grown in factory farms.
38. I owe this point to a conversation with Colman McCarthy.

Justice, Caring, and Animal Liberation (1992)

Brian Luke

Carol Gilligan has described justice and caring as two distinct moral frameworks or orientations to ethical concerns.[1] The *justice* framework is characterized by abstraction, the application of general rules of conduct, an emphasis on restraining aggression, and a concern for consistency and the fair resolution of conflicting claims and interests. The *caring* framework, on the other hand, is characterized by its focus on the concrete and particular, its emphasis on the maintenance and extension of connection, and by its concern for responsiveness and the satisfaction of needs. Animal liberation is often framed as a justice issue, though, I will suggest, it may more appropriately be understood in terms of caring.

By *animal liberation* I mean opposition to institutions of animal exploitation such as vivisection, hunting, and animal farming. Two prominent philosophical defenders of animal liberation are Tom Regan and Peter Singer. Both work exclusively within the justice framework, presenting animal liberation as a matter of consistency and fair treatment, rather than in terms of responsiveness and the satisfaction of needs. We can start to see how the justice approach is ill-suited for animal liberation by considering the arguments of Regan and Singer.

Regan attempts to move the reader from a commitment to the respectful treatment of humans to a like commitment to the respectful treatment of normal adult mammals.[2] Regan points out that we do not in general think it is justifiable to harm one human to bene-

---

[*Between the Species.* 1992, vol. 8, no. 2.]

©1992 John Stockwell. Expanded for this book. Published by permission of author.

fit others—we would object, for example, to killing a healthy man against his will in order to use his organs to save three sick persons. We do, however, think it appropriate to harm one animal to benefit other animals, human or otherwise; at least this is the way that vivisection, hunting, and animal farming are usually justified.

Regan argues that we are being inconsistent in treating humans and other mammals differently in this respect. The notion of inconsistency here is not self-contradiction but contradiction with the formal principles of justice, according to which like individuals should be treated alike. Now we protect humans against being vivisected, farmed, or hunted, presumably because such treatment would harm them through the infliction of pain and death. But Regan has shown in the first three chapters of his book that pain and death are also harms to normal adult mammals. So these animals are just as deserving of protection from vivisection, farming, and hunting as are humans. Because both humans and other mammals are harmed by pain and death, the two groups are relevantly similar, and we are inconsistent to treat them so differently.

The flaw in this argument I wish to emphasize is the move from same kinds of harms to relevant similarity. Most of us would admit that pain and death are harms for both humans and other animals. But this by itself does not show that humans and other animals are relevantly similar with respect to assessing the moral status of these common harms. Regan allows that certain capacities may be unique to humans, and it is conceivable that the presence of uniquely human capacities in an individual is relevant to the justifiability of harming that individual, even when the type of harm in question is one that can be imposed on nonhumans. In fact, according to Kantian theories, only rational individuals can be directly wronged. A Kantian could hold that killing is a harm both to humans and other animals, but that the wrongness of the harm arises only from its impingement upon the victim's rationality. Thus, killing a rational human would require special justification not needed for killing a nonrational animal, even though both are harmed by being killed.

I am not saying that I agree with Kantianism or with the idea that there are uniquely human capacities. I am only saying that as long as Regan's readers are willing to embrace these theories, they can without inconsistency reject Regan's move from "death and pain are harms for both humans and other animals" to "killing and inflicting pain require the same justification for both humans and other animals." Since this move is crucial to his argument as a whole, they can consistently reject Regan's case for animals' rights.[3]

Essentially the same type of maneuver allows rejection of Singer's argument for animal liberation. Like Regan, Singer attempts to move the reader, through considerations of consistency, from commitments concerning the appropriate treatment of humans to similar commitments concerning the appropriate treatment of animals.[4] Singer starts not with respect for humans but with opposition to racism and sexism. Singer argues that anyone who opposes racism and sexism does so on the basis of a principle of equal consideration, according to which we must give equal consideration to the interests of all people, regardless of their race or sex. But animals, at least all those capable of feeling pleasure or pain, have interests, so there is no reason, according to Singer, why they should be excluded from the scope of this principle of equal consideration. But animal farming and vivisection, Singer maintains, are considered acceptable practices only because we tend to give the interests of nonhumans much less consideration than the similar interests of humans. This devaluation of interests solely on the basis of species Singer calls *speciesism*, and he thinks his argument shows that we are inconsistent to oppose sexism and racism but not speciesism.

As with Regan, however, anyone willing to accept a Kantian view can reject Singer's entire argument without inconsistency. Singer presumes that opposition to sexism and racism must be based on the principle of equal consideration of interests. One could maintain, however, that sexism and racism are objectionable because they are disrespectful of the rationality of members of the oppressed races and sex. One could then consistently exclude nonhumans from moral consideration by holding that they lack the rational capacities of humans.

Again I emphasize that I am not endorsing Kantianism here. I am just showing that Regan's and Singer's arguments fail on their own terms. Both writers insist that they are relying on reason alone, and not emotion, to establish their animal liberationist conclusions. But the crucial step in their arguments, that humans and other animals are relevantly similar, cannot be established by reason alone.

Regan and Singer have the following response for Kantian rebuttals of their arguments.[5] Taking rationality as a necessary condition for moral considerability does give one permission to harm animals (if rationality is defined narrowly enough). But it also gives permission to harm many nonrational humans, such as infants, mentally retarded individuals, and people with brain damage or in comas. Thus, a commitment to protect these so-called marginal cases of humanity entails the rejection of Kantianism and the adoption of some more inclusive criterion of considerability. But any criterion broad enough to include marginal humans (for example, sentience or subjectivity) will also include nonhuman animals and thus support animal liberation.

This line of thought, called *the argument from marginal cases*, is no more successful than Regan's and Singer's main arguments in proving that animals have rights. On the one hand, the argument may be circumvented simply by giving up the commitment to protect marginal humans. R. G. Frey does this. He takes the marginal cases argument to present a dilemma: either oppose animal vivisection or condone the vivisection of marginal humans.[6] He then reasons:

> Very few people indeed would look in the face the benefits which medical research in particular has conferred upon us, benefits which on the whole have most certainly involved vivisection.... Therefore, we may find ourselves unable to make the choice in favour of antivivisectionism.... Accordingly, we are left with human experiments. I think this is how I would choose, not with great glee and rejoicing, and with great reluctance; but if this is the price we must pay to hold the appeal to benefit and to enjoy the benefits which that appeal licenses, then we must, I think, pay it.[7]

Frey forgets that "we" academics, presumably (hopefully?) escaping classification as marginal, would not be the ones to pay the real price for a choice in favor of vivisection.

Even those of us not quite able to match Frey's noble sacrifice of other humans to vivisection can still consistently evade the marginal cases argument, if we are so inclined. Suppose we "justify" the vivisection of animals by reference to their supposed lack of rationality. And suppose we allow that some humans also lack this rationality. This does not imply that we *must* vivisect marginal humans, only that we *may*. Thus, the protection of marginal humans could be made consistent with the vivisection of animals possessing comparable degrees of rationality by interpreting that protection as supererogatory. According to this line of thought we may vivisect marginal humans, because, like nonhuman animals, they lack a right to protection, but for nonbinding reasons we decide only to vivisect the nonhuman animals. This stratagem is employed by Bonnie Steinbock:

> I am willing to admit that my horror at the thought of experiments being performed on severely mentally incapacitated human beings

in cases in which I would find it justifiable and preferable to perform the same experiments on nonhuman animals (capable of similar suffering) may not be a moral emotion. But it is certainly not wrong of us to extend special care to members of our own species.[8]

So like their main arguments, Regan's and Singer's backup argument from marginal cases fails to show any unavoidable inconsistency in supporting the exploitation of animals in vivisection, hunting, and farming, while rejecting any similar exploitation of human. Animal liberation is not a matter of consistency.

As arguments, justice-based approaches to animal liberation fail. The justice orientation also fails to capture the moral outlooks of many in the animal liberation movement. Justice-oriented writers cast the issue as, fundamentally, a comparison between the treatment of humans and the treatment of other animals. According to Regan, we harm animals to benefit others, we do not do this to humans (generally speaking), but there is no relevant difference between humans and animals to justify the dissimilar treatment. Thus animals are treated unfairly by comparison to the treatment of humans. For Singer, the comparative unfairness is in opposing sexism and racism but not opposing speciesism, when again there is no relevant difference between humans and other animals to support the distinction. For both Regan and Singer, and other writers within the justice framework, the basic moral judgment concerns the discrepancy between the treatment of humans and the treatment of other similar animals. What is called into question is the fairness, or what they more often refer to as the consistency, of a society that treats two relevantly similar groups of individuals in such totally different ways.

The emphasis on the consistency of the agent and the focus on comparing the treatment of humans and the treatment of other animals are quite distant from my motivations and those of others in the animal liberation movement. My opposition to the institutionalized exploitation of animals is not based on a *comparison* between human and animal treatment, but on a consideration of the abuse of the animals *in and of itself*. I respond directly to the needs and the plight of the animals used in hunting, farming, and vivisection. In objecting to these practices I am not comparing the treatment of humans and animals, and thinking "this is unfair because humans are protected from such usage." I am appalled by the abuses themselves—shooting, trapping, and poisoning; branding, castrating, forcibly impregnating, separating mother and young, tail docking, debeaking, confining, transporting in cattle cars, and slaughtering;

burning, cutting, gassing, starving, asphyxiating, decapitating, decompressing, irradiating, electrocuting, freezing, crushing, paralyzing, amputating, excising organs, removing parts of the brain, socially isolating, inducing addiction, and imposing disease—these acts are repellant because of what they do to the animals. My moral condemnation of the acts arises directly from my sympathy for the animals, and is independent of the question of whether humans are protected from such abuse. To the extent that humans are also treated in these ways I object to that, too, but again, out of sympathy, and not considerations of fairness.

Let me give some examples of discourse that clearly show the sort of direct responsiveness I am talking about. A 1983 study on the psychology of slaughter contains quotes from college students who worked on a farm as part of their curriculum. One 19-year-old woman wrote:

> The first time I went into the slaughter room I had just haltered and pulled a steer into the waiting line. I could tell that the steer sensed what was going to happen to him. He was doing anything to get away. Then when I walked to the slaughter room I was amazed at the amount of blood. It was an awful feeling to look at that steer with its eyes open and his feet pointing up, so I had to look at the ceiling. Mr. ———told me to cut off the head with a saw. I couldn't do it so I left. I guess slaughtering affects me more than the usual person because I raised calves for 4-H at home and became quite attached to them—but I *don't* butcher them.[9]

A 19-year-old man wrote:

> It's pretty gross. I don't like having the dry heaves all day. Plus, I feel really bad for the cow. It's bad seeing a big animal turned into hamburger.[10]

The reactions described here are not comparative judgments of justice, such as "cutting off this steer's head is wrong because we don't do that to humans," but rather revulsion at bloodshed, pity for an animal struggling for his life, memories of animal friends, a sense of the loss and the waste of "a big animal turned into hamburger"— all elements of caring. Now these students do not identify themselves as animal liberationists, but the reactions they describe do not differ essentially from the reactions on which animal liberation is often based. Consider the following statements by people who do support animal liberation, either partially or completely:

> The production-line maintenance of animals ... is without a doubt one of the darkest and most shameful chapters in human culture. If you have ever stood before a stable where animals are being fattened and have heard hundreds of calves bleating, if you can understand the calf's cry for help, then you will have had enough of those people who derive profit from it.
> I eat meat but rarely veal.... I could never bring myself to slaughter a cow. This is very difficult to do to any animal that one has taken care of for a long time.[11]

> Ninety percent of all pigs are now raised in indoor, near-dark, windowless confinement sheds.... I respond on an emotional level with horror at what each individual pig is subjected to and sympathize with each pig, whose extreme sociability is evidenced by these animals' increased popularity as pets.... As a lactating mother, I empathize with the sow whose reproductive freedoms have been denied and whose nursing experience seems so wretched. As a consumer and a vegetarian, I visualize this information when I witness people buying or eating "ham," "bacon," or "sausage."[12]

> I was one morning, while studying alone in the Natural History Museum, suddenly disturbed by a frightful burst of screams, of a character more distressing than words can convey, proceeding from some chamber on another side of the building. I called the porter in charge of the museum, and asked him what it meant. He replied with a grin, "It is only the dogs being vivisected in Monsieur Beclard's laboratory." ... Therewith he left me, and I sat down alone and listened. Much as I had heard and said, and even written, before that day about vivisection, I found myself then for the first time in its actual presence, and there swept over me a wave of such extreme mental anguish that my heart stood still under it.... And then and there, burying my face in my hands, with tears of agony I prayed for strength and courage to labour effectually for the abolition of so vile a wrong, and to do at least what one heart and voice might to root this course of torture from the land.[13]

No comparisons of human and animal treatment, or fixation on one's own consistency—upon seeing or hearing how animals are abused, there is an immediate reaction directed against that treatment, and based on that reaction, a moral judgment and decision to act.

In response to the criticism that their justice approach misses the fundamental importance of direct sympathetic responsiveness in the actual motivations of activists, Regan and Singer could point out that their work is not descriptive but normative—that is, that they are not trying to describe animal rights activists and their psyches[14] but, rather, to set out the best reasons we have for accepting the animal rights position. Such a response would be inadequate in two ways. First, it is doubtful that justice-based arguments do present the best reasons for animal liberation, given that those arguments are unsound, as I have shown above. More importantly, this response would incompletely characterize the projects Singer and Regan take for themselves, since, besides attempting to construct sound arguments, both writers explicitly indicate that they also want to further the animal liberation movement. This second part of their project, I would suggest, makes it incumbent upon them to attend to the actual motivations of activists. Arguments with little relation to the ethics of those who already affirm animal liberation are unlikely to bring new members into the movement or to help present activists maintain their commitment. Those of us who write or speak to move others should make presentations consonant with the real processes by which individuals come to reject animal farming, vivisection, and hunting.

In fact, Regan and Singer believe that they *are* taking these processes sufficiently into account in constructing their justice-based arguments. Each believes that sympathetic responsiveness to animals is an insufficient basis for the development of an animal rights perspective in most individuals. They feel that justice-based argumentation, or what they call *reason*, is necessary to augment people's sympathies. I will now describe why they believe this and why I think they are mistaken.

Regan questions whether an ethic of care can "go far enough."[15] He asks:

> What are the resources within the ethic of care that can move people to consider the ethics of their dealings with individuals who *stand outside* the existing circle of their valued interpersonal relationships? . . . Unless we supplement the ethic of care with some other motivating force—some other grounding of our moral judgment—we run the grave risk that our ethic will be excessively

Justice, Caring, and Animal Liberation (1992) | 85

conservative and will blind us to those obligations we have to people for whom we are indifferent.

Nowhere, perhaps, is this possibility more evident than in the case of our moral dealings with nonhuman animals. The plain fact is, most people do not care very much about what happens to them. . . .

And thus it is that a feminist ethic that is *limited to an ethic of care* will, I think, be unable to illuminate the moral significance of the idea that we (human) animals are not superior to all other animals.[16]

To remedy this supposed limitation of the caring approach, Regan suggests the marshaling of *consistency* arguments such as those I have already discussed.

Singer does "not think that an appeal to sympathy and goodheartedness alone will convince most people of the wrongness of speciesism."[17] He places his distrust of the caring approach within a sociobiological framework. In *The Expanding Circle* he argues that humans are disposed toward kin altruism, reciprocal altruism, and group altruism, and that these dispositions can be explained in evolutionary terms. Singer sees the capacity to reason and the practice of reason-giving as evolving independently of the evolution of our sympathetic dispositions. Reason, however, can act to override narrow sympathies, to expand our consideration beyond that yielded by kin, reciprocal, and group altruism. Singer argues:

> Altruistic impulses once limited to one's kin and one's own group might be extended to a wider circle by reasoning creatures who can see that they and their kin are one group among others, and from an impartial point of view no more important than others.[18]

So, for Singer, humans have evolved instinctive capacities to respond sympathetically only to a few individuals closely similar to or associated with themselves. Therefore reason, in the form of the principle of equal consideration of interests, must be applied for consideration to be extended to other clans, races, and species.

Given their low estimation of the human capacity to sympathize with nonhumans, we can understand why Regan and Singer might feel that their justice-oriented approaches to animal liberation are essential. If people do not care for animals, the supporters of animal liberation cannot presume that such affections are present in those they are trying to persuade. At best, they can assume the presence of some concern for humans and use this concern as a fulcrum, trying to impel their interlocutors to animal liberation through charges of inconsistency. This is precisely Regan's and Singer's justice-based strategy.

Now, I can understand how one might conclude that people do not care about animals, given the existence of such horrendous institutions as vivisection, factory farming, and sport hunting. Regan's and Singer's accounts, however, involve an oversimplistic understanding of the limitations of people's sympathies. For Regan it is a "plain fact" that people do not care about animals, while for Singer it is a genetic fact. On the contrary, I contend that this state of affairs is not "plain" but rather elaborate, and it is not genetic but socially constructed. Animal exploitation thrives not because people fail to care, but in spite of the fact that they do care.

The disposition to care for animals is not the unreliable quirk of a few, but is rather the normal state of humans generally. As Andrée Collard puts it: "Our common bond with animals is *natural* (of nature), *normal* (of the norm), and healthy *(wholesome)*."[19] If we shift our attention away from animal exploitation to other cultural phenomena, we can see the strength and depth of the human-animal bond. I will mention just four examples:

(1) *Animal companions.* The practice of befriending animals, in its cross-cultural prevalence and its frequently avid pursuit, demonstrates the strength and depth of human interest in and affection for nonhuman animals. Approximately half of all contemporary Americans and Europeans live with nonhuman animals, or "pets," at any given time. Many Westerners do keep animals merely as status symbols, objects of domination, emblems of masculinity, or even as pieces of furniture. More commonly, however, the animals we live with are seen as companions and family members. In one survey, for example, companionship, love and affection, and pleasure, ranked respectively as the top three self-reported "advantages of owning a pet."[20] Indigenous people also commonly befriend nonhuman animals. And as in the industrialized West, when they do so their animal companions receive great attention and affection, and are viewed as family and community members.[21]

(2) *Therapy.* Many people either socially withdrawn or in depressed states have been helped through the companionship of animals. These people were unable to interact positively with other humans, but could establish a connection with a friendly animal, often a dog or a cat.[22] This reinforces what most of us already recognize, that

bonds with animals are sometimes *easier* to establish and maintain than bonds with humans.

(3) *Rescue.* You may recall from 1988 the plight of three California gray whales off the coast of Point Barrow, Alaska. The iceholes through which the whales were surfacing to breathe were in the process of freezing over, which would result in the whales drowning. A rescue attempt was mounted, which ultimately cost $5.8 million and directly involved local subsistence whalers, professional biologists, environmental activists, 150 journalists, the oil industry, U.S. National Guard, and the U.S. and Soviet federal governments.[23] If we ask why the rescue was pursued at such great lengths, a cynical answer in terms of the self-interest of the participants would be to some extent correct. But to leave it at that would give a very superficial and distorted understanding of the final cause of the rescue. The participation of these groups in the whales' rescue served their interests only by virtue of a deep and widespread concern for the whales' well-being among people generally. The media, for example, cannot play to emotions people do not have: whale rescues boost ratings because people care about whales, especially whales who have become individualized through their special circumstances.

(4) *Expiation.* James Serpell describes the almost universal presence, in cultures that hunt or slaughter animals, of mechanisms for mediating the guilt that such exploitation engenders.[24] Mechanisms that soothe the consciences of those who harm animals take many forms. Consider the following: many African tribes perform elaborate cleansing and purification ceremonies after killing an animal, others apologize to the slain. Ancient Babylonian priests, as part of the rite of animal sacrifice, would whisper in the slaughtered victim's ear: "This deed was done by all the gods; I did not do it." The Nuer people of the Sudan justify their consumption of cattle blood by claiming that periodic bleeding is beneficial to the animals' health. The Ainu of Japan also claim to benefit the bears they eat by maintaining that bears want to return to the spirit realm from which they came.[25] Western civilization has its own expiatory myths, most outstandingly the biblical fable of divinely granted dominion over animals, and the scientific denial of animal subjectivity (originally expressed as *Cartesian animal automatism*, now more circumspectly maintained as *operational behaviorism*).

All these rituals and myths serve in some way to reduce the guilt feelings of those who harm animals. The general occurrence of guilt-mediating mechanisms around systems of animal exploitation contradicts the notion that humans are naturally indifferent toward animal welfare. People are generally inclined *against* harming animals: otherwise, there would be no need for social mechanisms that make killing somewhat more bearable—the exploitation of animals would be as straightforward as, say, drinking water or breathing air.

Attention to social phenomena such as befriending animals, therapeutic human-animal relationships, animal rescues and the ubiquity of expiatory mechanisms around animal exploitation brings a realization of the depth of the human-animal connection. This realization shifts the question, from Regan's and Singer's "How can we get people to oppose animal exploitation, given that they don't care?" to "How does animal exploitation continue, given that people do care?" The answer I would give to this latter question is that animal exploitation continues with great difficulty. Enormous amounts of social energy are expended to forestall, undermine, and override our sympathies for animals, so that vivisection, animal farming, and hunting can continue.

It is worth examining the mechanisms developed for subverting opposition to animal exploitation—the vast scope of these mechanisms underscores the continual threat human sympathies pose to the animal exploitation industries. Moreover, knowledge of the strategies used to block sympathetic opposition to animal exploitation focuses activism. Rather than constructing justice-based arguments with a view toward charging animal exploiters with inconsistency, we might better resist those corporate and personal manipulations deployed to forestall the expression of our sympathies for animals in animal liberationist politics.

Perhaps the most significant mechanism for forestalling opposition to animal exploitation in our society is reference to supposed divine permission. The idea of a biblical mandate to dominate animals can be applied in defense of any of the animal exploitation industries. Of course, this attempt to pass responsibility to God begs the question of our responsibility for choosing to affirm a nominally anthropocentric religion rather than an explicitly vegetarian religion such as Jainism. Also, Christians or Jews who might attempt to defer responsibility for animal exploitation to God are acting in bad faith, insofar as they are denying their responsibility for choosing to emphasize one biblical passage over another—for instance, Genesis 2:4–25 (in which animals are created after man, to be his helpers) rather than Genesis 1:1–2:3 (in which animals are created before humans, and are recognized as good independently of their relations with humans).

The deferral of responsibility for human exploitation of animals to God is naggingly incomplete without some suggestion as to why God would give "dominion" to humans. Men in the West have filled in this lacuna through the meticulous elaboration of a theory of nonhuman inferiority based on their supposedly deficient rationality. I argued above that if people are determined to maintain a notion of nonhuman inferiority, we cannot prove them to be inconsistent. In that sense we cannot prove that humans and other animals are moral equals. It is crucial to recognize the converse, however—namely, that neither can human superiority be objectively proven. Even if one could show that normal adult humans are more rational than nonhuman animals, there is still the insuperable problem of proving that beings of greater rationality have a right to exploit beings of lesser rationality.[26] The doctrine of human supremacy may be consistent, but so is its denial—justice-based arguments fail on *both* sides of the animal rights debate.

Regarding other animals as subhuman is thus more a choice than a recognition of some objective fact. In this context James Serpell's work is extremely significant.[27] He points out that regarding others as subhuman is a very potent mechanism for emotionally distancing ourselves from them. Moreover, he argues that only in cultures that have domesticated animals do people regard animals as subhuman. From these two observations he infers that we denigrate animals *because* we domesticate them—without this denigration, our sympathies would more seriously interfere with the work of slaughtering an animal who has come to trust us through a previously established relationship of feeding and protection. If he is correct here, then the notion of nonhuman inferiority is a thoroughly political doctrine propagated to facilitate animal exploitation. I noticed in my own case that once I became vegan, the idea of nonhuman animals as inferiors seemed not so much false as *meaningless*—since I no longer have a personal interest in the continuation of animal exploitation, the question of whether other animals are our inferiors is moot.

Divine permission and nonhuman inferiority are the most generally applied techniques for forestalling sympathetic opposition to animal exploitation. Each of the major animal exploitation industries—animal farming, hunting, and vivisection—also develops its own particular protective devices. Though these devices differ in their specific content, the various industries tend to follow a common set of strategies, such as: promulgating a cover story, denying the harm done to the animals, denying the animals' subjectivity, and derogating human sympathies for animals. Each of these strategies works through one of two processes: either by blocking some part of our awareness of what is happening so that sympathetic connection with the suffering animals cannot arise, or by providing strong disincentives for acting on any sympathetic feelings we may still have. The extensive network of academics, scientists, marketing experts, and popular writers who set themselves the task of easing the public mind shows that those in the business of exploiting animals have no doubts about the human tendency to sympathize with animals.

Cover stories. Industry cover stories work to disincline us from sympathetic intervention. They all say in effect, "Well, there may be animals being harmed here, but what we're doing is so important, you better let us continue." The cover story for the animal farming industry, of course, is that they are providing food for people. Human consumption of animal flesh is portrayed as an unremarkable given, leading to a consumer "demand" for meat that simply must be met. For example: "[slaughtering] work is honest and necessary in a society which consumes beef"[28] and "the most commonly reported justification for slaughtering ... was that people eat meat, so that slaughtering must be done by someone."[29] This story obscures the crucial facts that the taste for meat is culturally variable, not innate, that animal flesh is not a nutritional necessity for humans (indeed, the standard North American flesh-based diet is unhealthy), and that the animal farming industries do not passively respond to some mass insistence for meat, but rather actively construct markets for their products in order to accumulate profits.[30]

Animal vivisectionists similarly claim to be providing for significant human needs, in this case, our health needs. This story has successfully preempted sympathetic opposition to their routine confinement, injury, and killing of animals, inasmuch as most people who have awareness or concern about animal vivisection at all tend to oppose only the most egregiously cruel and useless experiments, but support the continuation of all the medical experimentation we have been told is so "necessary." Vivisectionists respond to any challenges to animal experimentation by publicly pronouncing that we would all be dying earlier if not for their work, as in the following public service announcement made by former U.S. Surgeon General C. Everett Koop for the National Association for Biomedical Research:

> When I was born there was no vaccine for polio, no antibiotics, no way to treat diabetes or heart disease. As a result our life expectancy was just 52 years. Today, thanks to animal-based research, that figure is more than 72 years, which means that even those against animal research live to protest at least 20 years longer.[31]

Such fear-mongering, though invaluable for maintaining funding and public support, is scientifically invalid insofar as crediting increased life expectancy to "animal-based research" ignores contributions from public health improvements and from non-vivisectionist research.[32] Koop's analysis also completely passes over the iatrogenic effects of vivisection—the many ways people have been harmed by medicines developed through animal experimentation. We really do not know whether the animal vivisection paradigm has been more beneficial than harmful to society as a whole. Modern medicine, including animal vivisection, is a hierarchically organized male-dominated practice oriented around the control and invasive manipulation of bodies. This practice has developed at the expense of and in opposition to the previously existing woman-centered healing practices that were holistic, noninvasive, and community-based.[33] We simply cannot say what the overall health of our society would be if the enormous resources poured into modern medicine over the last century had instead been used to support women's ways of healing.

Defenders of the hunting system have faced an even greater challenge than vivisectionists and animal farmers. How do you explain the social necessity of men killing animals for the sheer joy of it? So far, they have come up with two cover stories: hunters kill animals for meat, and we need the hunting system to control population levels. Both these stories are exact reversals of reality. In many U.S. states we are told that deer population levels are so high that we must have a hunting system. Apart from sliding over the fact that in the U.S. deer are only two percent of the animals killed by hunters (most of the animals killed are doves, rabbits, squirrels, quail, pheasant, and ducks,[34] and it is never claimed that they are overpopulated), this statement disingenuously obscures that deer population levels are high *because* men like to kill bucks. Wildlife managers manipulate flora, exterminate natural predators, regulate hunting permits, and even at times breed and release deer, all in order to maintain herd sizes large enough to insure what they call a "harvestable surplus" of the animals men most like to kill.[35]

Most Americans support hunting for meat, but oppose hunting for trophies.[36] This is understandable: since most Americans eat the flesh of slaughtered animals, to oppose those who purportedly hunt for meat would put them in the awkward position of opposing fellow meat-eaters who at least do their own killing. Hunters are well aware of this fact and use it to deflect criticism of their sport. One hunting defender supports a growing practice among wildlife managers by advocating the self-conscious control of terminology to shift the connotation of hunting from pleasure to food-procurement:

> Consider dropping the word "sport" to refer to hunting. Fish and game departments are quietly changing the vocabulary of hunting; for instance they are replacing an emotional word such as *kill* with *harvest*. The word *sport* has many negative connotations when it is used to describe hunting. I have heard that the California Department of Fish and Game is phasing out the term *sport hunting*.[37]

This hunter's concern with "emotional" vocabulary shows his awareness of what motivates animal liberationism.

It is not that hunters simply talk about eating their "harvest," as often as possible they in fact do eat the flesh of killed animals in order to excuse their blood sport to the public (and to themselves):

> Using venison as a basic source of food gives the sport of deer hunting a sound, utilitarian foundation. We must remember that the non-hunting public does not accept deer hunting for either recreational purposes or antler collecting; the non-hunting public, however, accepts hunting when it is done to put deer meat on the table. As an old buck hunter once exclaimed: "If you don't eat it, don't shoot it."[38]

A glance at any of the innumerable hunting magazines on the stands clearly reveals the primary reasons men hunt—for the thrill of a challenging conquest, for the male bonding derived through cooperative killing, and for the male status gained through "antler collecting." It is not that men hunt to get meat, just the reverse, they eat the meat in order to hunt—that is, in order to gain ex post facto legitimation for the hunt itself. Hunters admit this most often when talking to each other, as in the following statement from Ted Nugent's *World Bowhunters Magazine:*

> Nobody hunts just to put meat on the table because it's too expensive, time consuming and extremely inconsistent. Everybody bowhunts because it's FUN![39]

Denying the harms. Representatives of all the animal exploitation industries attempt to deny the harms done to animals. Toward this end there is routine and self-conscious use of euphemisms:

A recent edition of the British *Meat Trades Journal* recommended a change in terminology designed to "conjure up an image of meat divorced from the act of slaughter." Suggestions included getting rid of the words "butcher" and "slaughterhouse" and replacing them with the American euphemisms "meat plant" and "meat factory."[40]

Similarly, vivisectors do not kill their animal subjects, they "dispatch," "terminate," or "sacrifice" them; while hunters are only "harvesting," "bagging," or "taking" the animals they shoot to death. This manipulation of language becomes manifestly deceitful, as when a fur industry spokeswoman recently spoke of animals trapped or anally electrocuted in order to sell their fur for profit as being *euthanized,* a word that actually means "killed painlessly to relieve suffering."[41]

Vivisectors routinely hide their injurious work, by restricting tours of research laboratories to the holding facilities, by attempting to block media portrayals of animal vivisection[42] and, notoriously, by the process known as *debarking:*

> Recently I visited the compound where animals are "conditioned" for the ordeal of experimentation at the University of California laboratories at La Jolla. There were well over a hundred dogs, all large: collies, German shepherds, huskies, and others. But there was not a sound from the four rows of crowded kennels: the helpless victims had their vocal chords severed, which rendered them truly voiceless.[43]

If we cannot see them or hear them, we cannot sympathize with them, a point well appreciated by the founder of professional vivisection, Claude Bernard. He remarked that "laboratories are no less valuable to us for sheltering overly impressionable people."[44]

Hunters often attempt to minimize the harm they inflict by suggesting that death by bullet or arrow is less traumatic than the deaths these targeted animals would otherwise experience. This ignores the fact that human hunters specifically target large, healthy animals, exactly those least likely to die from disease, starvation, or nonhuman predation. One hunter, attempting to deflect sympathetic opposition to his sport, goes so far as to call deaths from bowhunting *peaceful:*

> if a bullet or broadhead [arrow] damages a vital organ, hemorrhagic shock will send a deer to a swift, painless, and peaceful demise. If

the general public was aware of this knowledge, their minds could be set at ease and a major argument against hunting would fall by the wayside.[45]

The general public should also be aware that for every deer killed and retrieved by a bowhunter, one is hit and wounded but not retrieved.[46]

Especially by the animal farming industry, for whom every person is a potential customer, there is an ongoing effort to deny the harms done to animals. In recognition of the potential business loss threatened by a growing movement that explicitly advocates vegetarianism based on compassion for animals, meat industry representatives are attempting to frame animal farmers as the true animal welfarists:

> Our research shows that we can prevent long-term erosion of public support for the livestock industry. . . . We've got to do a better job of communicating with consumers, and letting them know that we, not the animal rights groups, are the animal welfare experts.[47]

The above quote is from the videotape "Animal Welfare," produced by the National Pork Producers Council and distributed to pig farmers. The narrator of this videotape mentions that newspaper, radio, and television ads are being produced and placed to communicate a message:

> Livestock producers have always been dedicated to the humane treatment of the livestock in their care; first of all, it's good business. But more importantly, producers know it's the right thing to do.

The usual argument is that farmers have a business interest in maintaining the well-being of their "stock" since sick or unhappy animals do not grow as well or cannot be sold and therefore are not as profitable. In fact, today's factory farming systems (that is, farming systems in which animals are kept confined and immobilized for long periods of time) do turn a profit from animals generally unhealthy and in pain, since economies of scale allow the absorption of the early deaths of a small but not insignificant percentage of the animals. Pharmaceuticals are used to keep animals crowded in noxious conditions growing long enough to turn a profit.[48] Even in the most oppressive animal farming industries, such as egg laying by hens in battery cages, animal agriculturalists attempt to deny the harms to the animals: "Generally we try to provide exactly the environment which is most suitable for the bird."⁴⁹ One farmer, who keeps calves tethered for the entirety of their brief lives (so their unexercised flesh has the distinctive veal taste of a newborn), struggles to deny the cruelty:

> Some feel that it's rather cruel to the animals to keep them tied in there, but I point out that they're in a controlled environment, they, uh, the weather is, they never get real hot, or in the winter time it's never zero weather, there's no fly problem. And as a result, really, they've got a pretty good life in there ... although they are chained.⁵⁰

This description evokes the old halcyon picture of the farming family living in harmony and mutual affection with their animals. Even for traditional, less intensive animal farming, this picture erases the realty that farmers profit from the slaughter and commodification of farmed animals. The image persists, nonetheless, particularly in children's books. Animals, including farmed animals, are a favorite subject of children's books, but farmed animals are never shown being branded, castrated, debeaked, or slaughtered, they are always portrayed as protected friends.

For instance the book *The Midnight Farm* (described on its jacket as "a loving vision ... of nature and humanity in harmony"), after visiting the peacefully sleeping farmed animals, concludes with the poem: "Here in the dark of the midnight farm/Safe and still and full and warm/Deep in the dark and free from harm/In the dark of the midnight farm."⁵¹ Who are such images protecting from consciousness of the violent reality intrinsic to animal farming—children, or the parents who buy these books for them?

Denying animal subjectivity. In the second Genesis creation story, God created the animals as helpers for the lone first man, then brought them to the man, "to see what he would call them; and whatever the man called every living creature, that was its name" (2:19). Today some people call other living creatures "livestock," "game," "pets," "laboratory animals," "meat," and so forth, and in so doing they deny the animals' own subjectivity. Projecting human uses for these animals into their definitional essences forestalls sympathy by blocking our awareness that other animals have interests of their own that are systematically overridden by the animal exploitation industries.

Those who take an active role in exploiting animals—vivisectors, hunters, farmers, purchasers of meat—are particularly likely to apply the notion that the purpose of an animal's life comes from human interests. As one animal vivisector puts it:

> I grew up in the city, but we were very close to a farm community, and my values are farm values. I grew up thinking of animals as *for* something: some were for food, others were pets ... each type of animal had its purpose. I think of laboratory animals in the same way: they were bred for research; that's what they're for.[52]

The hunter and writer Archibald Rutledge expressed a similar "that's what they're for" philosophy: "certain game birds and animals are apparently made to be hunted, because of their peculiar food value and because their character lends zest to the pursuit of them."[53]

It can certainly smooth the exploitation process to heed the counsel of agricultural scientists: "Forget the pig is an animal. Treat him just like a machine in a factory." And "the modern [egg] layer is, after all, only a very efficient converting machine."[54] Animals come to be seen as voids, beings whose inherently empty lives are redeemed only through the imposition of human purposes. A veterinarian giving me a tour of a vivisection facility pointed to a group of beagle puppies in a cage and said, "Beautiful, aren't they? At least this way they have a purpose." One vivisection textbook defines "experimental animal" as "part instrument, part reagent, a complicated and incidentally sentient system."[55] The breeders who supply vivisectors further this view of animals as tools with advertisement headlines such as "Now available in standard and stripped down model" (referring to guinea pigs with and without hair), "Building a Better Beagle," and "Specific Disease Model Available."[56]

Apparently the mere erasure of animal subjectivity is not sufficient to allow us to accept the harms done to animals—in each of the exploitation industries we see a definite construction of the animals as *willing* victims. The day after the 1990 March on Washington for the Animals, I heard a National Public Radio reporter discuss a slaughterhouse tour she had taken to see for herself whether the animal liberationist call for vegetarianism had any merit. She declared that she could see in the terrified animals' eyes that they would willingly go to slaughter if they understood the human purpose being served. This fantasy of animals longing to end up dead on our plates is promulgated through industry advertisements, such as the long-running Charlie the Tuna campaign (in which the fish repeatedly tries to get hooked), and more recently, a Domino's Pizza billboard displaying winged bison stampeding toward the viewer over the caption: "Buffalo Wings—They Come When You Call."[57] Just for kids, the meat industry provides schools with coloring books that show steers grinning all the way to the "meat packing company."[58]

A study of the advertisements placed by breeders who supply vivisectors found that the animals are often portrayed as "team-players" who facilitate the researchers' work in much the same ways as colleagues or other employees.[59] Advertisement copy describes the animals as research collaborators (mice are said to be "stalking cancer," a guinea pig is called the "unsung hero of bronchial research"). Animals are posed so as to appear to like laboratory equipment such as cages and jars of chemicals. Sexist stereotypes are used to portray animals as wanting to please the vivisector: "Female animals are shown as subordinate and desiring to please. 'Real anxious to please you' reads the text of an ad that has a drawing of a pregnant hamster in a maternity dress."[60]

A portrayal of the hunted animal as willing victim is apparently fairly common historically. In his book *In Defense of Hunting*, James Swan attempts to revive this myth, pointedly asking animal liberationists "How do you know that the animals really support you?" and sympathetically citing the beliefs of several indigenous cultures that "the success of the hunter is not just a reflection of skill but the choice of the animal."[61] Significantly, Swan also notes that the modern hunter "is challenged not so much by fear as by overcoming guilt," echoing Ortega y Gasset's contention that "every good hunter is uneasy in the depths of his conscience when faced with the death he is about to inflict."[62] The ascription of uneasiness about inflicting harm makes sense, for how else can we understand the recurring image of the willing animal victim—an image in such blatant contradiction to the coercive intent of the cattle prod, the vivisectors' cages, the hunters' bullets, arrows, lures, and camouflage—except as a salve to the troubled conscience?

Derogating sympathies for animals. When harms to animals are effectively concealed or animals are convincingly portrayed as tools or willing victims, our sympathies cannot become engaged. But these strategies are not always successful.[63] When people do sympathize with exploited animals, the animal exploitation industries protect themselves by belittlement, intending that such sympathies never be taken seriously as the basis of individual action or public policy. An example of this is the characterization of antihunters as "Bambi-lovers." Many people have been emotionally affected by the movie *Bambi*, and it is true that the movie is biologically inaccurate (deer do not really speak). But the suggestion that opposition to hunting stems solely from exposure to anthropomorphic depictions of animals derides sympathies for targeted animals by implying that they are always irrationally based.[64]

The derogation of sympathies is typically done in gender-specific ways. Women's expressions of sympathetic concern are expected and tolerated, but they are not respected; rather, they are dismissed as female hysteria.[65] Men, on the other hand, are typically not allowed to express such feelings. For example, on one occasion at the annual live pigeon shoot in Hegins, Pennsylvania, a boy, about eight years old or so, was crying at the sight of pigeons being blown out of the air and then having their heads pulled off by "trapper boys." As this boy turned away in tears, his dad grabbed and twisted his head, forcing him to face the shooting, saying "you *will* watch."[66]

In the vivisection industry, founded by men and still male-dominated, compassion for animals has been simultaneously feminized and derogated:

> As a young graduate student, he was running an experiment with rats. The experiment was over, and he was faced with the problem of what to do with the animals. He approached his advisor, who replied, "Sacrifice them." ... "How?" asked my friend.... "Like this," replied the instructor, dashing the head of the rat on the side of the workbench, breaking its neck.... My friend, a kind man, was horrified and said so. The professor fixed him in a cold gaze and said, "What's the matter, Smith, are you soft? Maybe you're not cut out to be a psychologist!"[67]

In this environment "softness" is not allowed, so men who would be scientists must establish their hard callousness, and women who would be scientists must be like the men. Susan Sperling tells of her graduate work in the early seventies under the supervision of a "great man" and "famous scientist." Her severe emotional turmoil after dissecting eight guinea pigs led her to conclude that she "would disappoint the famous man."[68]

This traditional association of scientific capacity with masculine callousness can become a liability, however, when vivisectors, like hunters and animal farmers, choose to deflect outside criticism by depicting themselves as compassionate animal welfarists. In an article published by the trade journal *Lab Animal*, Arnold Arluke reports that of the 130 vivisectors he interviewed, only 10 percent immediately admitted to any guilt feelings about their work, but after being given ample space to examine their feelings, fully 90 percent expressed what most people would consider "guilty" feelings.[69] Rather than continue the traditional suppression of such sympathetic hesitations, however, Arluke recommends that vivisection facilities support the expression of these feelings and help to manage and "redefine" them through stress management workshops and individual counseling. Apparently, many vivisectors somehow believe that feeling guilty about their work means they may be doing something wrong. But Arluke suggests that institutions remedy this moral naivety by teaching vivisectors that "guilt is really an indicator that the lab workers' consciences are alive and well."[70] Arluke makes clear that improving vivisection's public image is the ultimate point of bringing vivisectors' uneasiness out of the closet:

> If [institutions] acknowledge and attend to the types of uneasiness that I discussed earlier, it is possible that scientists and technicians may become more human in the public's eye.[71]

Insofar as deep and recurring hesitations are not recognized as the basis for compassionate social change, they are degraded. Thus Arluke's strategy continues to degrade the human disinclination to harm animals, no longer as a feminine vice, but now as a commendable stress to be therapeutically managed in the course of animal exploitation business as usual.

■ ■ ■

To sum up: justice-based arguments for animal liberation fail. But my own experience and the reports of others lead me to believe that direct responsiveness to need is more central to animal liberationism than concerns about consistency anyway. And contrary to the suppositions of the justice-oriented writers, the capacity to respond to animals is a deep and recurring feature of human life. That is precisely why societies that institutionalize animal exploitation must and do find ways to override and to undercut our sympathetic capacities.

The lesson I draw from this analysis is twofold, part heartening and part sobering. Heartening is the realization that the ethical basis of animal liberation is very simple and generally moving. A straightforward presentation of what the animals are like and what is done to them by hunters, vivisectors, and farmers can stir people, especially if the ideologies that block sympathy are simultaneously debunked.

But sobering is a grasp of the nature of the social forces allied against a true perception of animals, against an understanding of what is done to them, against the possibility of acting from compassion. The substantial power of institutionalized animal exploitation sustains ignorance, promotes fear, rewards cruelty, and punishes kindness. So, though the ethics of animal liberation are inherently appealing, the obstacles placed in the way of radical social change based on sympathy are daunting. This is not to say that those obstacles are insurmountable. Moving away from unsound and irrelevant justice-based arguments, taking instead a caring perspective that expects a human-animal bond, and that challenges any hindrances to this natural, normal, and healthy bond, allows us to continue moving toward a society in which animals have been liberated from human tyranny.

Notes

1. Carol Gilligan, *In a Different Voice: Psychological Theory and Women's Development* (Cambridge: Harvard University Press, 1982).
2. Tom Regan, *The Case for Animal Rights* (Berkeley: University of California Press, 1983).
3. I should note that Regan does not neglect this response to his argument: section 5.5 of his book is a rejection of Kantianism. Close examination, however, reveals that his argument against Kantianism is question begging. See Brian Luke, "From Animal Rights to Animal Liberation: An Anarchistic Approach to Inter-Species Morality" (Ph. D. diss., University of Pittsburgh, 1992), 15–16.
4. Peter Singer, *Animal Liberation* (New York: Avon Books, 1975), chap. 1.
5. See Singer, *Animal Liberation,* and Singer, "The Significance of Animal Suffering," *Behavioral and Brain Sciences* 13 (1990): 9–12; and Tom Regan, "An Examination and Defense of One Argument Concerning Animal Rights," *Inquiry* 22 (1979): 189–220.
6. R. G. Frey, "Vivisection, Morals and Medicine," *Journal of Medical Ethics* 9 (1983): 94–97.
7. Ibid., 97.
8. Bonnie Steinbock, "Speciesism and the Idea of Equality," *Philosophy* 53 (1978): 256.
9. Harold Herzog, Jr., and Sandy McGee, "Psychological Aspects of Slaughter: Reactions of College Students to Killing and Butchering Cattle and Hogs," *International Journal for the Study of Animal Problems* 4 (1983): 129–30.
10. Ibid., 130.
11. Konrad Lorenz, *On Life and Living* (New York: St. Martin's, 1988), 113.
12. Carol J. Adams, "Ecofeminism and the Eating of Animals," *Hypatia* 6, no. 1 (1991): 134.
13. Anna Kingsford, quoted in John Vyvyan, *In Pity and in Anger: A Study of the Use of Animals in Science* (Marblehead, Mass.: Micah Publications, 1988), 122–23.
14. A la Susan Sperling, *Animal Liberators: Research and Morality* (Berkeley: University of California Press, 1988), or Keith Tester, *Animals and Society: The Humanity of Animal Rights* (London: Routledge, 1991).
15. Tom Regan, *The Thee Generation: Reflections on the Coming Revolution* (Philadelphia: Temple University Press, 1991), 95.
16. Ibid., 95–96.
17. Singer, *Animal Liberation,* 255.

18. Peter Singer, *The Expanding Circle: Ethics and Sociobiology* (New York: Farrar, Straus & Giroux, 1981), 134.
19. Andrée Collard with Joyce Contrucci, *Rape of the Wild: Man's Violence against Animals and the Earth* (Bloomington: Indiana University Press, 1989), 70.
20. Joseph Quigley, Lyle Vogel, and Robert Anderson, "A Study of Perceptions and Attitudes Toward Pet Ownership," in *New Perspectives on Our Lives with Companion Animals*, ed. Aaron Katcher and Alan Beck (Philadelphia: University of Pennsylvania Press, 1983), 271.
21. James Serpell, *In the Company of Animals: A Study of Human-Animal Relationships* (New York: Basil Blackwell, 1986), chap. 4.
22. See Alan Beck and Aaron Katcher, *Between Pets and People: The Importance of Animal Companionship* (New York: G. P. Putnam's, 1983), chap. 8.
23. Tom Rose, *Freeing the Whales: How the Media Created the World's Greatest Non-Event* (New York: Birch Lane, 1989).
24. Serpell, *In the Company of Animals*, chaps. 10 and 11.
25. Ibid., 145, 168, 153, 148.
26. See Elizabeth Dodson Gray, *Green Paradise Lost* (Wellesley, Mass.: Roundtable Press, 1979), chaps. 1 and 2.
27. Serpell, *In the Company of Animals*, pt. 4.
28. William Thompson, "Hanging Tongues: A Sociological Encounter with the Assembly Line," *Qualitative Sociology* 6 (1983): 215.
29. Herzog and McGee, "Psychological Aspects of Slaughter," 130.
30. See, for example, John Robbins, *Diet for a New America* (Walpole, N.H.: Stillpoint, 1987); Jeremy Rifkin, *Beyond Beef: The Rise and Fall of the Cattle Culture* (New York: Dutton, 1992); and Carol Adams, *The Sexual Politics of Meat: A Feminist-Vegetarian Critical Theory* (New York: Continuum, 1990).
31. "Animal Welfare" videotape, National Pork Producers Council.
32. See Robert Sharpe, *The Cruel Deception: The Use of Animals in Medical Research* (Wellingborough, Eng.: Thorsons, 1988).
33. See Barbara Ehrenreich and Deirdre English, *For Her Own Good: 150 Years of the Experts' Advice to Women* (Garden City, N.Y.: Anchor, 1978) and Marti Kheel, "From Healing Herbs to Deadly Drugs: Western Medicine's War against the Natural World," in *Healing the Wounds: The Promise of Ecofeminism*, ed. Judith Plant (Philadelphia: New Society Publishers, 1989), 96–111.
34. James Swan, *In Defense of Hunting* (New York: Harper, 1995), 8.
35. Ron Baker, *The American Hunting Myth* (New York: Vantage, 1985).
36. Swan, *In Defense of Hunting*, 9.
37. Ibid., 274.
38. Robert Wegner, *Deer and Deer Hunting: Book 3* (Harrisburg, Pa: Stackpole, 1990), 165.
39. Ted Nugent, "Fun. Good, Clean, Fun!" *Ted Nugent's World Bowhunters Magazine* 1, no. 3 (1990): 7.
40. Serpell, *In the Company of Animals*, 158–59.
41. NBC Dateline, 20 December 1994.
42. Vivisectors are not unanimously in favor of this tactic: see Deborah Blum, *The Monkey Wars* (Oxford: Oxford University Press, 1994), 160–62.
43. From a 1968 letter quoted in Vyvyan, *In Pity and in Anger*, 133.
44. Ibid.
45. *Deer & Deer Hunting*, October 1991, 51.
46. Glenn A. Boydston and Horace G. Gore, "Archery Wounding Loss in Texas," Texas Parks & Wildlife Department, unpublished report, 1986.
47. Norm Montague, Chairman of the Animal Welfare Committee, National Pork Producers Council, on the videotape "Animal Welfare," produced by the National Pork Producers Council, 1991.
48. Jim Mason and Peter Singer, *Animal Factories* (New York: Harmony, 1990).

49. "The Animals' Film," section on factory farming, available from People for the Ethical Treatment of Animals.
50. Ibid.
51. Reeve Lindbergh, *The Midnight Farm* (New York: Dial, 1987).
52. Quoted in Mary Phillips, "Proper Names and the Social Construction of Biography: The Negative Case of Laboratory Animals," *Qualitative Sociology* 17 (1994): 134.
53. Jim Casada, ed., *Hunting and Home in the Southern Heartland: The Best of Archibald Rutledge* (Columbia: University of South Carolina Press, 1992), 30.
54. From *Farmer and Stockbreeder* and *Hog Farm Management*, quoted in Mason and Singer, *Animal Factories*, 1.
55. Quoted in Collard, *Rape of the Wild*, 59.
56. See Arnold Arluke, "'We Build a Better Beagle': Fantastic Creatures in Lab Animal Ads," *Qualitative Sociology* 17 (1994): 143–58. The last example is from *Lab Animals* magazine.
57. "Buffalo wings" is an American locution for cooked chickens' wings served spicy as "appetizers."
58. Robbins, *Diet for a New America*, 128.
59. Arluke, "'We Build a Better Beagle.'"
60. Ibid., 154.
61. Swan, *In Defense of Hunting*, 121, 37.
62. Swan, *In Defense of Hunting*, 29; José Ortega y Gasset, *Meditations on Hunting* (New York: Scribner's, 1972), 88.
63. For example D. Lawrence Wieder, "Behavioristic Operationalism and the Life-World: Chimpanzees and Chimpanzee Researchers in Face-to-Face Interaction," *Sociological Inquiry* 50 (1980): 75–103,, points out that vivisectors must and do at times recognize animals as subjects, for without an awareness of the animals' subjective states they could not effectively manage them throughout the course of the experiment.
64. Matt Cartmill's book *A View to a Death in the Morning: Hunting and Nature through History* (Cambridge: Harvard University Press, 1993) contains a chapter on "The Bambi Syndrome" in which he concludes that "many hunting writers seem to think that if *Bambi* and other Disney products could somehow be suppressed, opposition to hunting would evaporate" (180).
65. I discuss these sexist dismissals and how animal liberationists might respond to them in "Taming Ourselves or Going Feral?: Toward a Non-Patriarchal Metaethic of Animal Liberation," in *Animals and Women: Feminist Theoretical Explorations*, ed. Carol J. Adams and Josephine Donovan (Durham, N.C.: Duke University Press, 1995).
66. Personal communication, Ingrid Newkirk.
67. Bernard Rollin, *Animal Rights and Human Morality* (Buffalo: Prometheus, 1981), 109–10.
68. Sperling, *Animal Liberators*, 5–8.
69. Arnold Arluke, "Uneasiness among Laboratory Technicians," *Lab Animal* 19 (1990): 33.
70. Ibid., 34.
71. Ibid., 38.

Caring for Animals (1992)

Rita C. Manning

I freely confess to being a bit tired of debates about animal rights. It seems to me that opponents of animal rights almost inevitably fall into the trap of begging the question against nonhuman animals and in favor of human animals.[1] Proponents spend so much of their time defending themselves against opponents that they don't get to spend enough time reflecting upon the real issues that confront us as we try to care for animals.[2] I am not criticizing the defenders of animals: I think that their work is crucial and effective.[3] I simply want to get on to the next stage.

In the first part of this chapter, I'm going to focus directly on concrete issues that confront us as we try to care for companion animals. I will not defend my descriptions of my companion animals' behavior, which rely on my assumption that they have a rich mental life. To those who object to my attributing intentional states to animals, I give the reply that Steve Sapontzis gives in his book on animal rights, go adopt a dog (or some other animal) and get to know it personally.[4] In the second section I will discuss other domestic animals. In the third section I will turn to a discussion of wild animals. In each of these discussions, I will be looking to extend, clarify and test an ethic of care. In the final section, I discuss the more general question of why we should care for any animals.

Caring for Companion Animals

Don't Fence Me In

Looking like a cross between a Chihuahua and a pit bull, Thorp made his appearance one evening out at the barn where I boarded

---

[From *Speaking from the Heart: A Feminist Perspective on Ethics* (Lanham, Md.: Rowman & Littlefield, 1992)]

© 1992 by Rita C. Manning. Published by permission of author and Rowman & Littlefield.

my horses. I continued to see him there scrounging food for a couple of days, but I resisted my son's pleas to take him home. Finally, my hand was forced. The owner of the barn got tired of seeing him hanging around and resolved to take matters into his own hands. When he locked Thorp up in a cage by the office while he went to get his gun, my son and I sprung him and brought him home.

It didn't take long for us to discover that he was a confirmed roamer. No fence could keep him in. We got him neutered, expecting it to change his behavior, but it made absolutely no difference.

For ten years he has "belonged" to us. During that time, he has racked up hundreds of dollars in fines for not being confined, while we tried everything we could think of to crimp his style. I reinforced the fence, tied him up, even moved to a house on two-thirds of an acre to give him room to run, but nothing seemed to help, though he did learn not to come when the dogcatcher called. The only thing that seemed to work was to keep him on a chain, but this seemed terribly cruel. I resorted to it, for a time, when his roamings inevitably took him to my neighbor's front yard at 3 A.M., where he howled at passing deer.

Finally, I gave in and let him roam. I don't know how he spent his days and nights, but he came to visit us regularly. Sometimes he would spend most of his time with us, leaving for a day or two at a time. Later, he spent most of his time elsewhere, coming to visit us every couple of weeks and staying for a day or two.

This went on for a couple of years until one morning two little girls brought him home. He had an enormous swelling under his chin, and he was thin and miserable. I took him to the vet, who diagnosed him as having either a tumor or an abscess, and who suggested exploratory surgery.

The surgery revealed an abscess, which the vet drained. Thorp was placed on two-week confinement while his wound healed. While Thorp was at the hospital, he got a present and a card signed by half the kids in the neighborhood. Later when he was able to go out for walks on a leash, he would be greeted by almost everyone we met. Obviously, he'd had a rich social life in his roaming days.

I have gone back to crimping his style. I reinforced the fence again, keep him tied up when I'm not here, take him running every day, and got him a puppy. It seems to be working, at least for the most part. He has escaped a few times, but he stays gone for only a day or so.

I'm still not sure I'm doing the right thing keeping him confined. This question does not come up with our horses, who are pathologically reluctant to leave familiar surroundings, nor does it come up with our other dog, who stirs herself only if you wave a leash under her nose. But there are real questions that I want to raise in connection with Thorp.

If we asked Thorp what he wanted, I am convinced that he would choose to roam. He is a very friendly dog and obviously values his time away from home enough to go to great lengths to escape. (He was once seen scaling a tree to vault over our six-foot chain-link fence.) He does display some conflict, though. When he makes his getaway right under your nose and you call him to come back, he looks over his shoulder and gives you a very guilty look as he keeps running, tail between his legs.

But caring does not require that we simply accede to the wishes of the one cared for.[5] Rather, we should respond in the interest of the one cared for, insofar as furthering that interest is compatible with our abilities and where this response sustains the network of care that connects us. In doing so, I should be sensitive to the relationship, and open to the possibility of compromise and accommodation.

The number of well-wishers who phoned or came by when he was sick convinced me that he had established many strong and loving relationships while he was living away from home. This concerned me, since three claims about relationships are relevant to our obligations to care. The first is that persons are, to a large extent, identified and self-identified by their relationships. This is a metaphysical view, which Michael Sandel calls the "embedded self" and which he contrasts with abstract individualism.[6] Second, whether or not the embedded-self picture is correct, persons can only thrive in relations with others. Finally, relationships with others place special obligations on us. I don't intend to defend these claims here; instead I want to see if they can be applied to dogs.

I don't know what to say about how dogs develop a sense of self. I am not even sure that they can be said to have a sense of self, though I do think we can say that they have selves in the sense of having a center of awareness. The effect of training on dogs and other animals suggests that this limited self is highly influenced by the context in which it develops.[7] Still, I am not sure whether this first claim about relationships should be applied to dogs.

The second claim—that persons can only thrive in relationships with others—can be applied to dogs who are essentially social creatures who are miserable if left alone for long periods of time. The question for Thorp, though, is not whether it is permissible to isolate him totally, but whether it is permissible to sever some of his existing relationships and limit his ability to fashion future new ones.[8]

I am inclined to take seriously the moral import of restricting Thorp's relationships, but on balance I think that this is a permissible restriction. My assessment depends, in large part, on my sense that he is relatively happy with his present life, even though it is more restricted than his earlier life.

It seems obvious that obligations are imposed by relationships. What is not obvious is what relationships create obligations. It is not even clear what counts as a relationship. I will return to this question when I discuss horses. Here, I want to focus on the obligations that I recognize as following from my relationship with dogs. I recognize an obligation to protect; to provide food, shelter, and companionship; to provide veterinary care. In so doing, I recognize an obligation to allow the dog to live a dog's life, a life that allows the dog to satisfy its desires and independently experience its life. This cuts to the heart of my dilemma about restricting Thorp. In doing so, I am concerned that I am thwarting both his desires and his ability to independently experience his life. On balance, I have decided that my obligation to protect him takes priority here, though that does not mean that my obligation to let him be a dog ceases.

It is fair to say that Thorp has some obligations too. This is a common view among people who raise what are called "working dogs." The dogs are expected to work in exchange for the care they receive, and in so doing, they are expected to display certain virtues, notably loyalty. This seems to be a fair exchange, especially in view of the evident pleasure working dogs get from discharging their obligations. The problem with Thorp is that he simply hasn't enough work to do. Serving vaguely as a watchdog does not sufficiently engage his interest. I do expect loyalty, though, and his wanderings display a lack of this virtue. If our arrangement—protection and care in exchange for some light work done with a keen sense of loyalty—is fair, then I think I am justified in enforcing its terms.

One might argue that it is not clear how a deal can be seen as fair when one of the parties is unable to refuse. To compound the problem, it is not even clear how dogs can be said to consent. I think that this objection underestimates the dog. I believe that dogs can refuse. They can run away and refuse to return and they do so. It is true that most dogs accept the deal and that they sometimes put up with terrible conditions rather than strike out on their own. I certainly do not want to deny that a dog can be broken, can lose its capacity to refuse, as can a human, but this does not show that all dogs are incapable of refusing.

The final two values for an ethic of care which are relevant here are compromise and accommodation, and these two values must be explained in terms of each other. A compromise that merely splits the difference and leaves no one satisfied is not worth making. The ideal compromise ends by accommodating everyone. The spirit of compromise and accommodation is generous and fair, and pleasure is taken in the satisfaction of the desires of others. With this spirit, compromise is often easy and pleasant. I recognize that it is often impossible to fully satisfy everyone in cases of conflict, but a compromise that accommodates everyone is less rare than we think.

A focus on compromise and accommodation reminds us that obligations are not an all-or-nothing thing. I don't discover that it is morally permissible to restrict Thorp's wanderings and give the matter no further thought, and it is not morally permissible to restrict his wanderings without regard to the means. For example, it would be wrong to keep him tied up twenty-four hours a day, or to keep him in a crate. When I restrict Thorp's wandering, I must do so in a way that accommodates him and me. I must strike a compromise.

Out to Pasture

When Champ was fifteen, I was faced with the need to retire him. I simply could not keep him comfortable enough to ride him. He had lived his entire life in a stall and paddock, and would be content to live that way until he died. There were two problems, however. One was that constant light exercise is best for an aging, arthritic horse; living in a confined space only exacerbates arthritis. Second, a stall and paddock was more than twice as expensive as the pasture, and I wanted to be able to afford a horse that I could ride.

I was terrified about putting him out to pasture. It symbolized the end of our special relationship, it made me aware of his mortality, and I was afraid he would hate it. Being turned out in a field or arena is supposed to be horse heaven, but he always hated it. He would race up and down in a panic until I came to get him. I was afraid he would see being put out to pasture as abandonment, as being turned out and forgotten.

I was also afraid he would kill himself out there. Once, he had had an injury that required being turned out for six weeks. After less than a week he ran through the fence, and it took four hours to stitch him up. Clearly, he didn't want to be out in the pasture when he could be in the barn.

After agonizing over it for months, I finally turned Champ out. First, I made sure the pasture was as safe as a pasture can be. Second, I got a tranquilizer from the vet, who assured me that if I tranquilized him and put him out while he was still groggy, he would wake up out in the pasture and be fine. For five days, he raced around the pasture in a panic. The other horses beat him up, and they chased him away from the food and water.

Around that same time, I got back a twenty-year-old horse that had been leased out. Champ and Bernard had been stabled together for years, though they hadn't seen each other for at least four years. I made arrangements to put Bernard out in the pasture with Champ. To my great surprise, they remembered each other. When I unloaded Bernard from the horse trailer, he and Champ started calling to each other. When I turned Bernard out, he and Champ ran laps around the pasture together, and from that day on they were inseparable. There was only one fly in the ointment.

Champers is a very big horse, standing seventeen hands and weighing fourteen hundred pounds at his best weight. The other six horses in the pasture included my daughter's incredibly fat pony, Billy, who should weigh about seven hundred pounds tops, and five average-size horses who should weigh between nine and eleven hundred pounds. A horse's need for food depends upon his size, his metabolism, and his level of activity. Given his much larger frame and his metabolism, Champ needed almost twice as much food as the other horses, and four times as much as the pony. Unfortunately, in a pasture situation, you cannot separate the horses for feeding. Seven large flakes of hay were thrown to the horses twice a day. Champ, being at the absolute bottom of the pecking order, was getting thinner and thinner, while the horses at the top of the pecking order were getting fatter and fatter.

I found another stable which specialized in retired horses and brood mares, but I agonized over separating Champ and Bernard. I didn't want to move Bernard, because he was being used in lessons. Not only did it help to pay his way, but it kept him in shape, and this is very important for a twenty-year-old horse.

This story does have a relatively happy ending. I moved Champ. He is now out with one old mare, and he seems perfectly happy and healthy. Bernard has adjusted, though he does not have a best friend out in the pasture anymore. He is tolerated by the other horses, so his life is not unpleasant.

This story raises several questions. The first is whether it is permissible to confine horses. Champ is a perfect example of the folly of thinking that a natural environment is best for all horses. Horses in pasture live in herds, in which they establish a pecking order. Horses on the bottom are sometimes mercilessly hounded. Some dominant horses are fair and generous, ruling with benevolence. Others are nasty and cruel, creating a dog-eat-dog atmosphere. Champ experienced both types of leaders while he was out with a herd. The first leader, who was nasty and cruel, was deposed by a new horse who came to live in the pasture. Luckily, he was fair and generous, and discouraged mayhem. Still, he did not protect Champ while he ate. He ate his own dinner and then did what dominant horses do—he chased the less dominant horses, including Champ, away from their dinners.

So a "natural" life is not always the best life for a horse. In a stall, a horse is protected from other horses; he gets to eat his meals in peace; he has a warm, dry spot to lie down in, and he has a soft bed to cushion him from the cold, hard ground.

Again, it is important to accommodate a horse. In keeping horses, we must be sensitive to their needs for companionship, for exercise, and for variety. A horse with a large stall and paddock, plenty of food and clean bedding, who can see and touch his stablemates while being protected from their biting and kicking, who is turned out regularly, and who is groomed and exercised several times a week is a happy horse. This type of horse-keeping accommodates a horse's needs for security, for comfort, and for movement.

This raises another question. If this is ideal horse-keeping, is it permissible to keep horses in less luxurious surroundings? In particular, am I cheating Champ of the comfortable retirement that he worked so hard to deserve? I must confess that I worry about this. I could have kept him in a stall and paddock, and had him turned out during the day. But doing so would have meant that I would have nothing to ride, since I could not afford to have two horses living in this style. Eventually, my craving for a horse to ride overcame my belief that I should focus all my attention on Champ. I could plead "ought implies can" here, but instead I will just admit to being human; adopting an ethic of care does not eliminate weakness of will.

The final issue I want to address in connection with this story is friendship between animals. While I don't think that horses can have the same kinds of friendships as humans can, I think it is clear enough that they do have friendships.

Aristotle described friendship as consisting of mutual good will, recognized by both parties.[9] Perfect friendship requires mutual trust, in addition to mutual good will.[10] Although horses lack the mental capacity to understand each other's good in the full-blown sense required by Aristotle for human friendship, I think horses can be friends.

There are three components of horse pairing that justify describing these pairings as "friendship." First, horses engage in behavior that resembles the behavior engaged in by humans as part of a friendship. They choose to be together. They often protect each other against more dominant horses. They seem to take pleasure in each other's company and display distress when they are separated. Second, the best explanation for this behavior is that they feel affection for each other. Third, these ties of affection are not based on mere habit or instinct, but on preference.

The close attachments horses form with other horses is not just a matter of being thrown together. Horses who are stabled next to each other are as likely to hate each other as love each other. Friendship in horses seems to be based on affection, and the object of the affection is uniquely favored.

Horses in a pasture will usually group themselves into pairs. The pairing may or may not be between geldings and mares, so a biological explanation based on sexual attraction is not the explanation for all of these pairings. Horse pairs seem to enjoy each other's company, though it is not unusual to see a pair, often a gelding and a mare, where the affection seems to be all on one side. The gelding is either more dominant than the mare and forces her to put up with him, or so in love with her that he follows her around even though she makes it clear that she does not want his company. I suspect that these pairings are based on sexual attraction, but I don't think that is the explanation for all horse pairings. Champ and Bernard are both geldings, and it is not at all unusual for geldings to pair. These pairs are often deeply and mutually devoted, as Champ and Bernard are. They spend the entire day together, often protecting each other from more dominant horses.

I am sure that explanations based on instinct or self-preservation could be offered for these pairings, but this is also true of human friendships. Although in both cases there is a biological basis, horses and humans both being social animals, I would argue that the burden of proof is on the person who claims that friendship in either case is based on mere instinct. Most would agree that human friendship is not based merely on instinct, and I think that the preference shown by two horses for each other's company is sufficiently similar to the preference of two humans for each other's company to justify calling these horse pairings friendship.

Even if I am wrong about this, the fact that the horses want to be together and are clearly distressed when they are apart is a sufficient reason for some moral concern about separating horse pairs. Do we then have any obligations to accommodate horse friendships?

I want to suggest that we get some guidance here from our more settled intuitions about whether and when it is permissible to separate human friends. Since concerns about liberty cloud the issue in the case of competent adult humans, I propose that we look to our intuitions about the permissibility of separating children from their friends.

Changes in jobs or family situations, or a concern for the safety of the child, are perhaps the most common reasons for separating children from their friends. If we think that a child is a danger to another child, we will often act to separate the child from the danger. Parents are notoriously self-deceptive both about the real cause of the danger and the efficacy of the solution, but I think that we would all agree that in most cases we would be morally justified in separating a child from a friend if that friend constituted a danger, and the danger could be eliminated by avoiding the friend.[11]

The pursuit of career or changes in family arrangements create pressures to move, and moving often necessitates the sundering of childhood friendships. My intuition here is that the importance of the career move or the need to accommodate a new family arrangement ought to be balanced against the harm to the child. This harm can be measured by appeal to two factors. The first is the strength of the bond, and the second is the difficulty of establishing similar bonds after the move. Younger children seem to have an easier time establishing new friendships and seem to grieve less at the sundering of old friendships. Adolescents seem to find the experience particularly traumatic. Even if I am wrong about the relative ease with which children make a move, I think that this is the right criterion for deciding whether a move is sufficiently harmful to outweigh the considerations in favor of the move.

Horses resemble younger children more than they resemble adolescents with respect to friendship. They do seem distressed at being separated from a friend, sometimes profoundly so, but in most cases, as with young children, they will settle down as long as they can make a new friend.

In Champ's case, the need to protect him from the more dominant horses precipitated the move, and my desire to have Bernard continue in a relatively active life necessitated separating them. But again, we have not settled the case by deciding where the right lies. In doing the permissible or even the obligatory act, we must do it in the right way. We must compromise with an eye to accommodation. In this case, I felt obligated to make sure that both Champ and Bernard either found a new friend or at least an accepting gang. I first turned Champ out with one gelding. In two days, it became clear that this pairing would never be a friendship. Next, we moved him in with a very submissive gelding and mare. Champ beat up the gelding, so we moved the gelding and let Champ have the mare to himself. Within a few days, it was clear that Champ had bonded to the mare, and, though the mare seemed less than enthusiastic, she seemed to accept him. Without the responsibility of protecting Champ against the more dominant horses, Bernard slipped into the herd. Though neither of them has the same relationship with any other horse that they once had with each other, they seem to be doing reasonably well and Champ has put on weight.

The Old Gray Mare

When I decided to retire Champ, I began to look for another horse. Clover, an eight-year-old mare boarded in our barn, was for sale. She had raced for two years and then sustained a fairly serious injury. She was not given the recommended treatment, but instead turned out to a pasture. Luckily, the injury healed reasonably well on its own. Eventually, she found her way to an agent for sale. At first, Clover was a basket case, but the agent was a kind and patient woman who worked with her until she was relatively tame. She was sold to a beginner, but returned when she proved to be too green for the green rider. When I tried her out, she was a model of kindness and trust. I loved riding her. She was incredibly willing and responsive.

I had her on approval for two weeks before I had her vetted. Unfortunately, the vet discovered arthritic changes in her ankle that made her unsuitable for my purposes because he doubted that she would stay sound for long. Since I already had one lame horse, and I didn't want to gamble with having two, with great sadness I decided not to buy her. At this point, the agent realized that she would be hard to sell. The only thing the agent wanted was a good home for her, but even that was questionable with the diagnosis of unsoundness. Months went by. Every time I walked past her stall, I felt guilty. Eventually, someone bought her. I have no idea if she is still sound, or where she will end up if and when she does go lame, but I sincerely hope she is doing well.

Three questions arise here. The first is, is it morally permissible to use animals when the use poses a risk of injury or death? The second question, which also comes up in connection with my story about Champ, is, does an animal have a right to life and, if so, what does this entail? The third is, how and when does someone become responsible for the care of an animal?

Describing an interaction with an animal as a "using" implies that the animals have not clearly consented to the interaction. It doesn't follow that the animals resent the use or that they find it unpleasant. Some would argue that any use of an animal is wrong.[12] Though I have some sympathy for this view, I think that one consequence of ending all uses of animals would be to sever many of the relationships and ties of affection that exist between humans and animals. This would be a tragedy, not just for the humans but for the many animals who flourish in these relationships.[13]

Yet I worry about the moral status of riding horses, because I am aware of the potential for injury that this practice involves. Horses die in traumatic accidents or they are killed ("put down") when it is decided that the injury will never heal well enough to warrant continued use. The more common scenario is a stress injury, caused by continued stress on a bone or a joint. These injuries often leave horses unable to be ridden ("unsound"), and often in pain.

We can do a great deal to reduce the incidence of both traumatic and stress injuries, but we cannot prevent them entirely.[14] Although I think it very likely that we would greatly reduce the incidence of both types of injuries by not riding horses, even horses in pasture suffer both kinds of injuries. The only sure cure is to stop breeding horses. I think this would be a great tragedy both because horses make wonderful friends and because they are unique parts of the natural world. They are exemplars of majestic values: beauty, dignity, strength, courage, speed, endurance, and agility. Although these qualities would continue to exist in the wild horses who would likely continue to survive, we would have far fewer encounters with horses.

One could argue that horses are not only willing partners, but sometimes more committed to the endeavor than their riders. Race horses, for example, are often praised for their heart, for their desire to run. The tragic death of Go For Wand at the 1990 Breeder's Cup was described as caused, in part, by the filly's incredible desire to run in front.[15]

If caring for animals requires that we take their good as a starting point, that we respect them as partners in the relationship, then I think that we have to stop using them in ways that pose a clear risk of serious injury. The death of Go For Wand was not an anomaly. Horses die every day on tracks all over the country. We race two-year-olds whose bodies and minds are three years from maturity. We race them on good and bad footing, we race them when they are sore and we throw them away when we are through. There are good people in racing, people who love horses, but the industry itself leads to the death of far too many horses. The factors that lead to this include the great cost of keeping a horse in training, the industry's inability to oversee the many horses running and training, the technical difficulties in identifying the many and constantly new drugs given to horses, and the proliferation of lower-rung tracks. Horses that were once retired to a good life as riding horses now race till they are completely used up. At that point, if they are lucky, they are humanely destroyed.

If racing is clearly beyond the pale, then what about other horse sports? What do we say about eventing which requires tremendous efforts of horse and rider at the advanced level? What about show jumping, dressage, cutting, and endurance riding? Each of these sports poses a risk of injury to horse and rider.

It does seem to me that an ethic of care requires that we actively seek to avoid risk of injury insofar as we can. This might require that we refrain from all use except gentle trail riding. In any case, we can do much to reduce injury: training systematically and carefully, providing the best footing we can, shoeing our horses regularly, and not letting our horses get overtired and susceptible to injury. We should be sensitive to our horse's own talents and weaknesses. However, none of these precautions can prevent all injuries. In the event of an injury, we must provide for the appropriate care, in the best interests of the animal. Finally, we should never have a horse killed merely to save on the feed bill. A horse injured enough to be unsound through our use deserves a loving retirement.

This leads to my second question, does a horse have a right to life? If a horse does have a right to life, is it a negative or positive right?[16] Horses bred for human use are often unable to survive in the wild. They might have feet that require shoes, a body size that requires more food than forage alone could provide, a coat that must be supplemented by blankets. For these horses, any meaningful right to life must be a positive right. But meeting the needs of a horse is a demanding and costly enterprise.

An ethic of care would be silent about the abstract right to life, whether positive or negative, though it could shed light on particular cases. Our intuitions about these particular cases generate rules of thumb to help us think about similar cases. I want to think about Champ and Clover here.

I have no doubt that Champ is entitled to my care until his life is more painful than pleasant. I take it that I owe him this much, since he probably sustained his arthritic changes through my use. But I have no intention of letting him suffer; when I judge that he is no longer enjoying his life, I will put him down. I think that I must do this if my care for him is to be guided by what is in his interest.

Although I think Clover is also entitled to this kind of care when she is no longer sound, I am not convinced that I am obligated to provide it. Here I turn to my final question: When am I obligated to care?

The answer to this question turns on four factors—need, ability to fill needs, existence of other avenues for filling needs, and relationship. With Champ the need is clear. It is also clear that I can fill this need. Next, no one else is available to fill this need; no one in his/her right mind would be willing to take on an unsound horse who required so much care. Finally, Champ and I have a relationship; he matters to me and I think I matter to him. We have a history together. In this case, the need was caused, in part, by me, but this need not be the case. Horses get old even if they never become unsound. Even in those cases, the strength of the relationship creates an obligation to care.

Clover was a different case. Her situation was not so bleak; the vet was optimistic that she could do well as a trail horse. As a result, I was not the only person who could fill her needs. Finally, she and I did not have the same kind of relationship that Champ and I had. The difference turned, in part, on the absence of a ritual transferring her to me. In the case of horses, the ritual is the economic transaction involved in buying a horse: the prepurchase exam, the bill of sale, the check. This ritual has a significance among horse people; it conveys a new sense of responsibility toward the animal.

But a new question presents itself here: Why should I be sensitive to these rituals? Why should *I* care what they signify? This hints at the larger question: Why *should* I care about animals?

One might point to the similarities between some animals and human animals, or to the role of animal care in building human character. We see both of these appeals in the classic tradition of horsemanship, which has many contemporary spokespersons:

> First of all, horses are like people. . . . As a group, they are probably more generous, more forgiving, and less neurotic than people, but they are all different, and all living. This means that our relationship with each of them will be different from our relationship with every other, and that it will be a dynamic relationship, subtly or perhaps not so subtly changing every day.[17]

> When Alexander the Great tamed Bucephalus he succeeded, not because of the Macedonian prince's firm seat, but because of his mental attitude, for he had thought his way into the horse's soul.[18]

> The attitude of an equestrian must change and grow to include patience, humility, tolerance, optimism, consistency, and empathy with the horse. . . . Without them no outstanding achievement is possible in riding, which is a character-improving art form.[19]

A second reason might be that some animals, at least, are as valuable as humans, and thus legitimately entitled to care. Anyone who thinks that humans are more valuable than horses, for example, needs to provide an account of what makes this so. I would be tempted to add that this account ought to make sense to my horse as well as to me. This account should include a list of characteristics a good creature ought to have. I suspect that such an account will not be forthcoming, because an account of what a good X is requires that we say what Xs are about; what role they are asked to play in the natural world. If we spell this out, we can see how to talk about a good horse or a good person, but it is not clear to me that we will be able to say that a good person is more good than a good horse.

The Ethics of Magic[20]

I draw one general conclusion from these stories and that is that we need a new understanding of our place in the universe.[21] I see my place as a member of the natural world.[22] As such, I must face my fellow creatures with humility. I have already referred to this sense of connection to the natural world. Here I want to discuss and defend it in more detail. I am adopting Starhawk's use of the term "magic" to convey this sense of the place of humans in the universe.

"Magic" is a word that has been revalued and reclaimed in much the same way as "witch" has been revalued and reclaimed. Starhawk, a witch, feminist peace activist, and ecofeminist, describes magic thus:

> Magical techniques are effective for and based upon the calling forth of power-from-within, because magic is the psychology/technology of immanence, of the understanding that everything is connected.... Magic is art—that is, it has to do with forms, with structures, with images that can shift us out of the limitations imposed by our culture in a way that words alone cannot, with visions that hint at possibilities of fulfillment not offered by the empty word. And magic is will—action, directed energy, choices made not once but many times.[23]

Magic involves two elements. The first is the recognition that everything is connected, that the earth is a living body, that it and all its parts are sacred. The second is the way we come to this realization, and how we transmit it to others. Here, visions, rituals, and involvement with the natural world are the media.

Horses have been my teachers. Through my relationships with horses, I have come to see the world as a living body and I have come to view it as sacred.[24]

The destruction of the earth has been encouraged by images of the earth as a machine to be manipulated or as a woman to be raped. It is perfectly obvious that the animals do not enjoy being tortured and that the earth is a less lovely place now than it was before being raped. If we begin to think of the earth as a living body of which we are a part, we will not be able to continue with our policies of wanton destruction.

Starhawk, in a recent talk, invited the audience to think of our own bodies as our culture thinks of the earth.[25] Here is a spot on my back. I don't use it very much; I can't see it. I might as well use it as a sacrificial area and put out cigarette butts here. How is this different, she asked, from setting aside a part of the earth as a repository for nuclear waste? If the earth is a living body, no parts will be sacrificial areas. When I practice magic, she said, I see the earth as a living body; I see it as sacred; I see its parts as sacred.

So far we have seen that companion animals matter to humans because we can have rich and complex relationships with them; relationships characterized by communication and ties of affection, relationships that deepen our sense of connection to the natural world.

We have also seen why this sense of connection to the natural world is valuable. This provides further support of an ethic of care. Let us now turn to other domestic animals.

Other Domestic Animals

J. Baird Callicott argues that domestic animals, which he describes as human artifacts, have less value, all things considered, than wild animals.[26] This follows from his commitment to a land ethic, first articulated by Aldo Leopold, which holds that things are right when they tend to "preserve the integrity, stability, and beauty of the biotic community."[27] Domestic animals are plentiful and in competition with wild animals for resources. There is a crucial difference, however, between a land ethic and an ethic of care: while both assume underlying and fundamental connection between all parts of the natural world, an ethic of care puts a premium on the relationships between humans and other members of the biotic community, both human and nonhuman.

As Mary Midgley points out and as I hope my examples illustrate, our relationships to some domestic animals are rich and complex, and deepen our sense of connection and commitment to the rest of the biosphere.[28]

I think there are important differences between animals raised for food and animals that are primarily companion animals. My hunch is that tending cattle or pigs doesn't provide the same complex relationship and concern for nature that tending companion animals does. This is not to suggest that tending these animals always, or even usually, prompts a concern for nature. I also agree that watching wild animals can provide a powerful experience of connection with and concern for nature. But companion animals seem to matter to us in a more immediate way. This suggests that an ethic of care would provide a unique place for them in our moral universe. But does it give us any guidance about other domestic animals?

Eating Pismo

My sister and brother-in-law, who teaches agriculture, bought a piglet with the intention of rearing it for food. They named it Pismo, and they and their three children took excellent care of it until it was time to slaughter it. Shortly after the deed was done, we came to visit. Gracing the dinner table that night was Pismo. As they ate, they commented on what a good pig Pismo was. They spoke of him with affection even as they lifted his flesh to their mouths.

I must confess that this only deepened my commitment to not eating meat, but the question I want to ask here is, is eating meat consistent with an ethic of care toward animals? Can I be acting to further the interests of an animal by killing it and eating it? I think the answer to this question is no. But I think it is possible to give an animal care that is sensitive to its interests up to the moment of slaughter. In this sense, Pismo was cared for.

In a world where humans needed meat to survive (and perhaps other animal products as well), this would not seem so paradoxical. I have in mind here some of the Native American rituals of slaughter. In such rituals, killing is entirely compatible with a sense of the sacredness of the animal , and a sense of connectedness to the animal. What is curious about the claim that Pismo was cared for even though he was destined for the freezer was that we know that we don't need meat to survive. Interestingly enough, they never raised another pig or any other "meat" animal. I take it that this is evidence of the difficulty of truly caring for an animal destined for slaughter.

Wild Animals

The Cats in Golden Gate Park

One day while walking through the Japanese Tea Garden in Golden Gate Park, I came upon a very sick cat sitting in the middle of the path, shivering and drooling. I was afraid to pick it up because I suspected it had rabies, so I called animal control. They were short-handed, so they suggested that I put it in a box and bring it in. In the meantime, the cat slipped back into the bushes and I was unable to find it. There are hundreds of cats in Golden Gate Park, and virtually every other park in the area has its share. They live on mice and trash and handouts from humans, and I suspect that their lives are much shorter and certainly much harsher than their domestic cousins. There are two questions I want to raise here. The first is, what makes an animal a companion animal as opposed to a wild animal? The second is, what are our obligations to wild animals?

Callicott argues that domestic animals are mere human artifacts, products of hundreds of years of selective breeding, too stupid to survive on their own. He concludes on the basis of this that they are less valuable than wild animals because they are too numerous and compete with wild animals for resources. Let us suppose that he is right that they are human artifacts. Doesn't this suggest that we have special obligations to domestic animals? After all, their stupidity and inability to get along without us is our fault.

According to Callicott's analysis, the cats in Golden Gate Park are domestic animals, since they or some of their ancestors are the results of human breeding programs. He would decide what to do with them by appeal to the land ethic: are they contributing to the integrity, stability, and beauty of the biosphere? Here we would need to ask how they affected the other species in the park. If it turned out that they were not contributing to the biosphere in the appropriate ways, then we should get rid of them. There is nothing in Callicott's view that suggests that we cannot do this humanely, of course, but we can assume that most of these "wild" cats will never be suitable for companion animals.

I think that it matters, from the perspective of an ethic of care, that these are descendants of companion animals and that we are in some sense responsible for their fate. The question is, what do we do with them? Do we treat them as wild animals? This brings us to my second question, what are our obligations to wild animals?

On one reading, the case of wild animals provides a reductio for an ethic of care. How can we maintain that our commitment is to an ethic of care and allow wild animals to exist in the cruel way they do in nature? In nature, animals often live short and painful lives. Predators prey on other animals, eliminating the old, the young, the sick, and the slow. Is this compatible with a vision of an ideal caring world? I shall begin to answer this question by telling another story.

The Wild Dogs

I recently watched a show narrated by Jane Goodall about her research on wild dogs of the African plain.[29] One of the wild dogs was a female who had a litter of puppies that were rejected by the pack. The mother tried to protect her puppies, but she was powerless against the pack. Finally, only one puppy was left. The pack moved on and the puppy, unable to keep up with the pack, was left behind. At this point, the Goodalls interceded and saved the pup. They were later able to successfully place the pup with another pack in the wild. I don't think that there was any question that the Goodalls were horrified by the killing of the puppies, but it did not occur to them to interfere. They explained this by pointing out that they did not know the significance of this event. Perhaps it was a way to protect the pack from overpopulation and the cruel deaths that could face them all if the pack grew beyond a manageable size. They were reflecting the sense of humility appropriate to a recognition of the vast ignorance that humans have about the natural world. But they were also expressing a hope that the natural world would "get it right," that somehow the way things worked out in nature were for the best.

I would give a similar answer to the criticism that an ethic of care provides counterintuitive advice about how we ought to treat wild animals. I don't think that an ethic of care requires that we interfere with nature, because we simply don't know the effects of such interference. Further, the attitude of humility and awe is the appropriate one to take toward the natural world. However, when we have some sense of how things will turn out, when we see the part we have played in creating cruelty in the natural world, then I think our intuitions are different. This brings me back to the feral cats. We think we know something about cats, having lived in very close proximity with them for perhaps thousands of years. Although we know they can survive, albeit in a limited way, in the wild, we feel some connection to them, and we feel responsible for their fate. Whether or not they are human artifacts (I favor the alternative explanation that we simply evolved together), our shared history creates a sense of obligation.

I don't mean to suggest that our obligations are exhausted by our attachments. Further, I recognize that there are many people who feel this same sense of attachment and obligation to other members of the natural world. The main point I want to make here is that an ethic of care is not incompatible with a respect for the workings of the natural world, even where they seem cruel.

Conclusion

What follows from all this about my obligations toward the natural world? The first thing I want to point out is that there is something odd about putting the question this way. It suggests two things: first, that I am not part of the natural world, and second, that I am in a superior position vis-à-vis the natural world. I get to make the decision about what the appropriate moral relationship between humans and the rest of the natural world should be. I would want to put the question differently: given that I am part of the sacred body of the earth, how ought I to acknowledge the other parts of this sacred body? It seems to me that I must recognize them as sacred. This requires, first of all, that I recognize them, that I look and see the other creatures that make up the body of the earth, that I look and listen and find the earth. I think that the appropriate moral attitude is humility and care.

There are no transcendent moral principles that should govern our behavior. This implies a dualism that magic rejects. There is no absolute to contrast with our finite, no soul to contrast with body, no God to command. We are the sacred body, we shape the consciousness of this body. There are many things that we will not do if we are informed by this vision of our place in the universe, and the state of the body and the damage to its parts will guide our moral actions.

We could appeal here to the argument that Thomas Nagel gives for altruism.[30] Nagel invites me to see other persons as standing in a morally similar relation to me as my future selves stand in relation to my present self. If I see myself as part of the living body of the earth, I will see myself as connected to other persons, animals, and the earth itself in a way very similar to my relationship to my future self.

Elsewhere I offered an argument for a general obligation to care.[31] We can extend this argument to defend an obligation to care for the creatures of the earth (and other things as well: communities, values, objects, and the like), but if one is convinced of the truth of magic, then one is committed to treating the natural order as sacred. This is simply an implication of the view; if I do not treat the natural order as sacred, then I do not understand the concept of the sacred. But I am willing to admit that not everyone shares this sense of the earth as sacred. The pitiful state of the earth and her creatures is testimony that this view is not the dominant one. How then can we argue that this is the view that should be adopted?

One strategy is to suggest that the consequences of not doing so are frightening. The problem is that the consequences are not as frightening to someone who does not share this conception. Someone who views the earth as exploitable and who views humans as the rightful dominators of nature will be concerned about the possibility of diminishing resources and the effect on humans of the diminished carrying capacity of the earth, but any reference to the sacredness of the earth becomes simply a metaphor to encourage us to improve the situation of human inhabitants of the earth. This does not require that we see the earth as truly sacred.

I would be inclined to take a different tack, and I would argue that those who have had a relationship with animals, with the earth, become, through these relationships, aware of the sacredness of the earth. I am willing to admit that this moral epistemology runs the risk of being circular. Farmers might point out that they are in contact with the natural world every day and that they have never seen the sacredness of a pig. I don't want to deny that this is possible; indeed, I suspect it is a common attitude for exploiters of the natural world. I am willing to argue here that the exploitive activity interferes with the recognition of the sacred. In short, exploiters are not truly relating to the natural world. Having a relationship with an animal or some other natural object then is a necessary and sufficient condition for recognizing the sacredness of the earthly body, but recognizing the sacredness of the earthly body is a necessary condition for having a relationship with the natural world.

The important epistemological questions become: How do I know that the earth is sacred? How do I know how to live even if I know that the earth is sacred?[32] To the first question I would say that you will come to know this if you make the attempt to relate honestly with the natural world. To the second question I would say that choosing a style of life requires an understanding of your proper role in the universe and deciding what to do in concrete situations requires reflecting upon that larger commitment and carefully listening to the creatures who are with you in that concrete situation. In deciding, remember that you are part of the sacred body and that you are shaping the consciousness of this body with your decisions.

Notes

1. R. G. Frey seems to be an example of this in assuming that the focus should be on whether animals have interests. See R. G. Frey, *Interests and Rights* (Oxford: Clarendon, 1980).
2. Peter Singer is a notable exception. His *Animal Liberation* (New York: Avon Books, 1975) was tremendously influential.
3. S. F. Sapontzis, *Morals, Reason, and Animals* (Philadelphia: Temple University Press, 1987), does an excellent job responding to criticisms of moral treatment of animals.
4. Ibid.
5. I needn't address the larger question of paternalism toward humans here since Thorp, being a dog, does not know about the dangers outside our yard and hence needs to be protected. He might have a better idea in some respects than I do of what's out there, having actually lived a dog's life on the streets. (During his convalescence, well-wishers told us stories of Thorp's life on the run, and he certainly found nice places to hang out. It appears that he had at least two other

families in addition to ours. He wasn't eating out of trash cans.) Still, though I think he does understand cars, mean dogs, and the dogcatcher, he does not understand illness and injury. He didn't bring himself home knowing that he needed veterinary care. And veterinary care is not something that he can find for himself the way he can find food, water, and shelter.
6. Michael Sandel, *Liberalism and Its Critics* (New York: New York University Press, 1984).
7. For a philosophically rich discussion of animal training, dog and horse training in particular, see Vicki Hearne, *Adam's Task: Calling Animals by Name* (New York: Vintage, 1982).
8. I think that this is an important question for humans as well, and I think it is curious that restrictions on one's actions are seen only as restrictions upon liberty and not as restrictions on relating. It seem to me that the most painful thing about prison would be the severing of relationships. The restriction on liberty might be merely instrumentally bad, in large part because it requires severing or crippling relationships.
9. Aristotle, *Nichomachean Ethics*, bk. 8, chap. 2 (Indianapolis and New York: Library of Liberal Arts, 1962).
10. Ibid., bk. 8, chap. 3.
11. The qualification is important here, because the danger might be caused through no fault of the child. For example, suppose I live in a racist society in which attacks on interracial pairings were common, should I separate my white child from his/her African-American friend? I am inclined to say no, depending upon the age of the child and the severity of the attacks, but I think this is an enormously difficult issue.
12. Some ecofeminists defend this view. Marti Kheel, for example, made this observation in conversation.
13. Mary Midgley describes in rich detail the relationships that can exist between humans and animals and asserts that our moral obligation to animals follows from the possibilities of such relationships. *Animals and Why They Matter* (Athens: University of Georgia Press, 1983).
14. Dr. James Rooney makes many suggestions for improving our horse management in order to reduce the incidence of injuries, especially on the track. See *The Lame Horse: Causes, Symptoms, and Treatment* (North Hollywood, Calif.: Hal Leighton, 1973).
15. *Sports Illustrated* describes the tragic death of Go For Wand in "Requiem at Belmont," November 5, 1990.
16. Although I use the language of rights here, I find it more natural to focus on my obligations to care. For a discussion that focuses on animals rights, see Tom Regan, *The Case for Animal Rights* (Berkeley: University of California Press, 1983).
17. William Steinkraus, *Riding and Jumping* (Garden City, N.Y.: Doubleday, 1961), 11–12.
18. Waldemar Seunig, *Horsemanship* (Garden City, N.Y.: Doubleday, 1960), 47.
19. Charles de Kunffy, *Creative Horsemanship* (South Brunswick and New York: A. S. Barnes, 1975), 15.
20. This is the title of chap. 3 of *Dreaming the Dark* by Starhawk (Boston: Beacon, 1989).
21. John Passmore offers a history of philosophical (and other) attempts to place a value on the world. *Man's Responsibility for Nature* (New York: Scribner's, 1974).
22. There is some tension here between my sense of self as member of the natural world and my sense of self as related to specific creatures. This tension is evident in the debate between animal rights defenders and environmentalists. See J. Baird Callicott, *In Defense of the Land Ethic* (Albany, N.Y.: SUNY Press, 1989) for a defense of an environmental ethic that does not require vegetarianism. See also

Aldo Leopold's classic defense of an environmental ethic, *A Sand Country Almanac* (Oxford: Oxford University Press, 1949).
23. Starhawk, *Dreaming the Dark*, 13–14.
24. Starhawk used this example in a talk at San Jose State, March 6, 1989.
25. Philosophers are understandably impatient with insights that are not discursive. Symbolic natural and artificial languages are the traditional language of philosophy. But here we face a dilemma. If we use magic, in speaking another kind of language with animals, in understanding our relationship with the earth, we must either say that we're not involved in an activity that can be characterized as philosophy and cannot even be discussed from a philosophical point of view, or we adopt the standards of philosophy and say that we are not really speaking with animals or understanding anything. But the second option has consequences. Philosophers like to think that they and they alone have the answers to many crucial questions: whether animals feel, whether they reason, whether the earth is a machine or a living body. These are not idle questions, for answering them tells philosophers whether these things have value. And, as the experts on these questions, philosophers speak for our culture. It is no accident that we call upon our philosophers to answer such questions: their historical commitments to a certain kind of discourse spell doom for the animals and the earth. Animals do not speak to us in any sense that philosophers understand, they do not have those properties that philosophers have singled out as conferring value. Since it matters to me, to women, to animals, and to the earth that we begin to see the creatures of the earth as valuable, I want to take up the cultural space of the philosopher: I want to speak to this issue and I want to practice magic.
26. Callicott, *In Defense of the Land Ethic*, chap. 1.
27. Leopold, *A Sand Country Almanac*, 225–26.
28. Midgley, *Animals and Why They Matter*.
29. *The Wild Dogs of the Serengeti*.
30. Thomas Nagel, *The Possibility of Altruism* (Princeton, N. J.: Princeton University Press, 1970).
31. Rita Manning, *Speaking from the Heart: A Feminist Perspective on Ethics* (Lanham, Md.: Rowman & Littlefield, 1992), chap. 4.
32. Christopher Stone tries to answer this question in *Earth and Other Ethics* (New York: Harper, 1987).

The Caring Sleuth: Portrait of an Animal Rights Activist (1994)

KENNETH SHAPIRO

*M*anny Bernstein recalls the German shepherd who licked his toddler face when he fell off his tricycle, and the sadness he felt looking at a gorilla confined in a barren cage at the local zoo. Shortly after, at the age of six, Bernstein donned a Batman cape inscribed with the letters AP (for "animal pals") and liberated Goldie, his goldfish, into a nearby drainage ditch. Ingrid Newkirk, as a girl of fourteen in India, watched in horror through a window as an ox cart driver prodded his beast by thrusting his driving stick deep into the animal's rectum.

As adults, Bernstein and Newkirk are both animal rights activists. When he is not treating patients suffering from multiple personality disorder, clinical psychologist Bernstein edits and produces a journal on alternatives to animal-based research. In various arenas, he pressures research psychologists to alleviate animal suffering and, eventually, liberate their own Goldies. As founding director of People for the Ethical Treatment of Animals, Newkirk's window now opens onto the interior of a busy office complex, but she is still drawn to suffering. She oversees a sophisticated investigatory apparatus that can reach into the locked files of the posh headquarters of a Paris-based cosmetic firm to find and follow an intricate trail: from the sales records of a shampoo, to one of its ingredients, to a laboratory

---

[*Society and Animals* 1994, vol. 2, no. 2]

© 1994 by White Horse Press. Published by permission of author.

that tested it on the shaved skin or eyes of rabbits locked in stockades.

Who are the animal rights activists, both national leaders and grassroots workers? How do they live? What is their daily round? How did they get to be that way? This study attempts to answer these questions through the application of a method of qualitative analysis.

Neither Bernstein nor Newkirk is a "terrorist in a stocking mask," nor a "little old lady in tennis shoes." The latter discriminatory stereotype trivialized an earlier animal protection movement by portraying its adherents as ineffectual. More recently, the press's conferral of the terrorist image on contemporary animal advocates has threatened to discredit the current movement by marginalizing it as extremist.

Recent literature in the social sciences attempts to provide a more veridical understanding than does at least the sensational press. In his study of the activists who attended a major demonstration in Washington, D.C., Scott Plous found a diversity of viewpoints, lifestyles, and objectives that do not fit neatly into any one image or stereotype.[1] Susan Sperling found parallels between the contemporary movement and an earlier Victorian antivivisectionist movement.[2] Both arose in response to new scientific and technological developments viewed as dangerous or undesirable. In both movements, the concern with animal suffering is a convenient symbol for a broader evangelical and millenarian agenda. While distinguishing between welfarists, pragmatists, and fundamentalists, James M. Jasper and Dorothy Nelkin described the movement as a moral crusade.[3] Its members have genuine moral concerns and are on a well-intentioned quest. However, they also, particularly the fundamentalist subgroup, are quixotic and uncompromising. While not necessarily antiscience, their views of animals are not based on scientific understanding. Harold Herzog likened activists to religious converts, noting that they experience changes in fundamental belief and lifestyle, have a missionary zeal, and are often dogmatic in their positions.[4]

Other studies do not support the association of animal rights activism with fundamentalism. R. T. Richards and R. S. Krannich found that activists typically belong to several other socially progressive or liberal movements, notably civil rights, environmentalism, and feminism.[5] Robert Kimball found that liberal members of Congress vote for proanimal legislation more often than do conservative members.[6]

In his review of Sperling's work, Charles Magel identifies a pitfall of some of the social scientific literature:

> My last and most important criticism is that Sperling ignores the essential nature of the animal rights movement. In her analysis, animals [and animal experiments] are symbols of something else. Very much to the contrary, the animal rights movement is concerned about the *animals themselves*.[7]

Of course, these are not mutually exclusive possibilities—the animal as a symbol *and* as an object of concern in his or her own right.

However, in the present study, I try to stay close to the immediate experience, activities, and personal development of activists. While my approach may miss some of the historical backdrops, cultural contexts, and symbolic meanings of the movement, it hopefully provides a portrait of animal rights activists that captures how they manifestly relate to animals, the movement, and its opposition.

Method

The data consist of two sets of materials. First, a set of fourteen autobiographies of leaders of the movement, all save one published between 1986 and 1991 in *Between the Species: A Journal of Ethics.* As the distribution of this publication is largely within the movement, the personal accounts are probably more confessional than promotional or tactical in intent. All but three are U.S.-based.

The second set consists of twenty-one survey protocols of grassroots activists solicited at an animal rights conference in 1991. The survey consisted of two semistructured questions: (1) Describe the situation in which you first realized that you had a special interest in nonhuman animals. Estimate your age at the time. (2) What is it like to be an animal rights activist? Respond by describing a recent situation in which you clearly were being an animal rights activist. What was going on, what were you experiencing?

Consistent with other studies reporting on the gender constitution of the animal rights movement, the sample was predominantly female (23 of 35).[8] However, again consistent with other findings, the leadership was predominantly male (9 of 14). Most of the grassroots activists had at least a college education, and most spent at least thirty hours per week in their movement activities.

The analysis of data employed a modified version of a method developed in phenomenological psychology.[9] As described by Fred J.

Wertz, in this qualitative method the investigator "demarcates meaning units" in each individual protocol to arrive at a description from a "first person perspective, more or less in the subject's own language."[10] The investigator then performs a "psychological reflection" to describe each individual account "*as experienced, as behaved,* or more generally *as meant* by the subject."

Finally, through a second psychological reflection, the investigator arrives at a more generalized account of the structures of experience exemplified in the individual accounts. The primary finding of the study is a statement of this "general psychological structure." This description consists of the psychological meanings of the structure, and is not necessarily in the subjects' own language.

This method and form of results keys on the similar or common structures in the phenomenon under investigation. Of course, this does not exclude the existence of variations within the common constitutive or defining features.

Phenomenological psychology is an interpretive approach that accepts the necessity of investigator participation and denies the objectivistic ideal of detachment (compare participant observation in anthropology and ethnomethodology in sociology). It is, then, appropriate for the investigator to explicitly identify his or her point of view in approaching the study. In addition to being trained as a phenomenological psychologist and a clinical psychologist, for the past twelve years I have been involved in the animal rights movement at both the national and grassroots levels.

Results

Here I present a summary account of the experience of being an animal rights activist. The materials examined suggested organization into five themes. Following this description of the general psychological structure of this experience, the balance of the paper provides further exposition, discusses selected issues raised by the theme, and speculates about connections to other general psychological literature:

> *An animal rights activist is an individual (1) whose primary concern is caring about animals; (2) who is primed to see suffering in animals; (3) who aggressively seeks out and skillfully investigates situations in which animals are suffering; and (4) for whom such caring, seeing, and seeking become pervasive aspects of daily life, embodied in his or her lifestyle. (5) Tensions created by the appar-*

> ent contradiction between an attitude of caring and the aggressive exposure of human-originated animal suffering are resolved in one of several ways: embracing, suppressing, or losing touch with the caring.

Caring

Animal rights activists have a caring attitude toward nonhuman animals. Consider *attitude* here not as a specific belief about something—the earth is flat—but as something like the adolescent behavior of "copping an attitude." We are all familiar with the infuriating tone, disdainful gesture, slouching posture, and "cool" response to even the most serious situations that characterize teenagers. While limited to a particular developmental stage and most often transparently defensive, such an attitude is a pervasive personal style—a habitual way of experiencing and expressing the world through the body.

Caring about nonhuman animals is such an attitude. It means being attentive to them in a watchful and concerned way. More than just curiosity or interest, it is a positive inclining or leaning toward them, a sympathy for them and their needs. A caring attitude is one of continuous sensitivity and responsiveness, not a transitory awareness or a momentary concern.

Most activists report having some inkling of the attitude of caring in childhood, often between the ages of five and ten years old. Although not consciously adopted, for some it immediately becomes a habitual style, pervasively coloring most aspects of life. Others report a recrudescence, a more conscious adoption of the attitude in early adulthood, perhaps an intellectual awakening occasioned by reading Peter Singer's *Animal Liberation*.[11]

For other activists the moment of discovery is decidedly less cerebral. Like Newkirk's, the awakening of Helen Jones, founder of the International Society for Animal Rights, took place in an atmosphere of trauma:

> My first awareness of animal suffering was at the age of four or five. My mother took me to a zoo. As we entered we saw a large white rabbit, transfixed with fear, in a cage with a snake. Within a second or two the snake began swallowing the rabbit.... My mother never again entered a zoo. I did, many years later, only to collect evidence for a legal case.[12]

Michael Fox, senior staff member of the Humane Society of the United States, describes a very different experience:

> My first encounter with the miraculous and the mystical was as a child. I had a playground full of miracles. . . . Like the child in Walt Whitman's poem who went out into the world and became all that he perceived, I entered the mystical world of nature that my miraculous playground embraced, and became a part of everything . . . to play with a pond . . . to "mind" everything that I perceived in it, on it, and around it.[13]

Such first moments of absorption in other beings are an emotional and intuitive grasp of a relation rather than an intellectual justification of it. They are moments of the heart, not of the brain. The caring attitude is not itself a philosophical position, although it is the experiential bedrock for any philosophy that is more than sterile intellectual discourse.

For most people, however, the initial recognition is likely to involve a dog or a cat rather than a zoo animal or the amphibian denizens of Fox's boyhood Derbyshire pond. Adopting and living with a companion animal promotes a poignant awareness of the caring connection, one that is sometimes only fully realized in grief at the death of the animal. Tom Regan, author of the seminal work on animal rights philosophy, writes that although he entered the movement through Gandhi's views on nonviolence to animals, it was "the death of our dog that awakened my heart."[14]

A few activists report having what can be described as a conversion experience, a moment of sudden awareness that the path they have been following is strikingly uncaring. After years of research testing the toxic effects of radiation on primates, Don Barnes, now of the National Anti-Vivisection Society, dramatically discovered and adopted a view that made continuing this work utterly unthinkable.

However they occur, these are wrenching moments. There is shock in recognizing that it is possible, perhaps morally obligatory, to care about these others. It is as if one suddenly realizes that sitting in the next room is a family member whom one has somehow forgotten—or, at least, forgotten to love. Such moments are powerful. They bring about change at the level of basic attitudes—a person's consciousness is raised. He or she becomes, in the movement's term, an "animal person." Typically, he or she adopts a lifestyle that carefully avoids at least the grosser forms of animal exploitation.

Does an "animal person" only care about nonhuman animals? For many activists the caring connection extends beyond animals to various classes of oppressed humans and to ecosystems that include animals, humans, trees, and even rocks. A poll of subscribers to *Animals' Agenda*, a leading magazine of the movement, showing that the great majority are or have been active in other progressive social movements, supports this generality of the caring attitude.[15] John Broida, Leanne Tingley, Robert Kimball, and Joseph Miele found that undergraduates who take a position critical of animal research are more likely than uncritical students to have a personality profile associated with counseling, teaching, and other helping (caring) professions.[16]

In the other direction, Adelman M. Hills found that people who like people (people-oriented) also like animals, more than do thing-oriented people.[17] Historically, Henry Bergh, founder of the American Society for the Protection of Animals, also helped form the New York Society for the Prevention of Cruelty to Children. Frances Power Cobbe, a leader of antivivisectionism in late nineteenth-century England, was also a leading feminist.[18]

What is the developmental origin of this caring attitude? Our speculations here must take into account the fact that, according to the *Agenda* survey and other studies, roughly 75 percent of movement activists are women. We will consider three lines of argument.

The first has to do with social conditioning. Although child-rearing practices and cultural expectations are changing, girls' socialization still tends to foster nurturing, responsiveness, and caring behavior. Carol Gilligan has demonstrated that this difference in gender training affects not only behavior but the acquisition of a different moral framework.[19] Girls develop an ethic built on responsiveness to the needs of others in a personal setting, while boys forge a justice ethic based on abstract rules and universal principles.

A related explanation of individuals' participation in the movement is the nature of caring, which is itself based on an even more fundamental attribute, an empathic style of understanding the world. As a sympathetic response, caring is a judgment about someone else's neediness. Empathy, by contrast, is a feeling but not yet a judgment of need or an attempt to alleviate another's pain. It is a way of relating to the world that focuses on and directly apprehends the feelings, motives, and interests of other beings. Fox's boyhood play "minding" a pond, becoming part of the creatures that inhabit it, is an example of the empathic style in action, as are those exhilarating moments of self-forgetfulness induced by the performance of a great actor, dancer, or musician.

As a style of understanding, empathy is readily distinguishable from objective understanding, in which we try to stay outside an experience and our personal responses to it. The paradigm of objective understanding is experimental science.

A child's understanding of the world begins with something closer to empathy than to objective knowledge. After an early stage in which the child feels the mother's love or anxiety by a kind of immediate contagion—as if mother and child were one—he or she enters a stage Jean Piaget calls *animism*.[20] All objects—falling leaves, the toast popping up, as well as the meowing cat—are invested with intention. The toast wants to be eaten, just as the cat wants to be fed.

The first task of education is to "advance" the child, from this ensoulment of everything in the world that moves, to the more direct understanding provided by empathy. Later he or she is initiated into the task of constructing, primarily through inference rather than empathy, a world of impersonal objects related causally rather than intersubjectively.

This objective understanding is not gained without casualties. One cannot simultaneously infer and empathize, keep outside and go inside. Earlier empathic capabilities are subordinated and can grow rusty from disuse. Moreover, we are taught *not* to empathize with certain classes of objects. The deer we hunt, the chicken we eat, the mink we wear, and the frog we dissect are no longer individual subjects of a world we can empathically enter. They are objects, members of an abstract aggregate (the deer population), commodities for our consumption (meat or fur), or instruments for our learning (organism or laboratory preparation).[21]

Objective understanding, therefore, actively devalues emotional responsiveness and intersubjectivity—which threaten to create personal involvements and so violate the ideal of neutrality. In science's adoption of this ideal, these contaminate objective understanding by giving rise to bias. If, as we have described it, the caring attitude is a leaning toward, objective understanding cannot be caring. By contrast, empathy, although it is not yet a judgment or leaning, readily lends itself to caring. When I empathize with you, I experience, directly and intimately, what you need. We are close, if only for a moment and only imperfectly, for I have cohabited your world. If the paradigm of objective understanding is science, that of empathic understanding is care-taking.

The respective converses are also possible. I can exploit you more effectively by knowing your needs at the close hand provided by empathy; and I can care for you more effectively when I have coolly and objectively determined your needs. Nonetheless, it is clear, on psychological grounds, that empathy facilitates caring and, from the historical record, that objectification is the handmaiden of instrumental use—that is, of exploitation.

During childhood, both sexes learn to abandon the bald egocentrism of infancy. In general, girls are socialized to leave the self through immediate empathic involvement in another person, while boys are encouraged to assimilate the self to an objectified understanding of the wider world. It therefore follows that women in the animal rights movement outnumber men because they have been socialized to retain an empathic style of understanding and a personal style of relatedness—subject to subject rather than subject to object.

A third explanation of the origin of the caring attitude suggests that it is based on identification with the oppressed. According to this analysis, because women in Western culture are themselves oppressed, they are more likely than men to identify with other oppressed groups and so to predominate in numbers (though not in leadership roles) in progressive social movements. Moreover, women's identification with nonhuman animals may occur because their oppression shares certain structural and linguistic terms.[22] Both women and animals require "husbanding" (husband, husbandry); both can be a good piece of meat ("Are you a breast or a leg man?"—advertisement for Purdue chicken); and both are fair game (objects of the hunt).

Seeing Suffering

In the sketch of his childhood, Bernstein relates that even at the age of four or five, he saw the suffering of nonhuman animals. The ability to see suffering is characteristic of animal rights activists; their solicitous leaning toward animals positions them to notice their suffering.

But how does this distinguish them from anyone else? Surely everyone can see suffering? On the contrary, many, if not most people, do not see it. To understand how this is possible, we need to clarify what it means to see, exploring two different perspectives—one dealing with human perception and the second with its object, in this case nonhuman animals.

As there are different styles of understanding, so there are different styles of seeing. Two people look at a person wearing a fur coat. One sees elegance and beauty, the second sees dead animals, and the suffering and exploitation they underwent when alive. In spite of the movement's public exposés of the fur business, some people remain genuinely ignorant of the living and dying conditions of trapped and ranch animals; and, of course, individuals have different interests and values. Other people, however, literally do not perceive the suffering, because of a particular style of seeing akin to denial, an unwitting disavowal of certain emotionally laden themes or issues. Questioned directly, such individuals may indicate knowledge of these subjects, even though they are able to block full awareness of its emotional implications.

Another style of seeing, both subtler and more common, involves a distinction between *registering* and *reporting*, and leads to the claim that animal rights activists are people who consistently register suffering.[23] Consider, for example, a visit to the museum. It is crowded; you have not allowed enough time, and you rush through the exhibition. Do you see the Rembrandt? Yes, you see it, but you do not really take it in, fully take stock of it, appropriate it. You look at it, but, while aware that this is a Rembrandt and that a Rembrandt has certain striking and inimitable features, you are too hurried to grasp them fully or let them sink in. Your style of seeing in that moment is more like receiving a report of a Rembrandt than being fully present to one.

As a group, animal rights activists see suffering in a more robust and appropriative way: they register suffering. While not radically or grossly disavowing it, most other people are conscious of it somewhat vaguely, as they were aware of the nightly body count of famine victims in a far-off land, as reports of events remaining always at a distance. Even people interested in animals—the casual horseback rider, the owner of a purebred dog, the birdwatcher—are usually cognizant only of the problems of animals that are objects of their special interest.

Kim Bartlett, editor of *Animal People*, describes a moment in her life when a shift occurred in how she saw suffering: "Shortly after [going dove hunting], I went to a bullfight across the [South Texas] border. Nothing registered but the music. The blood didn't seem real."[24] But only a few years later:

> I received a piece of mail. . . . It was about fur and contained . . . pictures of a fox and rabbit caught in leghold traps. The look in their eyes pierced my soul. . . . I sat down and cried.[25]

A combination of institutional arrangements, linguistic sleights of hand, and defensive operations sustain this style of seeing as reportage. Animals in factory farms, fur ranches, and laboratories are located at remote distances and physically hidden from us. They are maintained in aggregates that make it difficult to relate to their individual suffering. As consumers, we see them packaged in ways that conceal their animal origins and any provenance of suffering. Animals are also concealed through language—"fruits of the sea." Cognitively, many people exaggerate the categorical distinctions between human and nonhuman species of animals. Such overdrawn distinctions then allow "outgroup biases" to come into play.[26] These further distance "us" from "them," and support the failure to register their suffering. A final style of seeing—abstract seeing or seeing past the suffering—is found both in the movement and among its detractors. It allows us to pass over the real animal or animals before us and move to a symbolic plane. We see injustice, speciesism, or the "death of nature," not the suffering animal. Of course, no one can stay constantly in the existential moment. The fully engaged seeing, registering, leaves us vulnerable to the suffering and injustices of the world, while abstract seeing deflects and softens their impact. Eventually, we must abstract, contextualize, integrate, make sense of things.

However, these modes can also function as blocks to perception. When we adopt them as a habitual style of seeing, we lose touch with the experiential foundations of our value systems. The hunter who sees past the death throes of the buck he or she has shot to the abstraction "the deer," a "population" that needs "culling," never sees the pain. Nor, occasionally, does the animal rights activist who sees past the frustration and boredom of hens in tiers of cages the size of this page. The caged animals become a symbol for something else—perhaps the transformation of traditional agriculture to factory farming.

In addition to styles of seeing that deflect us from directly registering suffering, a prior block may occur in the nature of animals. After all, we can only see suffering if it exists; and many people, in both laboratory and slaughterhouse, have long maintained that animals do not suffer—or, at least, that we cannot know whether they do.[27]

Some argue, for example, that suffering—a distinct emotional response characterized by fear and anxiety—while usually associated with physical pain, is not inseparable from it. The runner who painfully but elatedly extends him or herself to cross the finish line first is not suffering. According to this reasoning, animals could experience pain without suffering. Some researchers, in fact, suggest that suffering implies an awareness that pain or distress represents a threat to one's integrity or well-being. The questioning of nonhuman animals' capacity to experience such awareness further fosters styles of seeing that fail to register animal suffering.

In addition to these considerations of the nature of nonhuman animal experience, another backdrop to seeing their suffering is the human proclivity to take nonhuman animals as metaphors of ourselves. Although some deny animals the capacity to manipulate symbols, no one denies their ability to bear them. From Aesop's fables to Kipling's *Just So Stories* to Disney's animations, folk and modern cultures have required animals to bear a rich load of meanings to help us understand (or just stand) ourselves. As symbols they have served as repositories of both our valorized (wise as an owl) and our denigrated (animal or bestial) human characteristics. The symbols come to function as opaque layers, masking our perception of the real animals' true nature and immediate plight. If our perception of animals is so laden with metaphors of ourselves, how can we be sure that their suffering is not our own, projected? This symbolic density also allows us to limit our experience of their suffering to reportage rather than registration.

Caring *can* be sentimentalized, and sensitivity to suffering can be a projection of human characteristics onto nonhuman animals. There is a minority in the movement on whom childhood exposure to the early Disney has left a certain proclivity to the maudlin. As a group, however, the caring of animal rights activists is informed by a sophisticated understanding of animals, both their suffering and the institutional and ideological origins of that suffering.[28]

Armed with this knowledge, their empathy and caring, animal rights activists register the suffering of nonhuman animals. However, while a necessary condition, the registration of suffering is not a sufficient one, for it does not yet imply a commitment to action. Animal rights activists not only know that animals suffer, they live to do something about it.

Seeking Suffering

> But pain and suffering are often the hidden ingredients ... [so] we have to go behind the closed doors, behind the sanitized wrap.[29]

In an earlier era, a carter beat a horse until the welts were bloody and, exhausted and overheated from the burden of pulling a heavily laden carriage, the animal collapsed on the street. Today, a research assistant takes a baboon away from her or his protesting mother, and places the infant in a cage that will serve as experimental home and school in the ensuing (de)formative months of emotional and intellectual development. The first was a highly visible public event, while the second occurs behind layers of sanitized, justificatory, and obscuring wrap—federal regulations, institutional animal care and use committees, specialized scientific journal articles, high security lab facilities.

Even to the eye desensitized in the various ways I have described, public display of human induced suffering in animals is still available, and there is still individual abuse—acts defined by their aberration from norms of acceptable behavior. However, the modern era has brought its own forms of institutionalized exploitation (factory farms, "animal models" of every form of physiological and psychological disorder) and with them new norms of the acceptable and the aberrant. To some extent a difference between the contemporary animal rights movement and its late nineteenth-century predecessor is a shift in focus from policing individual abuse to the development of a radical critique of institutional practices. Indeed, part of the current debate within the movement (rights versus welfare) hinges on the philosophical and strategic merits of that shift. Yet even beneath the surveillance of individual abuse by traditional humane society officers and the desire of some to focus on improving animal welfare within present institutions, lies a common impulse to effect still more fundamental structural changes.

What has shifted is less the locus of critique than the visibility of its object. The contemporary animal rights worker must actively seek suffering. To find it typically requires an investigatory posture combining classic Holmesian analysis of direct physical evidence with the use of sophisticated technological tools.

Today's activist is a skillful sleuth who has learned to follow trails through the labyrinths of democratic and bureaucratic political processes, to hear hints in diplomatic pronouncements, to defog regulatory smoke screens, to "search" online abstracts of biomedical research proposals. Holmes's magnifying glass is of little use here, for the animals are nowhere in sight. Investigative work begins with reading texts rather than with deductions from physical evidence. Even the texts, however, do not refer to animals and certainly not to their suffering. In a trade report on agricultural production, in place of animals there are numbers of pounds of meat and their market value. The animals are an absent referent, not even present by allusion. the relation between meat and living animals is unspoken as the animals who suffered and died within this productive enterprise were from the outset meat on the hoof.

Suffering is also hidden in time: in a past traced from the eggs in the cake back to the factory farm. Or it is a future event presaged by a notice of a proposed marine park and the consequent capture of dolphins to reside there to entertain us.

To the animal rights activist, these are all bloody trails—as bloody as that literal trail left by the blood and sweat of the exhausted carthorse. To discover and follow them, our latter-day Sherlock Holmes is trained in politics, diplomacy, science, economics, high-tech information retrieval; she possesses a skill in textual interpretation worthy of a postmodernist scholar. Primed by caring and sensitivity to suffering and equipped with a range of approaches, committed activists dedicate themselves to seeking and exposing suffering behind closed doors—suffering implicitly present between the lines of a bowdlerized text, beneath the red tape of a Byzantine political process, in a future only adumbrated or a past reconstructed like a revisionist history, from fragments and clues disregarded by others.

Pervasiveness of the Seeking

> People who have an affinity to nonhuman beings are drawn like magnets to places where these individuals are suffering. It's a horrible thing—your car steering wheel turns to the right and off you go because down that lane there is a slaughterhouse or something.[30]

Moreover, sleuth work is insidious, for it is difficult to stop seeking. What begins as a certain sensibility to suffering crystallizes into an avocation—volunteering at the local shelter—then becomes a vocation and, finally, turns into a way of life. Without intending it, animal rights activists find that they are increasingly and, eventually, perpetually on call:

> To devise a political strategy is one thing. To live everyday life is another.... It means to walk in the streets and see butcher shops, pharmacies, furrier shops, perfumeries, or to sit in restaurants not far from people eating animal flesh. Or to love and cherish persons who help to perpetuate the exploitation. Or to enjoy the beauty of spots and the enchantment of towns that conceal the exploitation behind the serene facades.[31]

The workday of research, inquiry, and confrontation does not end neatly at the office door. Whether seeking them or not, the activist senses traces of animal suffering and exploitation all around. The street in which she walks is no longer an open road, a horizon of stimulating possibility and chance encounter, but a set of potential clues, hints, suspect provenances. All roads become part of a network of bloody trails. Paradoxically, what is everywhere hidden, forgotten, denied, erased, transmuted, manufactured is yet everywhere present. The shopping mall, the restaurant, the city, but not less the woods and the sea—each has its own network of bloody trails. For animal rights activists, there is meat in their soup, animal-based research in their medicine.... They can't stop seeing or seeking the suffering.

Tensions and Conflict

> It is just so very troublesome to be sensitive to the suffering of others.... It takes so much out of a person and sometimes I believe it takes too much happiness away.[32]

The preoccupation with seeking suffering colors the physical landscape of the world. When Fox returned to the hillsides of his childhood, he saw them differently. He could no longer glory in the "mystical world of nature" and the "sense of renewal" gained through "emotional connectedness" to it. Beyond the real changes in that environment (now overstocked with sheep) and the inevitable sobriety of maturity, his loss is an occupational hazard, which perhaps has comparable forms in every social movement committed to basic change.

This (dis)coloration of the natural and animal scene also extends to the human landscape. Being a careful sleuth involves looking for trouble. Whether in the conventional style of a probe of the political process, an inquiry under the Freedom of Information Act, or in the more activist style of surveillance and infiltration, investigators are viewed by the targets of the investigation as troublemakers. Information gained exposes and pressures those targeted to change.

On a more interpersonal level, seeing and seeking what others do not notice and do not want to notice promotes certain forms of social interaction, attempts to convince others of the presence of exploitative practices. Particularly at the grassroots level, activists often present themselves as witnesses to animal suffering, testifying to strangers, acquaintances, and intimates alike. Activists' styles vary from a cool, controlled presentation of factually and philosophically grounded arguments to an impassioned striving to find the one compelling image to cut through the rationalizations that justify suffering.

Whatever the style, these are emotionally loaded moments, and they can arouse strong feelings in even the most seasoned campaigner. Beneath the concern for the well-being of animals and the inevitable measuring of one's own effectiveness lies another set of emotional dynamics: seeking and finding suffering induce anger and indignation—at both suspected perpetrators and consumers who collaborate in exploitation. At times, the impulse to blame and treat people with scorn, or even vengeance, is difficult to resist.

Some activists throw blood on fur-wearers not so much to educate and induce change—or to tactically stigmatize a symbol of high fashion—as to transform them literally into dripping bloody trails. The desire to make the bloody trail visible merges with a wish to smear others with guilt. Moreover, the dynamics of this dramatic example can generalize to even casual encounters if chronic anger gives vent to an intolerance that is almost always counterproductive for the activist. Can these feelings be those of a caring person?

Caring and anger are not, of course, inherently contradictory. I have no doubt that I still love my son even in that moment when we are both taken aback at the strength of my outburst at the end of a long rainy Saturday afternoon. An anger laced with intolerance and entitlement, however, corrodes caring; sensibility and intolerance of others' insensibility cannot be bedfellows for long. Aggressive investigation, confrontation, protest, and demonstration often met by stonewalling and, more recently (as a result of the movement's effectiveness), by counteroffensives, can suppress caring.

These occupational tensions between caring and anger can even threaten the activist's motivation. The fact that most people go about their business as if the activist's agenda were irrelevant to the world's "real" problems—while others argue that it is wrong-headed, misguided, even dangerous and unethical—induces self-doubt. Uncertainties arise about one's competence and motives, about being peripheral or weird, about missing the pleasures of a conventional life in which work is left at the office. Doubts can undermine confidence in one's account of the world and the positions taken. Perhaps, after all, the suffering is necessary; perhaps exploitation is part of the natural order of things. Perhaps caring and aggressively exposing suffering are contradictory, and the caring is counterfeit or, on balance, hurtful.

One further twist is that the activist, in seeking out suffering, offends her own caring sensibility, incites her own pain and distress, disappointment and disillusionment. The activist is looking for trouble in the further sense that what is sought is suffering. Its discovery is itself troubling, particularly to a caring person who habitually registers that suffering. She is searching for something; she wants to find it and is committed to finding it *and* does not want to find it. The sense of accomplishment, even of exhilaration at finding it, is, at best, bittersweet and, at worst, heart-rending. In exposing the bloody trail, the animal rights activist creates her own bloody trail; human pain commingles with the animals' suffering.

In the last few years I have become increasingly aware of losing touch with something precious to me. I am standing on a cliff at the head of Linekin Bay on the coast of Maine, idly watching the sea. The tide is coming in, the breezes play on the water, fish jump at the surface, gulls careen above, an occasional osprey hovers. Idyllic, yes, but I no longer fully find it so. Something in the periphery of my awareness nags at me. I notice hundreds of parti-colored buoys polka-dotting the bay, and now I recognize what distracts me. These buoys mark the death-row cells of countless lobsters and crabs who have found their way into but not out of the sunken traps. I remember a more innocent and fully engaged participant in such panoramas, myself as I wandered through the fields and gardens of my childhood and discovered nature and animals for the first time. My first sighting of a bluebird was stunning in a way irretrievably lost to me, for bluebirds now appear in an ecology of insecticides, introduced species, habitat destruction, and managed bluebird trails.

Between the sadness and the self-questioning, an impulse to remain uninvolved, to tend one's own garden, can gain momentum.

Resolutions

How do activists deal with the melancholy, the self-doubts, and the potential alienation from the wider society? How do they choose, among the coping styles available, one that will be most constructive for the individual and for the animals?

The most common resolution, in this and other social movements, is the constitution of a community of like-minded individuals brought together through investigations, exposés, demonstrations, and conversations. As individuals and as a community, animal rights activists are privileged to live fulfilling lives in which dedication to the well-being of others extends beyond the traditional pales of family, ethnic group, or even nation. As members of the animal rights community, activists have a sense of belonging, of sharing common values and purpose. They are "at home"—with themselves, in their relations with other people and animals, in a world that they both belong in and help to form. After the rugged natural beauty of Maine with its white-water canoeing and hiking was transformed for me into a landscape booby-trapped—as my neighbor's effort to rid his garden of "nuisance" animals one day resulted in the trapping of my own beloved dog—I helped found a new home in Maine. A small group of us formed a more neighborly group who would work together to lobby against trapping, to expose mistreatment in unmarked warehouse poultry "farms," and to provide students the right to alternatives to dissection.

Ours was a community in the fullest sense of the word. Activists share not simply a workplace or a job or even a set of values but a concrete way of life embodied in daily activities. Just as nonhuman animal suffering pervades society, so every aspect of activists' lives—diet, dress, diversions—is designed to expunge the taint of animals exploited for human ends. They embrace caring for animals by bearing witness at every mundane turn to the possibility of living their caring within a mutually supportive community.

Yet, if this sense of community can offset the disaffection often felt with respect to the larger society, it also has its pitfalls. It may result in a heightening of insularity and, consequently, in diminished effectiveness through a pattern of preaching to the converted. It may even reduce one's usefulness to animals by the phobic constriction of one's life (for example, to avoid driving because insects are killed against the windshield) or to become obsessively preoccupied with one's own purity. (Is it acceptable to eat honey from free-ranging bees?)

A second resolution involves suppressing the caring. Paola Cavalieri states: "The extent and pervasiveness of animal exploitation are such that only by closing your eyes a little can we keep the hope of affecting realty, and the grit to do it."[33] Newkirk expresses the temporary suspension of caring through a metaphor of building a "protective wall." Only by "steeling" herself, showing no emotions, is she able to do her work as a "conscientious investigator" of animal cruelty. Others suppress caring more systematically—distancing themselves from direct contact with suffering by conducting a campaign at some remove from the actual scene of the exploitation, developing and administering an animal rights organization, or writing on the issues.

A third resolution or style of coping occurs when self-righteous indignation creates an attitude more hateful than caring. More than suppressing or suspending caring, here the activist actually loses touch with it. Such a person can be a liability to the cause, playing into the efforts of vested interests in animal exploitation to polarize the movement into revolutionist and reformist camps. Often this posture of indignation involves a rigid adherence and preoccupation with principle. In place of caring and the registration of suffering, the knee-jerk application of a philosophy reduced to slogans can support an unforgiving bearing. Unwittingly, the activist collaborates with the press's readiness to oversimplify issues. The public is asked to choose between such extreme alternatives as whether or not to sacrifice a single mouse to save a million human lives, or to accept as reform a measure that allows a veal calf enough space to turn around in his crate.

To some extent, these three styles of dealing with the particular tensions inherent in this movement appear at different stages in the career of an activist. In an early stage, an individual often experiences an extended period of enthusiastic embracing of the community of caring. At a later stage, the activist realizes the depth of resistance to change and may move to a more self-protective position by suppressing the caring or by burying it beneath a rigid application of right and wrong.

Caring remains the foundation of the animal rights movement. The most accurate image of the animal rights advocate is that of a caring individual who persists in assertively and, when necessary, aggressively exposing animal suffering. A grassroots activist writes:

> I often look at things and situations in a very animal aware way. I see the degradation of animals in a lot of things. Being an animal rights activist, I feel a great urgency to change the world and I always have to deal with the fact that my ideas are not very popular.... Usually people are very defensive and annoyed when I talk about animal rights ... they feel it's an attack on them and their lifestyle and they don't see the bigger picture.[34]

Notes

1. Scott Plous, "An Attitude Survey of Animal Rights Activists," *Psychological Sciences* 2 (1991): 194–96.

2. Susan Sperling, *Animal Liberators: Research and Morality* (Berkeley: University of California Press, 1988).
3. James M. Jasper and Dorothy Nelkin, *The Animal Rights Crusade: The Growth of a Moral Protest* (New York: Free Press, 1992).
4. Harold Herzog, "The Movement is My Life: The Psychology of Animal Rights Activism," *Journal of Social Issues* 49 (1993): 103–21; Shelley L. Galvin and Harold A. Herzog, "The Ethical Judgment of Animal Research," *Ethics and Behavior* 2 (1992): 263–87.
5. R. T. Richards and R. S. Krannich, "The Ideology of the Animal Rights Movement and Activists' Attitudes toward Wildlife," *Transactions of the North American Wildlife and Natural Resources Conference* (1991): 363–71.
6. Robert Kimball, "Liberal/Conservative Voting Records Compared to Interest in Animal Protection Bills," *PSYeta Bulletin* 9 (1989): 7–9.
7. Charles Magel, "Animal Liberators are not Anti-Science," *Between the Species*, 6 (1990): 204–13.
8. Jasper and Nelkin, *Animal Rights Crusade*; Plous, "Attitude Survey."
9. Amedio Giorgi, *Psychology as a Human Science: A Phenomenologically Based Approach* (New York: Harper, 1970).
10. Fred J. Wertz, "Method and Findings in a Phenomenological Psychological Study of a Complex Life-Event: Being Criminally Victimized," in *Phenomenology and Psychological Research*, ed. A. Giorgi (Pittsburgh: Duquesne University Press, 1985), 168.
11. Peter Singer, *Animal Liberation* (New York: Avon, 1975).
12. Helen Jones, "Autographical Notes," *Between the Species*, 4 (1988): 70.
13. Michael W. Fox, "Autobiographical Notes," *Between the Species* 3 (1987): 98–99.
14. Tom Regan, "The Bird in the Cage: A Glimpse of My Life," *Between the Species* 2 (1986): 93.
15. Richards and Krannich, "Ideology."
16. John Broida, Leanne Tingley, Robert Kimball, and Joseph Miele, "Personality Differences between Pro- and Anti-Vivisectionists," *Society and Animals* 1 (1993): 129–45.
17. Adelman M. Hills, "The Relationship between Thing-Person Orientation and the Perception of Animals," *Anthrozoos* 3 (1989): 100–111.
18. Richard Ryder, *Animal Revolution: Changing Attitudes toward Speciesism* (Oxford: Basil Blackwell, 1989), 107, 174.
19. Carol Gilligan, *In a Different Voice: Psychological Theory and Women's Development* (Cambridge: Harvard University Press, 1982).
20. Jean Piaget, *The Child's Conception of the World* (1930), as cited in John Phillips, *The Origins of Intellect: Piaget's Theory* (San Francisco: W. H. Freeman, 1969), 109.
21. Kenneth J. Shapiro, "The Death of the Animal: Ontological Vulnerability," *Between the Species* 5 (1989): n.p.
22. Carol J. Adams, *The Sexual Politics of Meat: A Feminist-Vegetarian Critical Theory* (New York: Continuum, 1990).
23. Robert Sokolowski, *Husserlian Meditations: How Words Present Things* (Evanston, Ill.: Northwestern University Press, 1974).
24. Kim Bartlett, "Blinded by the Light: Or How Nature Triumphed Over Nurturance," *Between the Species* 6 (1990): 95.
25. Ibid.
26. Scott Plous, "Psychological Mechanisms in the Human Use of Animals," *Journal of Social Issues* 49 (1993) 11–53.
27. Ibid., 26–27.
28. Stephen Kellert, "Perceptions of Animals in America," *Perceptions of Animals in American Culture*, ed. R. J. Hoage (Washington, D.C.: Smithsonian Institution, 1989).

29. Theresa C. Corrigan, "A Woman is a Horse is a God is a Rat: An Interview with Ingrid Newkirk," in *And a Deer's Ear, Eagle's Song, and Bear's Grace: Animals and Women*, ed. Theresa Corrigan and Stephanie Hoppe (Pittsburgh: Cleis, 1990), 164.
30. Ibid., 163.
31. Paola Cavalieri, "Reflections," *Between the Species* 6 (1990): 156.
32. Emmanuel Bernstein, "Empathy toward Animals and Other Sentient Beings: A Very Personal Account," *Between the Species* 3 (1987): 152.
33. Cavalieri, "Reflections," 157.
34. From one of the survey protocols collected at the National Alliance for Animals Conference in 1991, Washington, D.C.

Attention to Suffering:
Sympathy as a Basis for
Ethical Treatment of Animals (1994)

JOSEPHINE DONOVAN

*M*any feminists, including myself, have criticized contemporary animal advocacy theory for its reliance upon natural rights doctrine, on the one hand, and utilitarianism, on the other. The main exponent of the former approach has been Tom Regan, and of the latter, Peter Singer. However different the two theories may be, they nevertheless unite in their rationalist rejection of emotion or sympathy as a legitimate base for ethical theory about animal treatment. Many feminists have urged just the opposite, claiming that sympathy, compassion, and caring are the ground upon which theory about human treatment of animals should be constructed. Here I would like to further deepen this assertion.

To do so I will argue that the terms of what constitutes the ethical must be shifted. Like many other feminists I contend that the dominant strain in contemporary ethics reflects a male bias toward rationality, defined as the construction of abstract universals that elide not just the personal, the contextual, and the emotional, but also the political components of an ethical issue. Like other feminists, particularly those in the "caring" tradition, I believe that an alternative epistemology and ontology may be derived from women's historical, social, economic, and political practice. I will develop this point further below.

In addition to recent feminist theorizing, however, there is a long and important strain in Western (male) philosophy that does not express the rationalist bias of contemporary ethical theory, that in fact seeks to root ethics in emotion—in the feelings of sympathy and compassion. Why this tradition has been overshadowed by rationalist theory is a question beyond my scope. What I would like to do here is, first, summarize the main components of this sympathy tradition; second, extend recent feminist theorizing on the subject; and third, conclude with the idea that what we need is a refocus in our moral vision—a shift in the cultural ethical episteme—so that people will begin to see and attend to the suffering of animals, which is happening all about them. Here I will rely on theorizing about "attentive love" developed principally by Iris Murdoch (under the influence of Simone Weil), but anticipated by over a century of sympathy theory expounded by such major Western philosophers as David Hume, Arthur Schopenhauer, Martin Buber, Edmund Husserl and other phenomenologists, such as Max Scheler and Edith Stein. Murdoch indeed exhibits a thorough awareness of this tradition—especially of the contribution of Hume and Schopenhauer—in her latest book, *Metaphysics as a Guide to Morals* (1992).

It was Immanuel Kant who formulated the rationalist rights-based ethic that has dominated the contemporary field. In his Preface to the *Fundamental Principles of the Metaphysics of Morals* (1785) Kant rejects feeling or inclination as a morally worthy motive for ethical action. Rather, he stipulates, for an action to be ethically significant it must be performed out of a sense of duty. Indeed, "an action done from duty must wholly exclude the influence of inclination."[1] Kant's rejection of sentiment or sympathy as a base for moral decision-making or action seems to reflect three concerns: one, emotions are volatile (what one feels today one may not feel tomorrow) (276); two, the capacity for sentiment is not evenly distributed (and thus those who exhibit sympathy may act more morally by inclination than those who do not) (277); three, for these reasons a sentimental ethic is not universalizable—one cannot establish thereby universal ethical laws (281). The second and the third point suggest that an ethic based on sentiment or sympathy or care is incompatible with the claims of justice—that everyone be treated equally and fairly. Most defenses of and attacks on a sympathy-based ethic revolve around these points.

Kant also formulated what has become the dominant Western view of animals: that they are instrumental to human interests—are means to human ends but not ends in themselves worthy of moral consideration. Because Kant's views have been extensively criticized by animal-rights theorists, notably Tom Regan in his *Case for Ani-*

mal Rights, I will not further treat them here. Schopenhauer, however, sounded the keynote of this critique when he exclaimed: "genuine morality [is] outraged by the proposition . . . that beings devoid of reason (hence animals) are *things* and therefore should be treated merely as means":[2]

> I regard such propositions as revolting and abominable. . . . Thus, because Christian morality leaves animals out of account . . . they are at once outlawed in philosophical morals; they are mere "things." . . . They can therefore be used for vivisection, hunting, coursing, bullfights, and horse racing, and can be whipped to death as they struggle along with heavy carts of stone. Shame on such a morality . . . that fails to realize the eternal essence that exists in every living thing, and shines forth with inscrutable significance from all eyes. (96)

Kant's objection to an ethic rooted in emotional response, or sympathy, betrays a conception of emotion that construes it as irrational, uncontrollable, and erratic. Like other rationalists, Kant seems to imagine that emotional experience necessarily obliterates rational thinking. Kantian theorist Tom Regan follows in this vein when he accuses "ethic-of-care feminism" of "abjur[ing] the use of reason."[3]

But a considered and sophisticated response to such charges has been developed by sympathy theorists. They argue that experiencing sympathy is a complex intellectual as well as emotional exercise. Philip Mercer, for example, in his very useful study *Sympathy and Ethics* (1972), claims that in fact sympathy includes "a *cognitive* element."[4] Like Max Scheler (see below), Mercer is careful to distinguish between empathy and sympathy. Where the former may involve "losing oneself" in another's feelings, the latter requires keeping a certain distance so as to imaginatively construct the other's situation accurately and thereby to understand it intellectually as well as emotionally (9).

H. B. Acton in "The Ethical Importance of Sympathy" (1955) similarly argues that sympathy is a "form" of rationality.[5] It is not "as partial and impulsive" as critics have claimed (65); it is "not a primitive animal feeling but an exercise of the imagination requiring self-consciousness and comparison" (66).

In his phenomenological exploration of empathy, Husserl identifies it as an imaginative exercise that requires judgment and evaluation:

> I try to picture to myself, standing *here*, how I would look, how I would feel, and how the world would appear if I were *there*—in the

place of that body which resembles mine and acts as I might. My imaginative projection into the place of another, conjoined with the two types of data given by the senses [appearance and behavior] makes empathy possible.⁶

Mercer describes a similar imaginative construction but specifies that as a basis for ethical judgment and action, sympathy (again not empathy) should involve not projecting oneself into another's situation but rather figuring out how the other is feeling: "it is not enough that I should imagine how *I* should feel if *I* were in the other person's place; I have to imagine how [the other] feels" (9).

The most developed analysis of sympathy remains phenomenologist Max Scheler's *The Nature of Sympathy* (first ed., 1913; third rev. ed., 1926). Scheler elevates sympathy into a form of knowledge (*Verstehen* or understanding) that he proposes as an epistemological alternative to the objectification of the Cartesian scientific mode. Scheler indeed was a founder of the phenomenological school in the social sciences, which relies upon a method of "psychological sympathy" where the researcher attempts to imaginatively construct the reality of the subject, rather than objectifying him or her as data to fit mathematical paradigms.⁷ Scheler proposed his method not just for the social sciences, however, and not just for humans. Rather, he contends, "understanding and fellow-feeling [*Mitgefühl*] are able to range throughout the *entire* animal universe.... The mortal terror of a bird, its sprightly or dispirited moods, are intelligible to us and awaken our fellow-feeling."⁸

Scheler argues that humans need to develop (or redevelop) their sympathetic intellectual capacities in order to decode the symbolic language of nature. Humans need to learn to read this language in order to truly understand natural life, including animals. "We can understand the experience of animals," he notes, by attending to their behavioral and expressive signs: these have as their referent the animal's emotional and psychological state. "For instance when a dog expresses its joy by barking and wagging its tail . . . we have here . . . a *universal grammar* valid for all languages of expression" (11).

Similarly, other forms of natural life have a "grammar of expression" that humans can learn to understand; this understanding is both intellectual and emotional:

> The fullness of Nature in its phenomenological aspect still presents a vast number of fields in which the life of the cosmos may find expression; fields wherein all appearances have an *intelligible co-*

herence which is other and more than mechanical, and which, once disclosed by means of the universal mime, pantomime and grammar of expression is found to mirror the stirrings of universal life within (104).

Thus, Scheler is proposing that animals and other natural forms have a "language" that is accessible if humans attend to it, one that is elided by the mathematizing pretensions of modern science:

> We must rid ourselves henceforward of our one-sided conception of Nature as a mere instrument of human domination.... We must learn once more "to look upon Nature as into the heart of a friend" [*Faust* I. 3220].... Hence the first task of our educational practice must be to revive the capacity for identification with the life of the universe, and awaken it anew from its condition of dormancy in the capitalist social outlook of Western man (with its characteristic picture of the world as an aggregation of movable quantities). (105)[9]

Thus, Scheler proposes an epistemological mode of sympathetic understanding as a valid tool of knowledge, which will reveal realities that are not seen or understood by the Cartesian mathematizing mode of science. St. Francis of Assisi is presented as exemplary; in his "emotional relationship to Nature ... natural objects and processes take on an expressive significance of *their* own, without any parabolic reference to ... human relationships" (87). Humans must develop this kind of sympathetic understanding *(Verstehen)* as a cognitive mode to decipher nature's *own* language, to see organic life *as it is*, not as translated into manipulable objects for human use. Scheler does not, therefore, see sympathy as a whimsical, erratic, and irrational response, but rather as a systematic investigatory tool, a form of knowledge.

An interesting recent exploration of how such an approach might work in practice is to be found in Kenneth Shapiro's "Understanding Dogs through Kinesthetic Empathy, Social Construction, and History" (1989). Shapiro (following Paul Ricoeur as well as Scheler) suggests that we need a new "interpretive science in which the object of study is an autonomous subject, more textlike than thinglike, and, hence, to be understood rather than explained."[10] By use of what he calls "kinesthetic empathy" Shapiro attempts to understand his dog Sabaka. He does this by imaginatively entering into the dog's bodily movements and reactions, thus deciphering the realities of the dog's "life-world" (to borrow a term from Husserl).

Edith Stein, who studied with Husserl, developed a similar concept, which she called "sensual empathy" (a "sensing-in" of the body of another).[11] Such an effort yields knowledge of another's suffering. "Should I perhaps consider a dog's paw in comparison with my hand. I do not have a mere physical body ... but a physical limb of a living body.... I may sense-in pain when the animal is injured" (55).

A somewhat similar approach is proposed by John A. Fisher in "Taking Sympathy Seriously: A Defense of Our Moral Psychology toward Animals" (1987). Fisher notes that "the sympathetic experience of ... animals entails some understanding of what it is like to be them—for example, of what it is like to be huge and to walk on four legs, to have a large trunk, and so forth."[12] (Here the terms *empathy* and *sympathy* are used somewhat interchangeably, and Stein and Shapiro tend to see the experience as a kind of visceral emotion, as opposed to Fisher; but what is important is that they all maintain that a sympathetic imaginative construction of another's reality is what is required for an appropriate moral response.)

Environmental ethicist Paul Taylor argues that such knowledge must be the basis of any environmental ethic. It is only by close study and observation of organisms that one can come to understand their reality, their telos, their needs:

> As one becomes more and more familiar with the organism and its behavior, one becomes fully sensitive to the particular way it is living out its life cycle.... The final culmination of this process is the achievement of a genuine understanding of its point of view and ... an ability to "take" that point of view.[13]

Such a process is not anthropomorphic, nor need it deny the separate and different reality of the other organism. Rather it is a process of learning—through careful attention and observation—what the other's reality really is, respecting that different reality, and developing an ethical response that is appropriate to that creature's reality (110).

All of these theorists are saying in answer to Kantian charges that sympathy is irrational that, on the contrary, it involves an exercise of the moral imagination, an intense attentiveness to another's reality, which requires strong powers of observation and concentration, as well as faculties of evaluation and judgment. It is a matter of trying to fairly see another's world, to understand what another's experience is. It is a cognitive as well as emotional exercise.

The ability to extend the moral imagination in this way is not, they argue, necessarily a natural gift (though some, notably Scheler and Schopenhauer assert that women are more able to exercise sympathetic understanding than men); rather, it is an intellectual and emotional practice that can be learned. As we have seen, Scheler contends that "the first task of our educational practice must be to revive the capacity for identification with the life of the universe" (105). Mercer, too, believes that people can and should be trained in emotional knowledge (105). Feminist theorist Rosemarie Tong even suggests that a Kantian mechanistic rules-based ethic may lead to a deadening of the moral imagination.[14] Perhaps the most extensive recent plea for a reinstatement of sympathy education into the school system comes from Nel Noddings, who believes that "the maintenance and enhancement of caring [should be] the primary aim of education." She advocates instituting such practices as "caring apprenticeships," for example.[15]

Sympathy theorists argue, moreover, that one can in fact have no morality, no justice even, without first having sympathy. Acton, for example, observes that "a certain amount of sympathy is required if anyone is even to *notice* that someone else is in need of help" (62). And without such attention, there would be no morality, "for without [sympathy] there would be no helping, and hence no beneficence, and help and beneficence are necessary for morality" (66).[16]

In arguing therefore that sympathy is the sine qua non of ethical decision-making and action, sympathy theorists contend that sympathy precedes justice. Such precedence obtains ontogenetically, some claim; logically, others claim; and metaphysically, yet others contend.

Scheler maintains that one's feelings of sympathy are rooted in earliest childhood, or in what Freudians call the preoedipal phase. One's first feelings are "the instinctive identification of mother-love" (98). Only gradually is this "replaced, in the later stages of childhood, by merely vicarious feeling," which remains as the undergirding of "fellow-feeling [Mitgefühl]" (98). In his introduction to Scheler's work, W. Stark amplifies this idea: "originally, the experience of self and the experience of others is in no way differentiated: the child feels the feelings and thinks the thoughts of those who form [her or his] social environment. It takes a long time before [perceptions are sorted out] as 'mine' and 'others'" (xxxix). Others, thus, "live in *us*" (xl), which forms the basis of sympathetic identification, preceding the emergence of egocentricity.

Brian Luke in "Justice, Caring, and Animal Liberation" (in this volume) claims that sympathy for animals is indeed a deep, primary disposition that is only obscured and repressed by a process of intense social conditioning. Noting the extensive guilt expiation ceremonies that attend animal killing in traditional cultures, Luke suggests that the existence of such guilt (along with other social practices) is testimony to "the depth of the human-animal bond" (86). The fact that laboratory experiments and slaughterhouse practices are kept hidden from the public suggests, once again, shame or guilt over the violation of the human-animal bond. "Enormous amounts of social energy are expended to forestall, undermine, and override our sympathies for animals, so that vivisection, animal farming, and hunting can continue" (88).

A number of eighteenth-century theorists—including Shaftesbury, Hutchinson, Hume, and Adam Smith—claimed that humans have an innate sense of sympathy and that this is the basis for moral awareness. The Third Earl of Shaftesbury maintained that there is an innate "moral sense" that is rooted in one's sense of kinship with others.[17] Francis Hutchinson extended Shaftesbury's idea that there is an innate moral faculty, contributing further to what Keith Thomas has labeled the "new sensibilities" that developed during the century, including sensitivities to animal cruelty (many of the humane societies originated as the result of this new emphasis on the feelings as a guide to moral action).[18]

David Hume, picking up on his predecessors, insists that there is a "natural sympathy" "implanted in our nature."[19] "Would any man, who is walking along, tread as willingly on another's gouty toes, whom he has no quarrel with, as on the hard flint and pavement?" (61). From such examples, Hume maintains:

> we must, a priori, conclude it impossible for such a creature as man to be totally indifferent to the well or ill-being of his fellow-creatures, and not readily ... to pronounce, where nothing gives him any particular bias, that what promotes their happiness is good, what tends to their misery is evil, without any further regard or consideration. (65)

"Morality," he concludes, "is determined by sentiment. It defines virtue to be *whatever mental action or quality gives to a spectator the pleasing sentiment of approbation;* and vice the contrary" (129). Moreover, "the approbation or blame ... cannot be the work of our judgment, but of the heart; and is not a speculative proposition or affirmation, but an active feeling or sentiment" (131).

Scientific credibility has been added to eighteenth-century theorists' claims for innate, natural sympathy by Charles Darwin and, more recently, the sociobiologists. They argue that natural selection has resulted in the phenomenon of "kin altruism," which is an innate concern about the survival of one's kin (and thus one's genes) found in most animals.[20] Darwin in fact claimed in *The Descent of Man* (1871) that in higher mammals such altruism was extended to nonkin (Rachels 157).

In a recent and interesting extension of this view, "Animal Liberation and Environmental Ethics" (1988), J. Baird Callicott suggests that since domestic animals have historically been part of the immediate human community (and thus in a sense "kin"), *kin altruism* establishes a natural base for human concern and emotional attachment. There is, he claims, a kind of "evolved and unspoken social contract" between these animals and humans.[21]

Writing in direct confutation of Kant's ethical theory, Schopenhauer, like Hume, also contends that morality is rooted in sympathy: "only insofar as an action has sprung from compassion does it have moral value" (144). And compassion, he maintains, requires a kind of empathetic identification so that one can understand the other's situation. "I suffer directly with him, I feel his woe just as I ordinarily feel only my own.... But this requires that I am in some way *identified with him*, in other words that this *difference* between me and everyone else, which is the very basis of my egoism, is eliminated" (144). (It should be noted that later sympathy theorists, such as Scheler and Mercer, criticized Schopenhauer and Hume, respectively, for relying on empathy rather than sympathy, and thus sanctioning a loss of self in the identificatory process, which Scheler and Mercer reject.)

Schopenhauer, however, emphasizes the emotional component of compassion. One understands another's pain through "the everyday phenomenon of *compassion*, of the immediate *participation* ... in the *suffering* of another.... It is simply and solely this compassion that is the real basis of all *voluntary* justice and *genuine* loving-kindness" (144).

"Boundless compassion for all living things is the firmest and surest guarantee of pure moral conduct" (172). Schopenhauer specifically includes animals in this moral community. In a compassion-based ethic "the *animals* are also taken under its protection. In the European systems of morality they are badly provided for, which is most inexcusable. They are said to have no rights ... [and be] without moral significance. All of this is revoltingly crude, a barbarism of the West" (175).

Schopenhauer's ethical theory is rooted in his metaphysics, which entails the Indian distinction between what he called (in his magnum opus) the "Will" and the "Idea." The Will is a kind of undifferentiated pool of Being to which all living creatures belong. It underlies the screen of appearances, of separate individuals, the *Māyā* or the Idea. It is through the pool of Being that we are linked to all other creatures, and it is through compassion that we know that connection; it breaks through the barriers of individuation and egoism (210).

Like Schopenhauer and Hume, succeeding sympathy theorists claim that sympathy logically precedes justice; that is, there must first be the experience of sympathy before there can be any justice claims. Indeed, it is sympathy that determines who is to be included under the umbrella of justice. As environmentalist Fisher notes, "sympathy is fundamental to moral theory in that it determines the range of individuals to which moral principles apply" (245, n.5). And it is "our sympathetic response to animals [that] makes them a part of our moral community" (228).

Mercer also explains: if we take as the fundamental maxim of justice that one "treat everyone alike," then it becomes a question of who counts as "everyone." That decision is determined by the extent to which one can sympathize with the entity (132). In elaborating, Mercer specifies that sympathy only occurs between creatures who can feel. "'Sympathy' has regard for 'the other' solely in respect of his [or her] capacity to feel and to suffer" (4). The sympathetic agent must be "a thinking and feeling being" and the object of sympathy must be "at least a feeling being" (5). The awareness that the other has feelings, or is a subject of feelings, means that one can no longer see that creature as an object. "If we actively sympathize with someone then we cannot treat him as an object, as an instrument for our own self-satisfaction; on the contrary we see him as a being possessing individual worth and existing in his own right" (124). In other words, sympathy engenders moral respect, and thus determines who deserves to be treated on equal terms. The concept of justice, therefore, according to Mercer, is relevant only to sentient beings (133).

Acton also maintains that sympathy establishes claims for equal treatment or justice. This is because sympathy requires treating another's needs as comparable with one's own. It leads one to realize that "the other['s] distress is at least *comparable* with [one's own], and the road has been opened up ... to the demand for equal treatment of equal needs. Sympathy requires that every sentient being shall *count*" (66). Scheler, like Schopenhauer, agrees that sympathy frees us from the "illusion" of "'egocentricity' ... the illusion of taking one's own environment to be the world itself" (58). "The dissipation of this illusion ... [enables] us to grasp how a [person], or living creature ... is our *equal in worth*" (60). Thus, again, sympathy is seen as opening up and determining notions of justice.

Scheler also maintains that an individual encounter with suffering should make us aware of suffering in general. Thus "the pure sentiment of fellow-feeling is released as a permanent disposition, spreading far beyond the occasion which first inspired it, towards *everybody and every* good thing" (60). This brings us to the third issue Kantian theorists hold against sympathy-based ethics, that it is nonuniversalizable.

In his recent book *The Thee Generation* (1991) Tom Regan criticizes "ethic-of-care" feminism for its failure to provide a means of universalizing the individual experience of caring and sympathy. "What are the resources within the ethic of care that can move people to consider the ethics of their dealings with individuals who *stand outside* the existing circle of their valued interpersonal relationships?" (95). In fact, he argues, "most people do not care very much about what happens to [nonhuman animals] ... their care seems to be ... limited to 'pet' animals, or to cuddly or rare specimens of wildlife. What, then, becomes of the animals toward whom people are indifferent, given the ethic of care?" (96). In short, how does one generalize beyond the individual particular instance of caring or compassion to include all creatures within an ethic of care?

Regan argues that such extension can only come through logic. One extends one's care for one's own children to one's neighbors' children because it is illogical and inconsistent not to do so. "Whether I care or not [emotionally for the neighbors' children], I ought to and it is logic that leads me to the realization of this 'ought'" (140). Regan's characteristic rejection of emotion or sympathy as a base for moral decision-making is apparent here. Isn't it also likely that if one's neighbors' children were in harm, one would sympathize with them and care enough to help them? And isn't it unlikely that one would stop to figure out principles of logic and consistency to determine an appropriate moral action, if say, those children were crying in pain? (Of course, one can conjure up qualifying circumstances that will affect one's decision whether to help the children or not, but that is irrelevant to the question at hand—which is whether one responds on a rational or emotional basis to the suffering of nonkin).

It is clear in fact that one can and often does feel sympathy for complete strangers. If I watch on television children starving in Somalia or hear about the brutal rape of women in Bosnia, people I know little about and certainly do not know personally, I nevertheless *feel* sympathy; I care about their plight and am moved to try to help them. Thus, I contend—along with Hume and other sympathy theorists—that sympathy is easily universalized.

Virginia Held argues in a recent critique of rationalist ethics that in its reliance on theory based on universal, abstract "persons," it neglects the experience of the "particular other," the personal emotional relationship one has with a real person. But, she contends, "particular others" need not be individual people one knows personally; rather, they can be "actual starving children in Africa with whom one feels empathy . . . not just those we are close to in any traditional context of family, neighbors, or friends. But particular others are still not 'all rational beings' or 'the greatest number'"—the latter allusions to Kantian and utilitarian abstractions, respectively.[22] It is a particular qualitative experience that is missing in contemporary rationalist theory, the emotional sympathetic understanding of another creature. It is this "personalist" dimension that sympathy theorists would restore to ethical theory.

We see now that sympathy theorists refute Kant by arguing that sympathy is in fact a form of knowledge that includes a cognitive dimension. It is not, therefore, whimsical and erratic, nor does it entail obliteration of the thinking or feeling self. It is easily universalized, although, as Luke points out, such extensions are often muted by powerful social and political institutions.

A number of feminists, including myself, have asserted that ethical theory about animal treatment should be grounded in what these earlier theorists called sympathy. In her important 1985 article "Liberation of Nature" (included in this volume), Marti Kheel called for "a recognition of the importance of feeling and emotion and personal experience in moral decision-making" (30–31) about animals. Noting that much evil is obfuscated through abstract rationalization, which serves to distance one from its actuality, Kheel suggests that personal experience of evil might bring its reality home. For example, those who "*think* . . . that there is nothing morally wrong with eating meat . . . ought, perhaps, to visit a factory farm or slaughterhouse to see if [they] still *feel* the same way" (27).[23]

Some feminists have developed Carol Gilligan's "ethic of care" as a base for animal defense theory. See especially Deane Curtin's "Toward an Ecological Ethic of Care" (included in this volume).[24] Though

Attention to Suffering | 159

it has received much criticism and amplification (see especially Larabee and Kittay and Meyers), Gilligan's *In a Different Voice* (1982) remains the classic statement of the care ethic. In this framework:

> The moral problem arises from conflicting responsibilities rather than competing rights and requires for its resolution a mode of thinking that is contextual and narrative rather than formal and abstract. The conception of morality as concerned with the activity of care centers moral development around the understanding of responsibility and relationships, just as the conception of morality as fairness ties moral development to the understanding of rights and rules.²⁵

Thus, Gilligan identifies an ethic that is rooted in the kind of sympathetic understanding proposed by the sympathy theorists introduced above.

Such an ethic, historically, has been confined largely to the domestic sphere and to women. Leaving aside the question of whether as mothers women are biologically predisposed toward caring for their young (I leave it aside because biological determinism is simply an inadequate explanation of human [and indeed much nonhuman animal] behavior), it is apparent that women's historical social and economic practice has been of a caring nature. In addition to maternal practice (see Sara Ruddick 1989 on this), women have nearly universally engaged in use-value production as their primary economic experience. Use-value production means the creation of products for immediate use or consumption by members of the household (clothes, food, and the like). It is a "caring labor," to use Hilary Rose's term.²⁶

A number of theorists (particularly Nancy Hartsock, Linda Nicholson, and Eli Zaretsky) have shown how in the West a division of moral labor accompanied the historical division between the public and private spheres with their divergent economic practices.²⁷ In an interesting recent exploration of the subject, "Eco-Feminism and Deep Ecology" (1987), Jim Cheney ties Gilligan's caring ethic to the gift-exchange economy characteristic of preindustrial societies:

> If we were to describe the ethical voices characteristic of people living within the two economies, they would be the two ethical voices described by Carol Gilligan, the (gendered) male voice associated with the market economy and the very different (gendered) female voices associated with the gift economy.²⁸

Cheney proceeds to argue that the Gilligan caring ethic should form the basis of environmental ethical theory.

Several theorists (in addition to Cheney, especially Virginia Held and Annette Baier) have pointed out that rights theory is rooted in the contractual relationships of a market economy. Baier in fact notes that rights theory and the Kantian rationalist ethic were developed for an elite of white property-holding males. Kant himself excluded women from the moral community of "rights-holders" (along with animals). Women, in fact, formed a kind of "moral proletariat" who carried on the necessary caring labor in the home, while men enjoyed the privileges and rights of public citizenship.[29] This is not to say that the notion of equal rights should be abolished or that ideas of justice are automatically specious; it *is* to say that, historically, Western women came out of a different ethical tradition than men, one that has been identified by Gilligan as the "caring ethic." It makes sense then that because there is much that is valuable in this ethic, feminists who are concerned about animal welfare would seek to locate an animal treatment ethic within this tradition.

To do so, however, feminists must insist that it be framed within a political perspective. Caring is an important ethical point of departure, but to be effective it must be informed by an accurate political view. A number of theorists (including especially Sara Ruddick and Deane Curtin)[30] have made this point. As a good example of how the caring perspective is enriched by a political framework, consider Marilyn Friedman's discussion of the famous Heinz hypothetical (that Gilligan among others discusses). Here the issue concerns a man, Heinz, whose dying wife can only be saved by a particular drug. The druggist's prices are unfairly high, so that Heinz cannot afford the drug. The ethical question posed in the hypothetical is what is the proper moral course for Heinz? Should he obey the law (and presumably let his wife die) or steal the drug and save his wife? Friedman points out that the real answer to this question lies in a political analysis of a system that denies health care to people who cannot afford it and that "allows most health care resources to be privately owned, privately sold for profit in the market place, and privately withheld from people who cannot afford the market price."[31] While the traditional Kantian response to the Heinz dilemma is that he should not steal (Kant: "I am never to act otherwise than *so that I could also will that my maxim should become a universal law*" [281]), and the ethic-of-care response is that he should steal, because in this particular context his responsibility is to his wife and because stealing is a lesser evil than death, a political ethic-

Attention to Suffering | 161

of-care response would include the larger dimension of looking to the political and economic context within which people must make moral decisions. Thus, the corporate-controlled health-care system becomes the primary villain in the piece, and the incident should serve to motivate action to change the system. This is the real ethical act that should emerge from the Heinz dilemma. On the other hand, a political ethic-of-care would not abandon Heinz in the abstractions of a political critique; it would also support him in obtaining the drug (by stealing, if indeed that is the only way to secure it, and if indeed the drug is as miraculous as it is supposed to be—ecofeminists are also skeptical of drug industry claims of efficacity—see Kheel's "From Healing Herbs to Deadly Drugs" [1989]).[32]

Carol Adams's *Sexual Politics of Meat* (1990) is a good example of a work that lays out the political (in this case, patriarchal) context of meat-eating. So, while a caring ethic focuses on the suffering of the animal, it is enlarged by an understanding of the symbolic cultural significances of meat-eating, which Adams explains (see also Jeremy Rifkin, *Beyond Beef*).[33] Such awareness of cultural ideologies enable the formation of appropriate ethical actions because they help to explain who profits from certain practices, such as meat-eating, and who therefore continues to promulgate propaganda on their behalf. It is important to understand the role of the meat lobby or the National Rifle Association (in promoting hunting, for example) in furthering institutionalized sanctions of these practices. Indeed, as Luke points out, massive institutional strategies have been mobilized on a national level to obscure the reality of animal suffering. Part of any ethical response must therefore be to counter these lies, to lift the veil on animal agony.

In addition to assessing power relations, a political perspective also involves a consideration of needs. On the individual level, the caring response must include a determination of a person's or animal's needs. As Rita Manning notes, caring requires "a willingness to give ... lucid attention to the needs of others."[34] This attitude, which some have labeled "attentive love" (see below), goes beyond just respecting the rights of another.

Within a political perspective, needs assessment has a wider scope. While relatively undeveloped in liberal political theory, some Marxist theorists have focused on this issue (see Braybrooke). Agnes Heller has analyzed the social construction of the artificial consumer needs that fuel a capitalist society in her *Theory of Need in Marx* (1974).[35] She proposes the concept of *radical needs* as a revolutionary force whereby people become aware of their qualitative, spiritual needs beyond reified manufactured needs, and demand their satisfaction.

In her analysis of the Gilligan ethic, Seyla Benhabib proposes (following Jürgen Habermas) a "communicative ethic of need interpretations."[36] This means an ethic where the oppressed have an opportunity to voice their needs and where ethical decision-making is conducted in a dialogic process. Unlike universalistic rights-based theories, such an ethic would not elide the reality of the "concrete other," which remains "the *unthought*, the *unseen*, and the *unheard* in such theories" (168).

"One consequence of this ethic ... is that ... moral theory is enlarged so that not only rights but needs" are addressed (169). An assessment of animal needs must therefore be a part of any caring ethic for the treatment of animals. Indeed, further extension of needs theory into the area of animal welfare should be developed.

No ethic, therefore, exists in a political vacuum, and thus while it is important to ground ethics in a personal sympathetic response, it is also important to take a larger view, placing the individual instance within a political understanding of the cause and an assessment of the needs of the sufferer. The individual response is thus generalized not in a Kantian sense but within the framework of political analysis.

No ethic can therefore be apolitical; nor can any epistemology. The way we see the world—what in fact we see—is shaped by our understanding of its power relations and by our values. Much of this is taught, passed on through the mechanisms that reproduce cultural ideology, such as the schools, the churches, the media. It therefore often reflects uncritically the viewpoint and interests of the dominant powers in society.

Some feminists, notably Alison Jaggar and Nancy Hartsock, have argued that marginalized people may have an alternative perspective or standpoint that is more valid than the dominant view because it sees realities—pain and need—that are elided by controlling ideologies, which are motivated to distort the truth to perpetuate the status quo.[37] Women may be seen therefore as providing an alternative perspective—that codified in the "caring ethic," which is rooted, as we have seen, in women's historical social and economic practices.

In a recent article entitled "Moral Understandings: Alternative 'Epistemology' For a Feminist Ethics" (1992), Margaret Urban Walker calls for "a profound and original rebellion against the regnant [ethical] paradigm,"[38] which she labels the *"universalist/impersonalist tradition"* (168)—in short, the Kantian rationalist/rights tradition noted here. In its stead she proposes "an *alternative moral epistemol-*

ogy, a very different way of identifying and appreciating the forms of intelligence which define moral consideration" (166). Components of this alternative epistemology include those elements of feminist ethics identified here, such as paying "attention to the particular," constructing moral issues in "contextual and narrative" (Gilligan 19) frames, and using a conversational or dialogical mode in moral decision-making (166). In an earlier article (included in this volume), I argued that an ethic for the treatment of animals must be grounded "in an emotional and spiritual conversation with nonhuman lifeforms" (52). Such a conversation can emerge only when attentive love is directed at the other.

Attentive love is an exercise of the moral imagination, as urged by the numerous sympathy theorists cited above. The term derives, however, specifically from Simone Weil who in 1942 stated:

> The love of our neighbor in all its fullness simply means being able to say to him [or her]: "What are you going through?" It is a recognition that the sufferer exists, not only as a unit in a collection, or a specimen from the social category labeled "unfortunate," but as [an individual], exactly like us, who was one day stamped with a special mark by affliction. For this reason it is enough, but it is indispensable, to know how to look at him [or her] in a certain way.
> This way of looking is first of all attentive.[39]

But it is Iris Murdoch who elaborated Weil's insight into a central moral idea, one that numerous feminists have seized upon as establishing the necessary epistemology for a caring ethic.[40] Murdoch developed the idea in several articles and in her book *The Sovereignty of Good* (1971). "Attentive love" is a moral reorientation that requires developing one's powers of attention. It is a discipline similar to that exercised by great artists or scholars (Weil used the idea originally in an essay on the discipline of scholarly study). As other sympathy theorists remarked, this reorientation breaks down solipsistic barriers; it forces attention without, to others and to what they are experiencing. Murdoch notes, "The direction of attention is, contrary to nature, outward, away from self which reduces all to a false unity, toward the great surprising variety of the world, and the ability to so direct attention is love" (66). In acknowledging Weil's coinage of the term, Murdoch says she meant by it "the idea of a just and loving gaze directed upon an individual reality" (34). Such attention, Murdoch urges, is "the characteristic and proper mark of the active moral agent" (34).

Like Mercer, Murdoch recognizes that actually seeing another's reality means constituting him or her as a subject with separate needs from one's own: "The more . . . [it is] seen that another . . . has needs and wishes as demanding as one's own, the harder it becomes to treat a person as a thing" (66).

Recognizing the other as a subject means constituting the other as a *Thou*, not an *It*, to use Martin Buber's celebrated distinction. While Buber's moral epistemology (which is rooted in the phenomenological existentialism of some of the sympathy theorists noted above), is usually assumed to apply only to humans, promoting a kind of moral humanism, in fact Buber himself applies it to animals and other living beings.

In a moving meditation on a tree Buber writes:

> I contemplate a tree.
> I can accept it as a picture. . . .
> I can feel it as a movement. . . .
> I can assign it to a species. . . .
> But it can also happen, if grace and will are joined, that as I contemplate the tree I am drawn into a relation, and the tree ceases to be an It. . . .
> Does the tree have consciousness, similar to our own? I have no experience of that. . . . What I encounter is neither the soul of a tree nor a dryad, but the tree itself.[41]

In his theory of environmental ethics, Paul Taylor calls for a similar attentiveness to the particular reality of individual organisms as the basis for a human relationship to nonhuman life-forms:

> As one becomes more and more familiar with the organism being observed, one acquires a sharpened awareness of the particular way it is living its life. One may become fascinated by it and even get to be involved in its good and bad fortunes. The organism comes to mean something to one as a unique, irreplaceable individual. . . . This progressive development from objective, detached knowledge to the recognition of individuality . . . to a full awareness of an organism's standpoint, is a process of heightening our consciousness of what it means to be an individual living thing.[42]

Taylor further maintains that we must be "'open' to the full existence and nature of the organism . . . let the individuality of the organism come before us, undistorted by our likes and dislikes, our hopes and fears, our interests, wants, and needs. As far as it is humanly possible to do so, we comprehend the organism as it is in itself, not as we want it to be" (120).

A feminist moral epistemology calls for the just and loving attention seen in these examples.[43] Rooting ethics in right seeing is nothing new. As Rosemarie Tong remarks, "even Aristotle said that ethical decisions rest in perception—in perceiving, in *seeing through one's experiences* to the moral truth beneath appearances" (228). But in the past, she argues, the great philosophers of the Western tradition "failed in their abstract moral vision because they failed in their daily moral vision. Not seeing the oppression that surrounded them, they shaped an abstract ethics that may have served to protect the interests of those in power" (229).

Sympathy theory of the past, long eclipsed, is now reinforced by a powerful new wave of ethical theory proposed by "ethic-of-care" feminists, who derive their ethic from the experience of the oppressed, urging that ethics be rooted in caring practice and an epistemology of attentive love. Such a focus need not—indeed must not—lose sight of the political context in which our moral awareness develops and our moral actions take place. But it also does not lose sight of the individual case. Contrary to Kantian rationalism, it envisages *both* the personal *and* the political.

Like Buber, people exercising attentive love *see* the tree; but they also see the logging industry. They see the downed cow in the slaughterhouse pen; but they also see the farming and dairy industry. They see the Silver Spring monkey; but they also see the drug corporations and university collaboration.

A political analysis is thus essential—particularly for formulating an effective and appropriate ethical response. But the motivation for that response remains the primary experience of sympathy. By redirecting the national focus to the suffering reality of individual animals, I believe we can reawaken the sympathetic response and reactivate the moral imagination, as outlined in this article. The animal defense movement need no longer rely solely on abstract utilitarian and rights-based claims of equal justice for animals. Rather it should recognize that a viable ethic for the treatment of animals can be rooted in sympathy, a passionate caring about their well-being.

Notes

1. Immanuel Kant, *Kant Selections*, ed. Theodore Meyer Green (New York: Scribner's, 1957), 279. Further references follow in the text.
2. Arthur Schopenhauer, *On the Basis of Morality* (1841) (Indianapolis: Bobbs-Merrill, 1965), 95. Further references follow in the text.
3. Tom Regan, *The Thee Generation* (Philadelphia: Temple University Press, 1991), 142. Further references follow in the text.
4. Philip Mercer, *Sympathy and Ethics: A Study of the Relationship Between Sympathy and Morality with Special Reference to Hume's Treatise* (Oxford: Oxford University Press, 1972), 8. Further references follow in the text.
5. H. B. Acton, "The Ethical Importance of Sympathy," *Philosophy* 30 (1955): 66. Further references follow in the text.
6. Frederick A. Elliston, "Husserl's Phenomenology of Empathy," in *Husserl: Expositions and Appraisals*, ed. Elliston and Peter McCormick (Notre Dame, Ind.: University of Notre Dame Press, 1977), 223.
7. See Floyd Matson, *The Broken Image: Man, Science, and Society* (Garden City, N.Y.: Anchor, 1966), 240; H. Stuart Hughes, *Consciousness and Society: The Reconstruction of European Social Thought 1890–1930* (New York: Vintage, 1961), 187–88, 311.
8. Max Scheler, *The Nature of Sympathy* (1913) (Hamden, Conn.: Archon, 1970), 48. Further references follow in the text.
9. Scheler erroneously sees the Western dominative attitude toward nature as "a legacy of Judaism" (105). While the Hebrew Bible does sanction human domination, the Christian tradition heavily reinforced this thesis, and the Cartesian epistemological basis for modern science can hardly be seen as Judaic in origin. (Scheler also, of course, strongly criticizes Christianity.) Schopenhauer also—in even more offensive terms—attributed the Western derogation of animals to Judaism (the *"foetor Judaicus"*) (*On the Basis of Morality*, 175, 177, 187). Schopenhauer's anti-Semitism, as well as his sexism, is, of course, abominable.
10. Kenneth J. Shapiro, "Understanding Dogs through Kinesthetic Empathy, Social Construction, and History," *Anthrozoös* 3, no. 3 (1989): 184.
11. Edith Stein, *On the Problem of Empathy* (1916) (The Hague, Neth.: Martinus Nijhoff, 1966), 54–55. Further references follow in the text.
12. John A. Fisher, "Taking Sympathy Seriously: A Defense of Our Moral Psychology toward Animals," in *The Animal Rights/Environmental Ethics Debate: The Environmental Perspective*, ed. Eugene C. Hargrove (Albany, N.Y.: SUNY Press, 1992), 233.
13. Paul W. Taylor "The Ethics of Respect for Nature," in *The Animal Rights/Environmental Ethics Debate*, ed. Hargrove, 109–10. A further reference follows in the text.
14. Rosemarie Tong, *Feminine and Feminist Ethics* (Belmont, Calif.: Wadsworth, 1993), 64. Further references follow in the text.
15. Nel Noddings, *Caring: A Feminine Approach to Ethics and Moral Education* (Berkeley: University of California Press, 1984), 174. Noddings seems ambivalent, however, on whether or to what extent human caring should be extended to animals. See *Caring*, chap. 7, and her "Comment" on my "Animal Rights and Feminist Theory" (in this volume) in *Signs* 16, no. 2 (winter 1991): 418–22. For my "Reply to Noddings," see *Signs* 16, no. 2 (winter 1991): 423–25.
16. See also John Kekes, "Moral Sensitivity," *Philosophy* 59 (1984): 3–19.
17. See Joseph Duke Filanowicz, "Ethical Sentimentalism Revisited," *History of Philosophy Quarterly* 6, no. 2 (April 1989): 189–206, for a recent reassertion of Shaftsbury's system as "a genuine and live option for contemporary ethical theory" (189).

18. Keith Thomas, *Man and the Natural World: A History of the Modern Sensibility* (New York: Pantheon, 1983), 175–76.
19. David Hume, *An Enquiry Concerning the Principles of Morals* (1777) (La Salle, Ill.: Open Court, 1960), 146, 67. Further references follow in the text.
20. James Rachels, *Created from Animals: The Moral Implications of Darwinism* (Oxford: Oxford University Press, 1990), 77, 147–57. Further references follow in the text. See also Helena Cronin, *The Ant and the Peacock: Altruism and Sexual Selection from Darwin to Today* (Cambridge: Cambridge University Press, 1991).
21. J. Baird Callicott, "Animal Liberation and Environmental Ethics: Back Together Again," in *The Animal Rights/Environmental Ethics Debate*, ed. Hargrove, 156. Callicott offers a two-communities theory here, claiming that human treatment of domestic animals should operate according to one ethic, and of wild animals, to another. Less successfully, he attempts to argue that a Humean sympathy ethic also undergirds deep ecology theory, in particular the "land ethic" of Aldo Leopold—a thesis he develops in "The Conceptual Foundation of the Land Ethic," in *Companion to "A Sand County Almanac": Interpretive and Critical Essays* (Madison: University of Wisconsin Press, 1987), 186–217—but such an abstract use of the term *sympathy* would seem to rob it of meaning. Sympathy must be rooted in feelings for the particular, the concrete other.
22. Virginia Held, "Feminism and Moral Theory," in *Women and Moral Theory*, ed. Eva Feder Kittay and Diana T. Meyers (Totowa, N.J.: Rowman & Littlefield, 1987), 118.
23. See also Linda Vance, "Ecofeminism and the Politics of Reality," in *Ecofeminism: Women, Animals, Nature*, ed. Greta Gaard (Philadelphia: Temple University Press, 1993), 136.
24. Karen Warren extends the idea of care to mean intense appreciation of nature. In a celebrated passage she explains how in rock climbing she developed an emotional, respectful—indeed caring—attitude for the rock: "At that moment I was bathed in serenity. I began to talk to the rock in an almost inaudible, child-like way, as if the rock were my friend.... Gone was the determination to conquer the rock. I wanted simply to work respectfully with the rock as I climbed.... I felt myself caring for this rock" ("The Power and the Promise of Ecological Feminism," *Environmental Ethics* 12 [summer 1990]: 134–35). Greta Gaard points out, however, that later in the same article Warren blithely sanctions the killing of a deer, to which she does not seem to extend the same caring attitude ("Ecofeminism and Native American Cultures: Pushing the Limits of Cultural Imperialism," in *Ecofeminism*, ed. Gaard, 296–97). The reason for Warren's inconsistency, I suggest, is that she is coming out of deep ecology theory, which notoriously elides the suffering of individual animals in its rush to embrace "ecoholism." Feminists Marti Kheel and Ariel Kay Salleh have criticized deep ecology theory (see Kheel "Ecofeminism and Deep Ecology: Reflections on Identity and Difference," in *Reweaving the World: The Emergence of Ecofeminism*, ed. Irene Diamond and Gloria Feman Orenstein [San Francisco: Sierra Club, 1990], 128–37, and Salleh, "Deeper Than Deep Ecology: The Eco-Feminist Connection," *Environmental Ethics* 6 [winter 1984]: 339–45). I will not review these critiques here except to reaffirm that a feminist caring ethic for the treatment of animals must be rooted in appreciation, understanding, and sympathy for the animals as individuals. Following Mercer (see above, p. 156) I contend that sympathy or caring obtains between *feeling* beings: "'Sympathy' has regard for 'the other' solely in respect of his [or her] capacity to feel and to suffer" (Mercer 4). Thus, Warren's use of the term *caring* is inappropriate. One can appreciate or respect a rock but one cannot feel sympathetic concern for it: such compassion is appropriate only for sentient or at least living creatures.
25. Carol Gilligan, *In a Different Voice: Psychological Theory and Women's Development* (Cambridge: Harvard University Press, 1982), 19.

26. Hilary Rose, "Hand, Brain, and Heart: A Feminist Epistemology for the Natural Sciences," *Signs* 9, no. 1 (autumn 1983): 83.
27. Nancy C.M. Hartsock, *Money, Sex, and Power: Toward a Feminist Historical Materialism* (New York: Longman, 1983); Linda Nicholson, "Women, Morality, and History," in *An Ethic of Care: Feminist and Interdisciplinary Perspectives*, ed. Mary Jane Larrabee (New York: Routledge, 1993), 87–101; Eli Zaretsky, *Capitalism, the Family and Personal Life* (New York: Harper, 1976).
28. Jim Cheney, "Eco-Feminism and Deep Ecology," *Environmental Ethics* 9 (summer 1987): 115–45.
29. Annette Baier, "The Need for More than Justice," in *Science, Morality, and Feminist Theory*, ed. Marsha Hanan and Kai Nielsen (Calgary, Can.: University of Calgary Press, 1987), 50.
30. Sara Ruddick, "From Maternal Thinking to Peace Politics," in *Explorations in Feminist Ethics: Theory and Practice*, ed. Eve Browning Cole and Susan Coultrap-McQuin (Bloomington: Indiana University Press, 1992), 141–56; Deane Curtin, "Toward an Ecological Ethic of Care," in this volume. Also see my own discussion in *Feminist Theory: The Intellectual Traditions of American Feminism*, rev. ed. (New York: Continuum, 1992), 199–200.
31. Marilyn Friedman, "Care and Context in Moral Reasoning," in *Women and Moral Theory*, ed. Kittay and Meyers, 202. Further references follow in the text.
32. Marti Kheel, "From Healing Herbs to Deadly Drugs: Western Medicine's War against the Natural World," in *Healing the Wounds: The Promise of Ecofeminism*, ed. Judith Plant (Philadelphia: New Society, 1989), 96–111.
33. Carol J. Adams, *The Sexual Politics of Meat: A Feminist-Vegetarian Critical Theory* (New York: Continuum, 1990); Jeremy Rifkin, *Beyond Beef: The Rise and Fall of the Cattle Industry* (New York: Dutton, 1992).
34. Rita Manning, "Just Caring," in *Explorations in Feminist Ethics*, ed. Cole and Coultrap-McQuin, 45.
35. Agnes Heller, *The Theory of Need in Marx* (London: Allison & Busby, 1978).
36. Seyla Benhabib, "The Generalized and the Concrete Other: The Kohlberg-Gilligan Controversy and Moral Theory," in *Women and Moral Theory*, ed. Kittay and Meyers, 168. Further references follow in the text.
37. Alison M. Jaggar, *Feminist Politics and Human Nature* (Totowa, N.J.: Rowman & Littlefield, 1983); Jaggar, "Love and Knowledge," *Gender/Body/Knowledge*, ed. Jaggar and Susan R. Bordo (New Brunswick, N.J.: Rutgers University Press, 1989), 145–71; Donovan, *Feminist Theory*, 89–90, 198–200.
38. Margaret Urban Walker, "Moral Understandings: Alternative 'Epistemology' for a Feminist Ethics," in *Explorations in Feminist Ethics*, ed. Cole and Coultrap-McQuin, 165–75. Further references follow in the text.
39. Simone Weil, "Reflections on the Right Use of School Studies with a View to the Love of God" (1942), in *The Simone Weil Reader*, ed. George A. Panichas (New York: David McKay, 1977), 51.
40. See especially Walker, "Moral Understandings"; Ellen L. Fox, "Seeing through Women's Eyes: The Role of Vision in Women's Moral Theory," in *Explorations in Feminist Ethics*, ed. Cole and Coultrap-McQuin, 111–16; Ruddick, *Maternal Thinking: Toward a Politics of Peace* (Boston: Beacon, 1989); Robin S. Dillon, "Care and Respect," in *Explorations in Feminist Ethics*, ed. Cole and Coultrap-McQuin, 69–81; Meredith W. Michaels, "Morality without Distinction," *Philosophical Forum* 17, no. 3 (spring 1986): 175–87; and Iris Murdoch, *The Sovereignty of Good* (New York: Schocken, 1971). I elaborated these ideas earlier in "Beyond the Net: Feminist Criticism as a Moral Criticism," *Denver Quarterly* 17, no. 4 (winter 1983): 40–57.
41. Martin Buber, *I and Thou* (1923) (New York: Scribner's, 1970), 57–59. See also Buber's discussion of his exchange of glances with a cat (144–46), and his treatment of a horse as thou in *Between Man and Man* (1947; rev. ed., New York:

Macmillan, 1965), 23. Another important work that argues for the "Thouness" of animals is Gary A. Kowalski, *The Souls of Animals* (Walpole, N.H.: Stillpoint, 1991).

42. Paul W. Taylor, *Respect for Nature: A Theory of Environmental Ethics* (Princeton, N.J.: Princeton University Press, 1986), 120–21. A further reference follows in the text.

43. Taylor, a rationalist, would probably resist the term *loving* here, even though his description comes very close to the Murdoch/Weil notion of attentive love, applied to natural life. In *Respect for Nature*, Taylor insists upon the Kantian distinction between acting out of rational duty and acting out of emotional inclination. He rejects the latter on familiar Kantian grounds (85, 90–91, 126–27).

Caring about Suffering:
A Feminist Exploration (1995)

CAROL J. ADAMS

> Those in power typically advocate rules and
> rationality, others, relatedness and caring.
> *Ellyn Kaschak*

*I*n the wake of the appearance of *The Sexual Politics of Meat*, attempts were made to determine my feminist stance on animal rights as a philosophy. *The Sexual Politics of Meat* did not offer any helpful clues on this subject. It was not my goal to approach the oppression of animals in the manner of Peter Singer or Tom Regan. Not only had this been done, but my work had a different source, and in the early years, I was working without the benefit of their major texts. My goal was to expose the roots of animal exploitation in the construction of the patriarchal subject. I needed to make visible the invisible—the lives of women and the experience of animals used by humans—while identifying the theoretical structures that maintained this invisibility. Neither the philosophical language of rights nor that of interest seemed to intersect with this goal—nor could they since their analysis of animals' status ignored the issue of human male domination.

Although the theoretical debates about claims on behalf of animals' rights and interests did not personally appeal to me, what, I wondered, was the appropriate theoretical approach to establish animals as having other than instrumental value? Rights, it seemed to me, at least said, minimally, "do not touch." And there are many times when that is exactly what I feel about the exploitation of animals. I want to intervene and proclaim this. But then I began more closely to study both the issue and myself. My own evolution toward animal defense was because of the sudden loss of a Welsh pony, and the feelings that I experienced when I tried to eat a hamburger the night of that pony's death. Certainly I knew firsthand how relationships can catalyze one into refusing to view animals instrumentally. Moreover, it seemed that it is because animal advocates *care* that many gravitate to the language of rights.

While writing *The Sexual Politics of Meat*, I was unaware of the "rights-care" debate. When I learned of the debate, I was worried because ethics of care discussions seemed to reinforce certain assumptions about women and our caregiving role in Western patriarchal culture.

Was caring a survival skill developed under oppression? If caring was necessitated by women's lack of power, and a negotiation from this position of powerlessness, then to reclaim it as the source for transforming people's relationship with animals would only further women's oppression. But jettisoning the ethic of care because caring was an aspect of our oppression seemed to be the wrong approach. My own evolution had occurred precisely because I cared about animals. Were the day to come when women's oppression was eradicated, would we also wish to eradicate caring for others? Would not some form of caring survive the transformation of women's status?

Then I came to realize—thanks to feminist analyses of care—that the male ideal of the autonomous individual, on which rights theory is based, is fraudulent. As feminist psychotherapist Ellyn Kaschak points out,

> It would seem that men have just as much difficulty separating and individuating as do women, and that the ideal of separation and individuality is a somewhat unnatural act which must be accomplished largely by illusion. If men define women, children, and even physical aspects of the environment as extensions of themselves, then their own difficulties with separation are made invisible. Men so often report experiencing women's reactions to their behaviors as an extension of their own that we must consider that men lack a good sense of where their boundaries end and women's begin.... The construction of a separate and individual self directly reflects the masculinist predilection to make invisible the context and interconnections between people and all living things. This is the same perspective that leads to perceiving concepts as universal rather than as contextually bound.[1]

Kaschak thus reorients the rights-care debate by pointing out that the notion of the autonomous individual (the ontology that accompanies rights) is dependent on the relational ontology of care, but it renders invisible the whole network of relationships that are sustaining the solitary individual. Given this insight, we have to recognize that the idea of the independent rights-bearer depends, without acknowledgment, on the ontology of care.

The articulation of animal rights philosophy presumes an autonomous individual, traditionally a "man of reason," the Enlightenment idea of the autonomous seeker in an agonistic and lone quest for knowledge. But, as noted, the idea of autonomy is an illusion, because it depends on the invisibility of women's caring activities.

> If we define being relational as feeling responsible for, and defining, one's self-worth by the success or failure of one's relationships and by being sensitive to the expressed and unexpressed emotional needs of others, then it would appear that women, in general, are more relational than are men, in general. However, if we consider that men's independence and separateness viewed contextually emerge as emotional and physical dependence upon women—wives, lovers, secretaries, graduate assistants, nurses, and so on—then men are certainly as relational as women, if not more so. (Kaschak, 115)

In short, the unacknowledged context for animal rights philosophy is the fact that we live in a patriarchal culture. An entire cadre of female support allows for the illusion of the autonomous rights-holder.

Consider, for instance, when Tom Regan writes "of a new generation, *The Thee Generation*." He describes it as,

> a generation of service: of giving, not taking, of commitment to principles not material possessions, of communal compassion not conspicuous consumption. If the defining question of the present generation is What can I get for me? the central question of this new generation is What can I do for thee?[2]

It may now be "the thee generation" for men but it has always been "the thee generation"—of sacrificial service to others—for women. Thus, Regan's construction fails to acknowledge women's caregiving—the exact problem that rights discourse has at the theoretical level.

I value nurturing and caring because it is good, not because it constitutes women's "difference." Similarly, I do not value animals because women are somehow "closer" to them, but because we experience interdependent oppressions. I support animals because they are oppressed and because I care about their experiences of harm, pain, and suffering: I wish to intervene to end their oppression.[3] Clearly, the animal advocacy movement is committed to ending animal suffering, as well. But, it has failed to engage a central question: What are the implications that animal suffering occurs within the context of a patriarchal culture?

Caring, Emotions, and Theory

Sexual inequality influences our attitudes toward and responses to suffering in numerous ways. To begin with, suffering itself, as an experience, is socially constructed as feminine. Furthermore, emotions are denigrated as untrustworthy and unreliable. They have long been viewed as invalid sources of knowledge. Moreover, they are equated with women, with being "womanish." Given the patriarchal mind/body dualism, the working assumption appears to be that caring about and emotionally responding to suffering are not trustworthy as the foundation of theory.

In accepting as two primary texts, Singer's *Animal Liberation* and Regan's *The Case for Animal Rights*—texts that valorize rationality—the animal defense movement reiterates a patriarchal disavowal of emotions as having a legitimate role in theory making. The problem is that while on the one hand it articulates positions against animal suffering, on the other hand animal rights theory dispenses with the idea that caring about and emotionally responding to this suffering can be appropriate sources of knowledge.[4]

Emotions and theory are related. One does not have to eviscerate theory of emotional content and reflection to present legitimate theory. Nor does the presence of emotional content and reflection eradicate or militate against thinking theoretically. By disavowing emotional responses, two major texts of animal defense close off the intellectual space for recognizing the role of emotions in knowledge and therefore theory making.

As the issue of caring about suffering is problematized, difficulties with animal rights per se become apparent. Without a gender analysis, several important issues that accompany a focus on suffering are neglected, to the detriment of the movement.

Animal rights theory offers a legitimating language for animal defense without acknowledging the indebtedness of the rights-holder to caring relationships. Nor does it provide models for theoretically engaging with our own emotional responses, since emotions are seen as untrustworthy.

Because the animal advocacy movement has failed to incorporate an understanding of caring as a motivation for so many animal defense activists, and because it has not addressed the gendered nature of caring—that it is woman's duty to provide service to others, while it is men's choice—it has not addressed adequately the implications that a disproportionate number of activists are women motivated because they care about animal suffering.

Animal rights theory that disowns or ignores emotions mirrors on the theoretical level the gendered emotional responses inherent in a patriarchal society. In this culture, women are supposed to do the emotional work for heterosexual intimate relationships: "a man will come to expect that a woman's role in his life is to take care of his feelings and alleviate the discomfort involved in feeling."[5] At the cultural level, this may mean that women are doing the emotional work for the animal defense movement. And this emotional work takes place in the context of our own oppression.

The Sex-Species System

Before we can explore the gendered nature of various responses to suffering, we must establish the social and political environment in which suffering and caring about suffering take place.

Feminism identifies this environment as sexist. Animal defenders see it as speciesist. Clearly, as I have argued in *The Sexual Politics of Meat* and *Neither Man nor Beast*, sexism and speciesism are interconnected, mutually reinforcing systems of oppression and ways of organizing the world. The species barrier has always been gendered and racialized; patriarchy has been inscribed through species inequality as well as human inequality. The emphasis on differences between humans and animals not only reinforces fierce boundaries about what constitutes humanness, but particularly about what constitutes manhood. That which traditionally has been seen to distinguish humans from animals—qualities such as reason and rationality—has been used as well to differentiate men from women, whites from people of color. Species categorization is one aspect of a racist patriarchy. "Man" (read: white man) exists as a concept and a sexual identity through negation ("not woman, not beast, not colored"—that is, "not the other").⁶

The best way to convey this analysis of the overlapping, interdependent relationship of sexual inequality and species inequality is by referring to our current racist patriarchy as instituting a *sex-species system*.⁷ An ecofeminist analysis of racist patriarchal dualisms identifies dyads that organize our world. These dyads include:

man	woman
human	animal
white	"colored"
mind	body
reason	emotion

It is not simply that the Western dualistic worldview has divided us from each other, from animals, from a sense of self that thinks and feels in a continuous, related way, so that it could be said that we think through our feelings, feel through our thinking. Nor is it only that the dominated side of the dualism is in service to the dominant side.⁸ It is also—and very specifically—that the inequality attributed to the colored-female-body-animal side is *sexualized*. That is, the colored, female, animal is the body that is constructed as available for sex. Kaschak explains:

> Several decades ago, Karen Horney noted that "the prerogative of gender [is] the socially sanctioned right of all males to sexualize all females, regardless of age or status"—to observe, evaluate, and use the female body for their own purposes. . . . Although not all men may choose to exercise this right actively, no woman can choose to opt out of this system. (68)

As Kathy Barry cogently argues in her new work *The Prostitution of Sexuality:*

> When society becomes sexually saturated, sex is equated with the female body—where it is gotten, had, taken. . . . Sexual saturation of society is a political accomplishment of male domination. . . . When sex is objectified and human beings are reduced to vehicles for acquiring it, sexual domination enters into and is anchored in the body.⁹

The sex-species system insures that white, "rational" men have access to female animal bodies. In *The Sexual Politics of Meat*, I explain how it is that nonhuman animal bodies of either sex are rendered female. "Prey"—from whales to foxes—are called "shes" whether they are male or female.[10] Similarly, women's bodies, especially the bodies of women of color, are seen as animal.

Racism is clearly a part of the sex-species system. Not only does it use an animalizing discourse about oppressed, disenfranchised, and marginalized people (imputing that they *are* animals, that they are *like* animals, or that they are *closer* to animals—that is, using a species hierarchy), but it sexualizes these now-animalized bodies, insisting on the availability of "colored" female animal bodies, and claiming that these sexed bodies sexually desire being violated as well as sexually desiring animals as partners.[11] Bestiality is often the pornographic focus characteristic of a speciesist racist patriarchy. Fixated on women of color, having sex with animals, such pornography actually reverses the agent: most acts of forced sex with animals involve men as agents. Yet, in pornography, the agent is frequently cast as a woman of color.[12] Here is the sex-species system at work: men taking/making sex with colored "female" animal bodies. This is racialized sexual oppression.[13] As Patricia Hill Collins argues:

> African-American women's experiences suggest that Black women were not added into a preexisting pornography, but rather that pornography itself must be reconceptualized as an example of the interlocking nature of race, gender, and class oppression. At the heart of both racism and sexism are notions of biological determinism claiming that people of African descent and women possess immutable biological characteristics marking their inferiority to elite white men. In pornography these racist and sexist beliefs are sexualized.[14]

Building on an analysis of Alice Walker's, Collins explains how it is that pornography depicts white women as objects and black women as animals:

> As objects white women become creations of culture—in this case, the mind of white men—using the materials of nature—in this case, uncontrolled female sexuality. In contrast, as animals Black women receive no such redeeming dose of culture and remain open to the type of exploitation visited on nature overall. Race becomes the distinguishing feature in determining the type of objectification

women will encounter.... Publicly exhibiting Black women may have been central to objectifying Black women as animals and to creating the icon of Black women as animals.... The treatment of all women in contemporary pornography has strong ties to the portrayal of Black women as animals.[15]

To support her claim that "in pornography women become nonpeople and are often represented as the sum of their fragmented body parts," Collins draws on the analysis of Scott McNall, who observes:

> This fragmentation of women relates to the predominance of rear-entry position photographs.... All of these kinds of photographs reduce the woman to her reproductive system, and furthermore, make her open, willing, and available—not in control.... The other thing rear-entry position photographs tell us about women is that they are animals. They are animals because they are the same as dogs—bitches in heat who can't control themselves.[16]

Because of the sexualizing of the nondominant side of the dyad (the colored-woman-body-animal), and because whiteness, on its own, does not intervene in the sex-species system solely as privilege, women of all races are seen as woman-body-animal. As a result, women's orifices are a part of the accessible environment available to men. As Catharine MacKinnon points out, we live "in a society of sex inequality—where sex is what women *have* to sell, sex is what we are, sex is what we are valued for, we are born sex, we die sex."[17]

The sex-species system appears to be deceptively divisible, seeming to be two different systems (women's issues on the one hand, animal issues on the other). This keeps us from making connections. Insisting that we recognize the sex-species system does not insinuate that this is *all* that we must recognize, it is simply insisting that without recognizing the interdependence of the sex-species system, our actions and analyses are fragmented and fractured.

This schema contributes the ecofeminist insight into the devaluation of the body to the radical feminist understanding of the specific sexual use of women's bodies. The sexualized female animal body is consumable when alive through sex acts and pornography,[18] and consumable, if nonhuman, when dead, as food or clothing or scientific material. The mobility of women in the sex-species system means that sometimes we may be unmarked humans in relationship to animals (especially as we benefit from their exploitation) and if we are white in relationship to people of color, while in relationship to those who are the generic humans (men), we are animalized.

A sense of entitlement accompanies men's status in the sex-species system. Psychotherapist Kaschak proposes that male entitlement means that men have extensive boundaries that subsume others. This is male privilege. For women and marginalized men, the boundaries we believed we established for ourselves and our bodies are not acknowledged or respected. Animals often are not seen as individuals and thus remain undifferentiated from each other. Thus, the concept of boundaries for animals—self-imposed or otherwise—rarely arises.

The suffering of women, the other animals, and disenfranchised, colonized peoples occurs within this sex-species system, which remains as well the unacknowledged context for animal rights philosophy and activism.

Is Suffering Generic?

We conventionally talk about human suffering and animal suffering as different phenomena. Elaine Scarry, in an otherwise cogently argued book, *The Body in Pain*, believes:

> a dividing line can be drawn between human hurt and animal hurt; for the displacement of human sacrifice with animal sacrifice (and its implicit designation of the human body as a privileged space that cannot be used in the important process of substantiation [the process by which we establish meaning]) has always been recognized as a special moment in the infancy of civilization.[19]

Most people agree with her, it seems, as we have a rather persistent hierarchy regarding pain and suffering: that it is different for human animals than for nonhuman animals.[20] However, many of the qualities of suffering are in fact nonspecies specific. As Bernard Rollin pointed out years ago, "the most eloquent signs of pain, human *or* animal, are non-linguistic."[21] Scarry confirms that the most prominent qualities of pain are its unsharability, its resistance to language, its active destruction of language. Indeed, pain brings "about an immediate reversion to a state anterior to language, to the sounds and cries a human being makes before language is learned."[22]

Pain, Scarry might have observed, thus eradicates one of the most firmly held demarcating points between humans and other animals: language use. Indeed, pain's "resistance to language is not simply one of its incidental or accidental attributes, but is essential to what it is."[23] It shatters language. In doing so, it transposes humans to an animal status. Does Scarry avoid stating the obvious—that it renders humans "animallike"—because she has so much conceptually invested (all of civilization!) in keeping human and animal pain separate?

James Rachels points out that

> we have virtually the same evidence for animal pain that we have for human pain. When humans are tortured, they cry out; so do animals. When humans are faced with painful stimuli, they draw back and try to escape; so do animals. Pain in humans is associated with the operation of a complex nervous system; so it is with animals.... Darwin stressed that, in an important sense, their nervous systems, their behaviours, their cries, *are* our nervous systems, our behaviours, and our cries, with only a little modification.[24]

But animals also express pain differently. This, too, is important to acknowledge. Feminist scientist Lynda Birke explains that "some species, particularly ungulates (hoofed mammals) do not usually whimper and squeal."[25] Bernard Rollin insists, "Animals do show unique pain behaviour. It just doesn't happen to be human pain behaviour. But, then why should it be?"[26]

The animal defense movement often ends up saying, "animals suffer like humans," thus gesturing toward a generic human suffering model. This is problematic in two ways: first, because it maintains anthropocentricity (animals suffer like human beings [rather than unpacking the idea and saying, "all animal bodies—ours included—suffer in many similar ways"]). Second, because it maintains androcentricity, male-centeredness. It does so because human suffering is much more likely to be conceptualized according to men's experiences rather than women's. In fact, because of the sex-species system, women's suffering and the harms we experience are different from men's.

Men's Suffering

Men's suffering (as men) is often construed to be purposeful. It is suffering for a good. Men's suffering has meaning and is attended to (consider the attention in past years to prostate cancer as opposed to breast cancer, or molested boys over molested girls). Suffering and dying in war is a primary example of suffering for a good. Also, men's suffering is often episodic, not chronic; it occurs in a situation that one is accidentally in, such as being injured or killed by random gunfire ("being in the wrong place at the wrong time"). On the other hand, men's suffering that is neither purposeful nor episodic is usually caused by a political ideological context, such as racism or homophobia. African-American men, Native men, and other men of color suffer for their biological markedness, their race, which makes their maleness conditional. Gay men suffer from homophobia, from being seen as an abomination of "nature's" intent for men, which is to have sex with female bodies.

Women's Suffering

Women's suffering similarly can be the result of our ideological context, i.e., sexism. Women *as women* suffer from a chronic violence that is ongoing, not episodic.[27] It is violence against women *un*modified (woman *qua* woman). This does not mean that women are "victims," but that we must anticipate that we will be victimized because we are women, because of the sex-species system that renders us sexed female animal bodies.[28] The sex-species system also renders other bodies, including at times certain men's bodies, as sexed female animal bodies. Catharine MacKinnon explains how "gender is a substantive process of inequality":

> To be victimized in certain ways may mean to be feminized, to partake of the low social status of the female, to be made into the girl regardless of biological sex. This does not mean that men experience or share the meaning of being a woman, because part of that meaning is that inferiority is indelible and total until it is changed for all women. It does mean that gender is an outcome of a social process of subordination that is only ascriptively tied to body and doesn't lose its particularity of meaning when it shifts embodied form. Femininity is a lowering that is imposed; it can be done to anybody and still be what feminine means. It is just women to whom it is considered natural.[29]

Not only is violence against women our context, rather than an episode, but our suffering from this violence is for no good reason. Unlike militarism, which offers ready explanations for men's suffering in times of military engagements, women's ongoing suffering from violence has no inherent redemptive qualities to it. Nor is it socially constructed as meaningful. Consequently it is not attended to; it is ignored. We women may and do spend many hours trying to figure out why sexual violence happened to us, but sexual violence is both ongoing and incomprehensible. Women's suffering could be stopped if our culture made a commitment to stopping sexually abusive and possessive behavior, mainly on the part of men. Unfortunately, our society has not done so.

The violence we suffer from is agential—that is, it is done by an agent. I refer to this, therefore, as *agential suffering*. But that agency—usually a particular man—is denied by language deriving from the sex-species system.[30] Our suffering is thereby mystified. Not wanting to acknowledge that deliberate violence is done by men, people use racist language and label acts of violence "dark,"[31] or they use speciesist language and label violence "animal." Such language suggests that violence is uncontrollably part of men's nature, the side one can't fathom (the dark side), the part one can't control (the beast within). But in reality men have not lost control when they act violently toward women, their violence is deliberate. Nowhere is this more apparent than when animals are harmed by woman-batterers. Men batter to gain control. Batterers can obfuscate why they batter when it is physical violence, (claiming "I 'lost' control and punched her"—the "dark" side explanation). They can confuse the issue of sexual assault (asserting "she was teasing me and said she wanted it"—the "it-brought-out-the-animal-in-me" explanation). But loss of control is harder to defend when an animal is the victim because the deliberateness of the violence is exposed in the description ("I 'lost' control and then cut the dog's head off and then nailed it to the porch"). There is not much leeway for a man to say he tortured animals and it was out of his control. It is clearly willful and deliberate.[32] But our culture does not want to recognize this willfulness, this deliberateness, or so far has failed to, and thus sexually abusive and possessive behavior is not stopped.

Why does our culture continue to sanction sexual violence? One explanation is offered by Robin West who, in a feminist law review article, explains:

> One reason that women suffer more than men is that women often find painful the same objective event or condition that men find pleasurable.... For the man, the office pass was sex (and pleasurable), for the woman, it was harassment (and painful); for the man the evening was a date—perhaps not pleasant, but certainly not frightening—for the woman, it was a rape and very scary indeed. Similarly, a man may experience as at worst offensive, and at best

stimulating, that which a woman finds debilitating, dehumanizing, or even life-threatening. Pornographic depictions of women which facilitate by legitimating the violent brutalization of our bodies are obvious examples.[33]

In other words, *our* harm is *their* pleasure.

Thus, suffering for men and for women is in certain respects different, because men and women are differently inscribed in the sex-species system.

Animal Suffering

Animal suffering is something else again. Sometimes it is said to be for a good reason; sometimes it is denied to be suffering; sometimes we do everything possible to avoid confronting reminders of animal suffering. Often their suffering is considered irrelevant, because one way or another it benefits humans. As their bodies are dematerialized as whole bodies to service our pleasures from fragmented body parts (leather, fur, meat, objects of scientific study), their suffering is rendered immaterial to assuage our conscience. To abet this instrumental use of animals' bodies, they are deliberately kept anonymous (don't name anyone you wish to consume). As opposed to efforts at memorializing slain anonymous humans, we are specifically not to remind people of slain anonymous animals. Nevertheless, despite all these obfuscations, it is clear that much animal pain is produced for human pleasure.

People often get upset when they are reminded of animal suffering and deaths, but a speciesist culture generally keeps people from being exposed to this upsetting information (see Luke in this volume). Thus, individuals are insulated from exposure to animal suffering, though their consequent emotional upset would be both valid and a valid foundation for theorizing. When I complained to an animal advocacy group that the graffiti-applied fur coats they were using in an advertising campaign might encourage the street harassment of furwearing women, I was informed that the city's bus system had refused to carry images that featured trapped furbearing animals. Steve Baker reports similar problems for British animal defense groups: "In 1990 the RSPCA found itself requested by the Advertising Standards Authority [ASA] to withdraw a press advertisement featuring a photograph of a dead horse suspended from a meat hook in an abattoir, as the ASA thought it likely to cause 'distress and revulsion' to the public." Antibullfighting posters were seen as too disturbing, so they were not allowed in British airports.[34]

The responses to individual cases of animal suffering that receive media attention, the outpouring of offers of assistance, the ongoing concern, the anger at perpetrators—reveal how intense awareness and action on behalf of an individual animal's suffering can be. Bernard Rollin observes, "to be morally responsive to pain in animals, one must ideally know animals in their individuality."[35] Of course, the cultural construction of animals is such that this is precisely what we are usually denied: knowledge of the individual animal being consumed for supper, knowledge of the individual animal being worn. Often, animals are never even seen as possessing individual identities.

It may be argued that even if we know the individual animal who is suffering, we cannot know the animal's experience of pain. But this is precisely the claim Elaine Scarry makes about human pain, that we cannot know another's pain. She explains:

> A person whose pain it is, knows it effortlessly, the person whose pain it is not, cannot know it even with effort.
>
> For the person whose pain it is, it is "effortlessly" grasped (that is, even with the most heroic effort it cannot *not* be grasped); while for the person outside the sufferer's body, what is "effortless" is *not* grasping it.

Scarry expands upon this insight in a way specifically relevant to this discussion of animals' suffering:

> It is easy to remain wholly unaware of its existence; even with effort, one may remain in doubt about its existence or may retain the astonishing freedom of denying its existence; and finally, if with the best effort of sustained attention one successfully apprehends it, the aversiveness of the "it" one apprehends will only be a shadowy fraction of the actual "it."[36]

The person in pain encounters pain that cannot be denied; the person outside of pain, encounters pain that cannot be confirmed. This is true whether we are speaking of human or nonhuman animal pain.

Should Suffering be Appropriated?

In *The Sexual Politics of Meat* I raised a concern about the way that the experience of animals under human oppression becomes a metaphor for peoples' experience—that is, the absent referent enables animals' experience of suffering to be appropriated.[37] We lose sight of the animal and focus on the violence, for instance, when we use metaphors about meat and butchering to protest the treatment of human beings, but do not see the terms as inherently troubling. Just so with using the Holocaust and other experiences of incomprehensibly immense suffering as metaphors. These metaphors attempt to make others' experience "borrowable."

It is not for us to compare suffering. We should *acknowledge* suffering, but not compare it. Acknowledging grants the *integrity* of the suffering, while comparing assumes the *reducibility*, the objectification of suffering. When the issue is animal suffering, the choice appears to be between asserting the basic unknowability of all pain (including that of animals') versus articulating anthropocentric examples of pain to convey animals' suffering. Clearly, when factory farms and slaughterhouses are compared to concentration camps, there is little question which choice is made. The standard is still human.

Just as the fact of women's suffering—and the suffering of marginalized men who are made to suffer as females—disappears when a heroic notion of men's suffering prevails, so animal suffering is ignored unless appropriated to human suffering to make it expressible. But this is anthropocentric. Why not talk about the way animals'—including us—suffer? Instead of saying, "animals' suffering is like human's," relying on metaphors, why not say animal suffering in their body is *theirs?* Since the experience of suffering is individual, a recognition of the individual is necessary before suffering can be acknowledged. But, once we do recognize the specific character of suffering, we must learn to cope with this sensitivity because such knowledge is wrenching. It interferes with human pleasure.

Our Own Suffering

How one has dealt with one's own pain influences one's ability to care about and respond to another's suffering.

Gendered Responses: Stoicism versus Sacrifice

The very idea of long-suffering or ongoing suffering is that it is a female experience—that it is unmanly. It is manly not to succumb to suffering or even to admit its existence. To deny its existence is seen as admirably manly personal stoicism. But denial creates an inability to sympathize with others' suffering, blocking empathy, and it also often prevents men from acknowledging their own suffering.

On the other hand, as noted above, women are socialized as the primary caretakers and nurturers of the family.[38] Women are therefore socialized to the role of being sensitive to others' needs and suffering.

Constriction and Dissociation

Traumatic dissociation or "constriction" may characterize a victim's response to ongoing violence:

> when a person is completely powerless, and any form of resistance is futile, she may go into a state of surrender. The system of self-defense shuts down entirely. The helpless person escapes from her situation not by action in the real world but rather by altering her state of consciousness. Analogous states are observed in animals, who sometimes "freeze" when they are attacked.[39]

For instance, survivors report how, during an attack—especially if it was part of a chronic situation of violence in which they lived with or knew their abuser well—they left their body and watched what happened to them from the ceiling. The developed ability to dissociate may mean that cues regarding impending danger may be neglected. It separates us from our bodies, and our time/space. We may literally lose hours that cannot be accounted for. Can we connect to others' bodies if to survive we must actively disconnect from our own?

Survivors and Victims

Kaschak explains that boundaries say "this is where I end and you begin" (131). Boundaries involve "knowing who one is and who one is not" (131). Being a survivor means that one has integrated one's own suffering and restored one's ability to maintain boundaries. But to fully recover more needs to be done. Judith Herman observes that "where there is no way to compensate for an atrocity, there is a way to transcend it, by making it a gift to others."[40] A survivor's mission involves recognizing that she has been a victim, understanding the effects of her victimization, and then transforming the meaning of this victimization "by making it the basis for social action."[41] Herman comments that "although giving to others is the essence of the survivor mission, those who practice it recognize that they do so for their own healing."[42] Some animal defense activists are engaging in their own survivor's mission; some, however, are still being victimized themselves. Some activists, especially those who are women, may be participating in victims' missions, where self-sacrifice is confused with the ethic of care. The self needs to be taken care of too.

A victim is someone currently still undergoing abuse or who has not successfully integrated past abuse. Past abuse needs to be rendered conditional, rather than determinative, in nature. But if our violation occurs when we are young, we are often deprived of the ability to create boundaries for ourselves. The result, especially for survivors of child sexual abuse, is that "many survivors have such profound deficiencies in self-protection that they can barely imagine themselves in a position of agency or choice. The idea of saying no to the emotional demands of a parent, spouse, lover, or authority figure may be practically inconceivable."[43] In a movement, such as the animal defense movement, where the majority of the grassroots activists are women and the majority of national leaders are men, this problem of saying no to authority figures may militate against some activists setting protective boundaries for themselves.

For women who have not integrated the experience of their own victimization, their intervention on behalf of animals can be fraught with problems. They have not restored or perhaps have not been allowed to establish adequate boundaries for saying to another "you stop here." While not saving themselves (and perhaps being unable to do so given the cultural structures that protect abusers), they nevertheless still try to save others.

How do we respond effectively to the numbingly uncalculable numbers and intensity of animal suffering while protecting our own selves? If I feel so deeply the suffering of animals, where does the "I-that-is-I" stop? In the face of failure to respond to animals' suffering by the vast majority of people, the question often seems to be, "If I don't care for this animal, who will?"

Animal defense activists often insist to other activists "the animals need you." When this happens, suffering *for* the animals is valorized. Because caring is so marginalized theoretically, there is little attention to equipping activists to be self-protective in response to immense suffering. A singular focus that gives attention to only one part of the sex-species system (in this case, the experience of the other species), will reinforce women's sacrificial way of saving others rather than working against our own oppressions. We put our oppression aside to address someone else's.

The challenge for women is to define our own boundaries, so that we are simultaneously saying "I will care for myself" as we care about and respond to the suffering of others. We must do all this while also learning to recognize men's definitions, sexuality, and needs not as part of ourselves but as part of the sex-species system, which is the context of our lives.[44]

Suppression

With suppression, all of one's emotional energy is given over to dealing—or in fact, not dealing—with one's own pain. To protect oneself from feeling one's own pain, one cannot feel anyone else's pain either. It may be that no one else's pain compares to what these individuals are experiencing or have experienced. They cannot experience suffering in ways that are redemptive, because they have made themselves incapable of recognizing (their own) suffering. They use all available energy to suppress recognition of their own suffering. It is a refusal to identify, by those who suffered or continue to suffer, with others who suffer.

Identification with the Aggressor

To avoid caring about suffering, an individual may identify with those causing the suffering, with those in power.[45] Consequently, one identifies with the consumer, not the consumed. Additionally, since dominance is eroticized, the harm/pleasure dialectic pertains (our harm is their pleasure, others' harm is our pleasure). In other words, identifying with the aggressor may offer certain hedonic rewards.

Deprivation

We may be confused about what our suffering constitutes. Sometimes, loss of a privilege feels like suffering. I call this *subjective suffering*[46] because to the person experiencing it, it is unpleasant, even though it may not seem significant to others. Unable to recognize that this privilege had been gained through the sex-species system, for instance, the privilege of using pornography or eating meat, men may conclude that this loss constitutes significant suffering.

Losing access to what one feels entitled to may indeed cause pain, but this is not comparable to agential suffering (suffering deliberately caused by another). Loss of pleasure may subjectively feel unpleasant. As a result, challenges to privilege and entitlement are often received hostilely (being against pornography is cast as antisex, puritanical; being against the consumption of animals is ascetic, self-denying). In this accusation, the loss of pleasure is acknowledged. But what remains invisible is the sex-species system. It is this that establishes the privileged to take pleasure in harm to others' bodies.

Why Do We Fail to Care about and Respond to the Suffering of Others?

We may not respond to the suffering of others because of denial, in order to avoid our own pain. However, societal forces also discourage responding.

Denial of Our Own Emotions

In a radically dualistic patriarchy such as ours, minds are not supposed to feel. Hyperationality rationalizes the suffering of others by denying it, disengaging from it, refusing to acknowledge it. As we have seen, part of the training to manhood is that men are not supposed to feel, are not supposed to acknowledge that others' suffering matters. Because emotions are felt to be untrustworthy, many men feel all negative emotions as anger.[47] Because men are socialized in this way, the complex feelings of sadness, depression, horror, and other emotions, including anger, that arise in response to caring about animals' suffering and exploitation, all become funneled into the feeling of anger alone.

Several animal advocacy men have told me that they spent years insisting they did not care for animals, because they did not feel caring was an appropriate response. They needed to appear rational, "in control," distanced from animals. With the appearance of ecofeminist writings on animals, they felt such relief because they now had a language that legitimated the idea that one might care for animals and that this was an appropriate motivation for activism.

Besides the constraint on men *qua* men caring about another's suffering, gay men may feel a constraint on expressing their emotions out of a fear that that might reveal them to be gay. They may fear that acknowledging to others that they care about animals will "out" them or, if out, that people will respond to some stereotype of gayness and emotionality rather than to themselves as individuals.

I have been aware as I rear two vegetarian sons how our emphasis on caring about animals demarcates them from the boys who are their friends. They are encouraged to explore a range of emotions in response to their awareness of animals' experience under human oppression.

We May Not Respond to Others' Suffering, Because the Harm to an Individual is Not Seen

Why is the harm to an individual not seen? First, *the individual may not be seen, because the victim has been dematerialized.* In other words, no individuality remains to identify with. For instance, animals' bodies are literally dematerialized as a whole, complete body. Similarly, the victim of pornography may be dematerialized, both literally—because of shots that focus on certain body parts—and by the argument that pornography is about "ideas," not about women and our bodies.

Second, *the harm to an individual is not seen, because of ideological construction.* The victims (because of the way that species, race, sex, and sexual identity are constructed in the sex-species system) are viewed as too inconsequential to matter. Because the victims have been trivialized, the issue can be trivialized as well. We can see this operating in queries about animals that pose the question, "Why else are they here?"

Third, *the individual is so devalued that the harm is not seen.* This occurs when a group of persons is chronically harmed, and thus constructed precisely as violable, as victims. Speaking of Linda Marchiano ("Linda Lovelace"), Catharine MacKinnon observes:

> It is apparently difficult to carry on about the ultimate inviolability of the person in the face of a person who has been so ultimately violated.... If it happened and it hurt her, she deserved it. If she didn't deserve it, either it didn't happen or it didn't hurt her. If she says it hurt her, she's oversensitive or unliberated.[48]

What results is a double standard of harm: "the degradation of women stigmatizes women to the point where that degradation is taken as evidence that there was nothing of value to which harm could be done; a raped or pornographed person is damaged goods hardly worth the respect a recognition of her harm would bring."[49] As a result of such circular reasoning, harm to a now-degraded individual does not require our attention.

We May Not Respond to Others' Suffering, because the Harm Is Invisible

Harm may not be acknowledged as harm. For example, Catharine MacKinnon observes that pornography "makes harm to women invisible by making it sex."[50] If the harm is acknowledged, it is seen as simply a part of the structures of society, acceptable in part because it benefits those with privilege. We need to remember that "an aspect of the power of privilege is to ignore."[51] Sarah Hoagland points out, "much ignorance is the result of ignoring."[52] Elsewhere I have argued that as a rule vegetarians know a great deal more about the process of producing "meat" to be eaten, than do those who eat animals.[53] Similarly, when pornography is thought to be about "sex," then the sexual inequality that pornography promotes and benefits from simply disappears.

Rationalizations: Animals Exist to Be Eaten and Women Choose to be Porn Objects

Various rationalizations may confuse an attempt to recognize harm. For instance, many meat eaters hold to a comforting notion that it is only because of their meat eating that certain animals exist. They believe that animals are luckier to have been born than never to have existed at all, and credit the existence of the animals to their demands for the bodies of dead animals to consume. Of course, one who is not born cannot actually regret one's nonexistence.[54] If confused ideas of existence palliate the fact of harm, notions of free will provide permission to ignore the oppressive nature of pornography and prostitution: "Those women chose to do this, didn't they?" Such ideas presume that the equality feminists seek has already been achieved.

If one knows one is being inconsistent—that is, that someone is being harmed for one's own pleasure—the response may be to defend oneself against one's inconsistencies rather than to acknowledge that one is being inconsistent. Awareness of harm is displaced by the desire to protect one's pleasure. Joel Kovel summarizes this thought process, "Since this set of ideas is inconsistent and will stand neither the test of reason nor of my better values, I am going to distort it, split it up, and otherwise defend myself against the realization."[55] The structure of the absent referent, which I introduced to explain the interdependent oppressions of women and animals in *The Sexual Politics of Meat*, functions in part to relieve one of dealing with one's own inconsistencies. Through the functioning of the absent referent, the individual may be recognized but the harm is absent, or the harm is acknowledged but the individual being harmed is invisible. In either case, pleasure is protected.

Saving Animals Is Not Enough

The context for animal suffering is a sex-species system that establishes interdependent oppressions. Further, gender construction influences our experience of and responses to this suffering. These two interrelated insights raise basic questions about the current assumptions of the animal rights movement.

Because men in our society are programmed to perceive all negative emotions as anger, those who feel only anger in response to animal suffering, rather than the complex of emotions that accompany anger, may experience animal defense as a battle rather than as a process. Of course, if animal defense is seen as a war, men's feelings of suffering about the other animals are rendered comprehensible. But the referent is no longer the animals, it is the battle. This maintains the hyperrationality that disengages from feelings. And it provides a heroic, male-identified framework for one's work to "save the animals."

Animal defense activism emphasizes "saving the animals." Activists, whether they allow themselves to experience emotional responses to the suffering of animals or not, and whether or not they then feel these emotions solely as anger, may see themselves as the "saviors" of animals. This language encourages a determined single-mindedness for both women and men in response to very complex sex-species structural inequalities leaving men's roles and privileges intact. For instance, when feminists raise concern about various animal defense activities aligning with pornography (see example below), a predominant response is "We are too busy saving the animals. You can discuss this all you want, but we need to spend our energy saving the animals."

This approach privileges animal suffering as the sole criterion for activism. We cannot save all the animals from suffering. Animals literally die by the millions every day. What this appeal to animal suffering does, however, is to keep the notion of human suffering unproblematized. This means that women's suffering is not stipulated as being different from men's suffering. The comment "You can discuss this all you want, but we need to spend our energy saving the animals" de facto includes another: "other humans' suffering is not important enough for us to consider compared to what animals suffer." It also implies the justification: "To save animals, I can cause other humans' suffering." What results is that animal defenders may violate women's boundaries to protest the use of animals by our culture. An example is in order.

What began initially as an advertisement campaign in which naked supermodels proclaimed "I would rather go naked than wear fur" expanded into joint receptions hosted by People for the Ethical Treatment of Animals and *Playboy* magazine. Many animal defense activists were pleased by the media attention this alignment with pornography produced, including interviews in *Penthouse* magazine. But to its critics this media campaign announced precisely the problem with the current state of animal rights activism and theory that leaves gender unproblematized.

The animal defense movement may end up using sexualized images of women and aligning with pornographers such as *Playboy* and *Penthouse* because of people's responses to the representation of animal suffering. Recall that people's reactions to stark images of animal suffering resulted in the banning of these images. Precisely because emotions are both feared and seen as untrustworthy, and precisely because animal suffering prompts emotional reactions, the animal rights movement is prevented from using images of animal suffering. What remains to be used?

Recall, as well, that harm to women through pornography is invisible, because it is constructed as sex. Representations of harm to animals are de facto made invisible through lack of access to outlets for billboards and advertisements. As a result, harm to women through a pornographic "I'd-rather-go-naked-than-wear-fur" ad becomes the acceptable way to raise the issue of harm to animals. Ironically, this compromise results in a focus on naked women's bodies rather than harmed animals, and thus actually upholds, rather than disturbing, the sex-species system.[56]

In the sex-species system, speech that harms and silences women—pornography—is protected speech. In fact, pornography is now the most prosperous media category in the United States. But the *representation* of harm to animals that documents suffering and is framed politically ("this should not be") is *not* protected speech.[57] Images that remind people of animals' suffering are banished, animals in traps or being tortured cannot be shown. Yet pornography documents women in traps, women being tortured, and this is protected speech. Harm to women through pornography gives great pleasure. Representations of harm to animals give little pleasure.

When naked female supermodels appear in advertisements that challenge furwearing, male entitlement is undisturbed. Our concern should not be that women can be sexy and attractive without wearing fur, but that women's status as sexy, attractive objects for men needs to be challenged. The message to men appears to be: you can still have objectified bodies in your life—they simply cannot be the bodies of nonhuman animals. Thus, a humanocentric focus continues: the issue of fur is presented as being about sexy women instead of the oppression of furbearing animals. The individuality of animals, and thus the individuality of their suffering, is never acknowledged. Instead, men's definitions, sexuality, and needs are identified as of primary concern to the animal defense movement. Meanwhile, the task for women remains for us to recognize men's definitions, sexuality, and needs *not* as part of ourselves but as part of the sex-species system, which is the context of our lives. Our caring about animals occurs in this context.

Caring for Bodies

Attention to suffering makes us ethically responsible. Only oppressors can deny the importance of suffering to the individuals who suffer or who respond to that suffering. However, as we have seen, gender construction influences our experience of suffering and our responses to this suffering. This remains unacknowledged within animal rights theory and activism. The failure to incorporate a gender analysis exposes the limitations of animal rights. When we incorporate a gender analysis, we move beyond animal rights.

Elaine Scarry observes that power "is always based on distance from the body."[58] A relationship exists between reclaiming the body and its full range of feeling, and reclaiming animals' bodies, including women's. A feminist care ethic for the treatment of animals offers the possibility of such reclamation.

Notes

An earlier version of this essay was presented as a keynote at Ecofeminist Perspectives: The Twenty-Second Annual Richard R. Baker Philosophy Colloquium, University of Dayton, April 1, 1995. Thanks to Chris Cuomo, Marie Fortune, Greta Gaard, Lori Gruen, Susanne Kappeler, Irena Klaver, Brian Luke, Barbara Noske, Kim Stallwood,

John Stoltenberg, and Noel Sturgeon for their insights and conversations. In thinking about rights and care, I have been deeply influenced by conversations over the years with Marti Kheel, Batya Bauman, Susanne Kappeler, Tom Regan, Linda Vance, Karen Warren, and especially by Josephine Donovan, whose careful reading of earlier drafts of this essay was invaluable to my thought process.

1. Ellyn Kaschak, *Engendered Lives: A New Psychology of Women's Experience* (New York: Basic Books, 1992), 136, 150. Further references follow in the text. The epigraph to this chapter is from Kaschak, 125.
2. Tom Regan, *The Thee Generation* (Philadelphia: Temple University Press, 1991), 3.
3. Thanks to Susanne Kappeler for her help in articulating this position.
4. For a discussion of emotions as legitimate sources for theory, see Carol J. Adams, *Neither Man nor Beast: Feminism and the Defense of Animals* (New York: Continuum, 1994), 185–88.
5. Dick Bathrick, Kathleen Carlin, Gus Kaufman, Jr. and Rich Vodde, *Men Stopping Violence: A Program for Change* (Atlanta: Men Stopping Violence, 1987), 39.
6. On this, see Adams, *Neither Man nor Beast*, esp. 9–13.
7. Thanks to a conversation with John Stoltenberg for provoking this insight. I am not subsuming race here but arguing that race becomes a mobile discourse under this system.
8. See Val Plumwood's excellent analysis in *Feminism and the Mastery of Nature* (New York: Routledge, 1993).
9. Kathleen Barry, *The Prostitution of Sexuality* (New York: New York University Press, 1995), 26.
10. On this, see Carol J. Adams, *The Sexual Politics of Meat: A Feminist-Vegetarian Critical Theory* (New York: Continuum, 1990), 72–74. The cultural feminizing of prey animals does not preclude the possibility that certain works of fiction may focus on the maleness of some animals *(Moby-Dick, The Bear)* as an essential aspect of its plot.
11. See my analysis in *Neither Man nor Beast*, chap. 4, "On Beastliness and a Politics of Solidarity."
12. It is hard to determine percentages for any specific form of pornography over against any other kind simply because one cannot survey all the pornography now available, especially because of the proliferation of computer-mediated pornography. See Carol J. Adams, "'This Is Not Our Fathers' Pornography': Sex, Lies, and Computers," in *Philosophical Perspectives on Computer-Mediated Communications*, ed. Charles Ess (Albany, N.Y.: SUNY Press, forthcoming).
13. I am indebted to the analysis of Kimberlé Crenshaw on the racializing of sexual harassment for my understanding of this. See Kimberlé Crenshaw, "Whose Story Is It Anyway? Feminist and Antiracist Appropriations of Anita Hill," In *Race-ing Justice, Engendering Power: Essays on Anita Hill, Clarence Thomas, and the Construction of Social Reality*, ed. Toni Morrison (New York: Pantheon, 1992), 412.
14. Patricia Hill Collins, *Black Feminist Thought: Knowledge, Consciousness, and the Politics of Empowerment* (Boston: Unwin Hyman, 1990), 170.
15. Collins, *Black Feminist Thought*, 170, 171, 172.
16. Ibid., 172, quoting Scott G. McNall, "Pornography: The Structure of Domination and the Mode of Reproduction," in *Current Perspectives in Social Theory*, vol. 4, ed. Scott McNall (Greenwich, Conn.: JAI Press, 1983), 197–98.
17. Catharine A. MacKinnon, "Liberalism and the Death of Feminism," in *The Sexual Liberals and the Attack on Feminism*, ed. Dorchen Leidholdt and Janice G. Raymond (Elmsford, N.Y.: Pergamon, 1990), 10.
18. On this, and the harm of pornography generally, see Catharine MacKinnon, *Feminism Unmodified* (Cambridge: Harvard University Press, 1987), and idem, *Toward a Feminist Theory of the State* (Cambridge: Harvard University Press, 1989); Catherine Itzin, ed., *Pornography: Women, Violence, and Civil Liberties* (Oxford:

Oxford University Press, 1993); Susanne Kappeler, *The Pornography of Representation* (Minneapolis: University of Minnesota Press, 1986); Andrea Dworkin, *Pornography: Men Possessing Women* (New York: Perigee, 1981); Laura Lederer, ed., *Take Back the Night: Women on Pornography* (New York: William Morrow, 1980).

19. Elaine Scarry, *The Body in Pain: The Making and Unmaking of the World* (New York: Oxford University Press, 1985), 148.
20. Pain, harm, and suffering are not precisely interchangeable concepts, yet they are often used interchangeably. In the context in which I am placing pain—that is, pain caused by an outside agent—pain announces that harm has been done. But pain is not necessarily experienced for harm to have occurred. Because of dissociative states, one may no longer feel the pain caused by harm. Tom Regan unpacks what he sees as the implications of Bentham's posing the question about animals as being preeminently a question about suffering:

    The question is, Can we cause them pain so intense and long-lasting as to make them suffer? That is a more central moral question since, if we can cause animals to suffer, then what we do to them not only can hurt them, it can harm them; and if it can harm them, then it can detract from the experiential quality of their life, considered over time; and if it can do that, then we must view these animals as retaining their identity over time and as having a good or ill of their own. For Bentham to put the question in terms of suffering rather than pain suggests that he recognizes a deeper and ... a truer resemblance between us and them than that we both may be hurt. It is that we both may be harmed. (Tom Regan, *The Case for Animal Rights* [Berkeley: University of California Press, 1984], 96.)

21. Bernard Rollin, *Animal Rights and Human Morality* (Buffalo, N.Y.: Prometheus, 1981), 32.
22. Scarry, *The Body in Pain*, 4.
23. Ibid., 5.
24. James Rachels, *Created from Animals: The Moral Implications of Darwinism* (Oxford: Oxford University Press, 1990), 131.
25. Lynda Birke, *Feminism, Animals, and Science: The Naming of the Shrew* (Buckingham, Eng., and Philadelphia: Open University Press, 1994), 91.
26. Bernard E. Rollin, *The Unheeded Cry: Animal Consciousness, Animal Pain, and Science* (Oxford, Oxford University Press, 1990), 146.
27. The idea that suffering for men is episodic and suffering for women is contextual is the insight of feminist theologian Mary E. Hunt.
28. For statistics on violence against women, please consult Carol J. Adams, "Toward a Feminist Theology of Church and State," in *Violence against Women and Children: A Christian Theological Sourcebook*, ed. Carol J. Adams and Marie M. Fortune (New York: Continuum, 1995).
29. Catharine MacKinnon, *Feminism Unmodified*, 234, n. 26.
30. See my discussion of the words *battered woman* and *meat* as examples of this nonagential language in *Neither Man nor Beast*, 101–2.
31. See, for example, *The Dark Side of Families: Current Family Violence Research*, ed. David Finkelhor, Richard J. Gelles, Gerald T. Hotaling, Murray A. Straus (Beverly Hills, Calif.: Sage, 1983).
32. Michael Jackson's reflections enriched my understanding of this phenomenon. This paragraph draws on my article, "Woman-Battering and Harm to Animals" in *Animals and Women: Feminist Theoretical Explorations*, ed. Carol J. Adams and Josephine Donovan (Durham, N.C. Duke University Press, 1996).
33. Robin L. West, "The Difference in Women's Hedonic Lives: A Phenomenological Critique of Feminist Legal Theory," *Wisconsin Women's Law Journal* 3 (1987): 81.
34. Steve Baker, *Picturing the Beast: Animals, Identity, and Representation* (Manchester, Eng., and New York: Manchester University Press, 1993), 234.
35. Rollin, 152.

36. Scarry, *The Body in Pain*, 4.
37. For a discussion of the absent referent, see Adams, *The Sexual Politics of Meat*, 40–44.
38. Carol S. Pearson, *The Hero Within* (New York: Harper, 1989), 99.
39. Judith Herman, *Trauma and Recovery* (New York: Basic Books, 1992), 42.
40. Herman, *Trauma and Recovery*, 207.
41. Ibid.
42. Ibid., 209.
43. Ibid., 112.
44. I am drawing on Kaschak, *Engendered Lives*, 87, in this sentence.
45. Thanks to Gus Kaufman, Jr., for suggesting this as a response to suffering.
46. Lori Gruen suggested this term to acknowledge that people losing privilege are indeed suffering, though it may not be socially constructed as such.
47. See John Stoltenberg for a discussion of "Why Can I Feel Nothing When Someone I Love Feels Pain?, in his *The End of Manhood: A Book for Men of Conscience* (New York: Penguin, 1993), 182–88.
48. MacKinnon, *Feminism Unmodified*, 13.
49. Katharine T. Bartlett, "MacKinnon's Feminism: Power on Whose Terms?", *California Law Review* 75 (1987): 1562.
50. MacKinnon, "Liberalism and the Death of Feminism," 11.
51. Sarah Lucia Hoagland, *Lesbian Ethics: Toward New Values* (Palo Alto, Calif.: Institute for Lesbian Studies, 1988) 207.
52. Ibid.
53. See *Neither Man nor Beast*, 25–36.
54. See my discussion of this issue in *Neither Man nor Beast*, 69–70.
55. Joel Kovel, *White Racism: A Psychohistory* (New York: Vintage, 1971), 19.
56. Despite the fact that it is the radical feminist analysis that establishes how the sex-species system oppresses animals, to defend the use of pornography and the association with pornographers to further animal rights, animal defenders must resort to a liberal feminist argument. Liberal feminism is the feminist analysis least amenable to arguments regarding the necessity of intervening to stop animal suffering (or nature's exploitation). Within the context of liberal feminism, efforts for vegetarianism and against harm to women in pornography and prostitution are greeted as puritan, legislative, controlling. This is because, as I argue above, a radical political analysis is missing: one that establishes that a preexisting privilege permits "apolitical" pleasure.
57. See Maria Comninou for an insightful discussion of free speech protection for pornography, but not for hunt protesters. "Speech, Pornography, and Hunting," in *Animals and Women*, ed. Adams and Donovan.
58. Scarry, *The Body in Pain*, 46.

Selected Bibliography and Suggestions for Further Reading

Note: This list includes only books and is limited to those centrally concerned with the ethic-of-care tradition in philosophy, relevant works in feminist and animal defense theory, and works dealing with women's connections with animals.

Adams, Carol J. 1990. *The Sexual Politics of Meat.* New York: Continuum.
———. 1994. *Neither Man nor Beast: Feminism and the Defense of Animals.* New York: Continuum, 1994.
———, and Josephine Donovan, eds. 1995. *Animals and Women: Feminist Theoretical Explorations.* Durham, N.C.: Duke University Press, 1996.
Allen, Paula Gunn. 1986. *The Sacred Hoop: Recovering the Feminine in American Indian Traditions.* Boston: Beacon.
Balbus, Isaac D. 1982. *Marxism and Domination: A Neo-Hegelian, Feminist, Psychoanalytic Theory of Sexual, Political and Technological Liberation.* Princeton, N.J.: Princeton University Press.
Benhabib, Selya and Drucilla Cornell, eds. 1987. *Feminism as Critique: On the Politics of Gender.* Minneapolis: University of Minnesota Press.
Birke, Lynda. 1994. *Feminism, Animals, and Science: The Naming of the Shrew.* Buckingham, Eng., and Philadelphia: Open University Press.
Blackwell, Elizabeth. 1909. *Essays in Medical Sociology.* London: Longmans Green.
Buber, Martin. 1970 (1923). *I and Thou.* New York: Scribner's.
———. 1965. (1947) *Between Man and Man.* Rev. ed. New York: Macmillan.
Burtt, Edwin A. 1939. *The English Philosophers from Bacon to Mill.* New York: Modern Library.
Callicott, J. Baird. 1987. *Companion to "A Sand County Almanac": Interpretive and Critical Essays.* Madison: University of Wisconsin Press.
Capra, Fritjof. 1983 (1975). *The Tao of Physics.* New York: Bantam.
Carrighar, Sally. 1973. *Home to the Wilderness.* Boston: Houghton Mifflin.
Cavendish, Margaret. 1653. *Poems and Fancies.* London: J. Martin and J. Alestrye.
———. 1664. *Philosophical Letters.* London: n.p.
———. 1655. *The World's Olio.* London: J. Martin and J. Allestrye.
Cobbe, Frances Power. 1899. *The Modern Rack.* London: Swann, Sonnenschein.
———. 1875. *The Moral Aspects of Vivisection.* London: Williams & Margater.

Code, Lorraine. 1991. *What Can She Know? Feminist Theory and the Construction of Knowledge.* Ithaca: Cornell University Press.
Cole, Eve Browning, and Susan Coultrap-McQuin, eds. 1992. *Explorations in Feminist Ethics: Theory and Practice.* Bloomington: Indiana University Press.
Coleman, Sydney H. 1924. *Humane Society Leaders in America.* Albany, N.Y.: American Humane Association.
Collard, Andrée, with Joyce Contrucci. 1988. *Rape of the Wild: Man's Violence against Animals and the Earth.* Bloomington: Indiana University Press.
Collins, Patricia Hill. 1990. *Black Feminist Thought: Knowledge, Consciousness and the Politics of Empowerment.* Boston: Unwin Hyman.
Corea, Gena. 1985. *The Mother Machine: Reproductive Technologies from Artificial Insemination to Artificial Wombs.* New York: Harper.
Corrigan, Theresa, and Stephanie Hoppe, eds. 1989. *With a Fly's Eye, Whale's Wit and Woman's Heart: Relationships between Animals and Women.* Pittsburgh: Cleis.
———. 1990. *And a Deer's Ear, Eagle's Song and Bear's Grace: Animals and Women.* Pittsburgh: Cleis.
Cronin, Helena. 1991. *The Ant and the Peacock: Altruism and Sexual Selection from Darwin to Today.* Cambridge: Cambridge University Press.
Diamond, Irene, and Gloria Feman Orenstein, eds. 1990. *Reweaving the World: The Emergence of Ecofeminism.* San Francisco: Sierra Club.
Donovan, Josephine. 1992. *Feminist Theory: The Intellectual Traditions of American Feminism.* Rev. ed. New York: Continuum.
———. 1989. *The Demeter-Persephone Myth in Wharton, Cather, and Glasgow.* University Park: Pennsylvania State University Press.
Fossey, Dian. 1983. *Gorillas in the Mist.* Boston: Houghton Mifflin.
French, Marilyn. 1985. *Beyond Power: On Women, Men and Morals.* New York: Summit.
Frye, Marilyn. 1983. *The Politics of Reality: Essays in Feminist Theory.* Trumansburg, N.Y.: Crossing.
Fuller, Margaret. 1971 (1845). *Woman in the Nineteenth Century.* New York: Norton.
Gaard, Greta. ed. 1993. *Ecofeminism: Women, Animals, Nature.* Philadelphia: Temple University Press.
Gilligan, Carol. 1982. *In a Different Voice: Psychological Theory and Women's Development.* Cambridge: Harvard University Press.
Gilman, Charlotte Perkins. 1976 (1923). *His Religion and Hers.* Westport, Conn.: Hyperion.
Goodall, Jane. 1971. *In the Shadow of Man.* Boston: Houghton Mifflin.
———. 1986. *The Chimpanzees of Gombe: Patterns of Behavior.* Cambridge: Harvard University Press.
Gray, Elizabeth Dodson. 1979. *Green Paradise Lost.* Wellesley, Mass.: Roundtable.
Griffin, Susan. 1978. *Woman and Nature: The Roaring Inside Her.* New York: Harper.
Hanan, Marsha, and Kai Nielsen, eds. 1987. *Science, Morality, and Feminist Theory.* Calgary, Can.: University of Calgary Press, 1987.
Harding, Sandra. 1986. *The Science Question in Feminism.* Ithaca: Cornell University Press.
———, and Merrill B. Hintikka, eds. 1983. *Discovering Reality: Feminist Perspec-*

tives on Epistemology, Metaphysics, Methodology, and Philosophy. Dordrecht, Neth.: Reidel.
Hargrove, Eugene. ed. 1992. *The Animal Rights/Environmental Ethics Debate: The Environmental Perspective.* Albany, N.Y.: SUNY Press.
Harstock, Nancy C. M. 1983. *Money, Sex and Power: Toward a Feminist Historical Materialism.* New York: Longman.
Horkheimer, Max, and Theodor F. Adorno. 1972 (1944). *Dialectic of Enlightenment.* New York: Herder & Herder.
Hubbell, Sue. 1986. *A Country Year: Living the Questions.* New York: Random House.
Hume, David. 1960 (1777). *An Enquiry Concerning the Principles of Morals.* La Salle, Ill.: Open Court.
Jaggar, Allison, and Susan Bordo, eds. 1989. *Gender/Body/Knowledge: Feminist Reconstructions of Being and Knowing.* New Brunswick, N.J.: Rutgers University Press.
Kant, Immanuel. 1957. *Selections*, ed. Theodore Meyer Green. New York: Scribner's.
Kingsford, Anna. 1885. *The Perfect Way in Diet.* 2d ed. London: Kegan, Paul, Trench.
———. 1912. *Addresses and Essays on Vegetarianism.* London: Watkins.
Kittay, Eva Feder, and Diana T. Meyers, eds. 1987. *Women and Moral Theory.* Totowa, N.J.: Rowman & Littlefield.
Kowalski, Gary. 1991. *The Souls of Animals.* Walpole, N.H.: Stillpoint.
Lansbury, Coral. 1985. *The Old Brown Dog: Women, Workers and Vivisection in Edwardian England.* Madison: University of Wisconsin.
Larabee, Mary Jeanne, ed. 1993. *An Ethic of Care: Feminist and Interdisciplinary Perspectives.* New York: Routledge.
Lauter, Estella. 1984. *Women as Mythmakers: Poetry and Visual Art by Twentieth-Century Women.* Bloomington: Indiana University Press.
Leiss, William. 1972. *The Domination of Nature.* New York: Braziller.
McAllister, Pam, ed. 1982. *Reweaving the Web of Life: Feminism and Nonviolence.* Philadelphia: New Society.
McMillan, Carol. 1982. *Women, Reason and Nature.* Princeton, N.J.: Princeton University Press.
McCrea, Roswell C. 1969 (1910). *The Humane Movement: A Descriptive Survey.* College Park, Md.: McGrath.
Mercer, Philip. 1972. *Sympathy and Ethics: A Study of the Relationship Between Sympathy and Morality with Special Reference to Hume's Treatise.* Oxford: Oxford University Press.
Merchant, Carolyn. 1980. *The Death of Nature: Women, Ecology, and the Scientific Revolution.* New York: Harper.
Midgley, Mary. 1981. *Heart and Mind.* New York: St. Martin's.
———. 1983. *Animals and Why They Matter.* Athens: University of Georgia Press.
Miller, Harlan, and William Williams, eds. 1983. *Ethics and Animals.* Clifton, N.J.: Humana Press.
Moraga, Cherríe, and Gloria Anzaldúa, eds. 1981. *This Bridge Called My Back: Writings By Radical Women of Color.* Watertown, Mass.: Persephone Press.
Moss, Cynthia. 1988. *Elephant Memories: Thirteen Years in the Life of an Elephant Family.* New York: Morrow.

Murdoch, Iris. 1971. *The Sovereignty of Good*. New York: Schocken.
———. 1993. *Metaphysics as a Guide to Morals*. New York: Viking Peguin.
Nagel, Thomas. 1970. *The Possibility of Altruism*. Princeton, N.J.: Princeton University Press.
Noddings, Nel. 1984. *Caring: A Feminine Approach to Ethics and Moral Education*. Berkeley: University of California Press.
Noske, Barbara. 1989. *Humans and Other Animals: Beyond the Boundaries of Anthropology*. London: Pluto Press, 1989.
Parham, Barbara. 1979. *What's Wrong with Eating Meat?* Denver, Colo.: Ananda Marga.
Plant, Judith, ed. 1989. *Healing the Wounds: The Promise of Ecofeminism*. Philadelphia: New Society.
Plumwood, Val. 1993. *Feminism and the Mastery of Nature*. New York: Routledge.
Rachels, James. 1990. *Created from Animals: The Moral Implications of Darwinism*. Oxford: Oxford University Press.
Regan, Tom. 1983. *The Case for Animal Rights*. Berkeley: University of California Press.
———. 1991. *The Thee Generation: Reflections on the Coming Revolution*. Philadelphia: Temple University Press.
———, ed. 1982. *All That Dwell Therein: Essays on Animals Rights and Environmental Ethics*. Berkeley: University of California Press.
———, and Peter Singer, eds. 1984. *Animal Rights and Human Obligations*. 2d ed. Englewood Cliffs, N.J.: Prentice-Hall.
Rifkin, Jeremy. 1992. *Beyond Beef: The Rise and Fall of the Cattle Culture*. New York: Dutton.
Robbins, John. 1987. *Diet for a New America*. Walpole, N.H.: Stillpoint.
Rollin, Bernard. 1981. *Animal Rights and Human Morality*. Buffalo, N.Y.: Prometheus.
———. 1990. *The Unheeded Cry: Animal Consciousness, Animal Pain, and Science*. Oxford: Oxford University Press.
Ruddick, Sara. 1989. *Maternal Thinking: Toward a Politics of Peace*. Boston: Beacon.
Ruether, Rosemary Radford. 1975. *New Woman/New Earth: Sexist Ideologies and Human Liberation*. New York: Seabury.
———. 1983. *Sexism and God-Talk: Toward a Feminist Theology*. Boston: Beacon.
———. 1992. *Gaia and God*. San Francisco: Harper.
Ryder, Richard. 1975. *Victims of Science*. London: David-Poynter.
Sanday, Peggy Reeves. 1981. *Female Power and Male Dominance: On the Origins of Sexual Inequality*. Cambridge: Cambridge University Press.
Scheler, Max. 1970. (1913). *The Nature of Sympathy*. Hamden, Conn.: Archon.
Scholtmeijer, Marian. 1993. *Animal Victims in Modern Fiction: From Sanctity to Sacrifice*. Toronto: University of Toronto Press.
Schopenhauer, Arthur. 1965 (1841). *On the Basis of Morality*. Indianapolis: Bobbs-Merrill.
Serpell, James. 1986. *In the Company of Animals: A Study of Human-Animal Relationships*. New York: Basil Blackwell.
Shiva, Vandana. 1988. *Staying Alive: Women, Ecology, and Development*. London: Zed.

Singer, Peter. 1990. *Animal Liberation.* 2d ed. New York: New York Review.
——, ed. 1985. *In Defense of Animals.* New York: Basil Blackwell.
Spretnak, Charlene, ed. 1982. *The Politics of Women's Spirituality: Essays on the Rise of Spiritual Power in the Movement.* Garden City, N.Y.: Anchor.
Starhawk. 1982. *Dreaming the Dark.* Boston: Beacon.
Stein, Edith. 1966 (1916). *On the Problem of Empathy.* The Hague, Neth.: Martinus Nijhoff.
Sunstein, Cass R., ed. 1990. *Feminism and Political Theory.* Chicago: University of Chicago Press.
Taylor, Paul W. 1986. *Respect for Nature: A Theory of Environmental Ethics.* Princeton, N.J.: Princeton University Press.
Thomas, Keith. 1983. *Man and the Natural World: A History of the Modern Sensibility.* New York: Pantheon.
Tong, Rosemarie. 1993. *Feminine and Feminist Ethics.* Belmont, Calif.: Wadsworth.
Tronto, Joan C. 1993. *Moral Boundaries: A Political Argument for an Ethic of Care.* New York: Routledge.
Turner, James. 1980. *Reckoning with the Beast: Animals, Pain and Humanity in the Victorian Mind.* Baltimore: Johns Hopkins University Press.
Vyvyan, John. 1988. *In Pity and in Anger: A Study of the Use of Animals in Science.* Marblehead, Mass.: Micah.
Walker, Alice. 1987. *Living by the Word: Selected Writings, 1973–1987.* San Diego: Harcourt Brace Jovanovich.
Weil, Simone. 1977. *The Simone Weil Reader,* ed. George A. Panichas. New York: David McKay.
Wollstonecraft, Mary. 1975 (1792). *A Vindication of the Rights of Woman.* Baltimore: Penguin.
Woolf, Virginia. 1963. (1938). *Three Guineas.* New York: Harcourt, Brace.
Zahava, Irene, ed. 1988. *Through Other Eyes: Animal Stories by Women.* Freedom, Calif.: Crossing.

Notes on Contributors

CAROL J. ADAMS is a feminist writer and activist. Her books include *The Sexual Politics of Meat, Neither Man nor Beast,* and *Woman-Battering.* She is currently working on a book that will examine images of women and animals, *The Meat Market.*

DEANE CURTIN is professor of philosophy at Gustavus Adolphus College where he directs the Community Development in India program, a national program for college students based in Madras. He has lived in Japan and India, recently returning from a semester in India spent studying the effects of the GATT agreement on indigenous peoples. His articles have appeared in journals such as *Hypatia, Environmental Ethics,* and *Philosophy East and West.* With Lisa Heldke he edited *Cooking, Eating, Thinking: Transformative Philosophies of Food.* He is currently at work on a book entitled *Seeds of Rebellion: Ethical Dimensions of North-South Conflict over the Environment,* forthcoming from Indiana University Press, on the ethics of environmental conflicts between the First and Third Worlds.

JOSEPHINE DONOVAN is the author of *Feminist Theory: The Intellectual Traditions of American Feminism,* rev. ed. (1992), and numerous other works. She recently co-edited, with Carol J. Adams, *Animals and Women: Feminist Theoretical Explorations* (Duke University Press, 1995). She is a professor at the University of Maine, and lives in New Hampshire with canine companions Aurora and Sadie.

MARTI KHEEL is a writer and activist in the areas of ecofeminism and animal liberation. Her articles have appeared in numerous journals and anthologies, including *Environmental Ethics, Between the Species, Woman of Power, Healing the Wounds: The Promise of Ecofeminism, Reweaving the World: The Challenge of Ecofeminism, Ecofeminism: Women, Animals, and Nature,* and *Animal Rights and Human Obligation.* She is co-founder of Feminists for Animal

Rights, and the creator of the FAR slide-show, "Women, Animals, and Nature Through an Ecofeminist Lens."

BRIAN LUKE lives in Dayton, Ohio, where he teaches philosophy at the University of Dayton, works for animal liberation with the local groups People/Animals Network and University of Dayton Students for Animal Rights, and co-parents two sons, Alex and Adam.

RITA C. MANNING teaches philosophy at San Jose State University when she is not on Sabbatical (who is a nine-year-old Appaloosa mare with a mind of her own).

KENNETH SHAPIRO is the author of *Society and Animals: Social Scientific Studies of the Human Experience of Other Animals;* founding co-editor of the forthcoming *Journal of Applied Animal Welfare Science (JAAWS),* and president of the Board of Directors of the Animal Rights Network, publishers of *The Animals' Agenda* magazine. Trained as a clinical and personality psychologist, he is author of three books, including a forthcoming critique of psychology's use of animals in research, "A Rodent for Your Thoughts: Animal Models of Human Psychology."

Index

absent referent, 191
  animals as, 71
  women and nature as, 58n.78
abuse and exploitation of animals
  and patriarchy, 170, 173–74
  types of, 81–82
  women's complicity in, 35–36, 53n.9
activists. *See* Animal activists
Acton, H. B., 149, 153, 156
Adams, Carol J., 41
  on the absent referent, 58n.78, 71, 191
  on meat eating, 161
  on oppression of women and animals, 70–71, 171–73, 183, 191, 196n.56
Adorno, Theodor, 41–43
advertisements
  animal exploitation justified in, 96–97
  suppression of, 182–83, 192–93
Allen, Paula Gunn, 41, 49, 51
altruism, 85, 122, 155
  See also Kin altruism
American Indian thought, 49, 116–17, 125n.25
anger, 141, 191
animal activists, 126–44
  caring attitude of, 130–34, 141
  coping styles of, 142–44
  described, 129–30
  stereotypes of, 127
animal advocacy theory. *See* Animal defense theory
animal-based research. *See* Vivisection
animal companions, 103
  owner's obligations to, 106–7, 114–15, 120, 123n.5, 124n.13
  owners' relationships with, 65, 86, 88, 115–17, 124n.8, 171
  See also Cats; Dogs; Horses
animal defense movement
  men's needs respected in, 193
  and pornography, alliance with, 191–92, 196n.56
  women in, 11, 128, 132, 134, 186
animal defense theory, 11, 12
animal experimentation. *See* Vivisection
animal farming, 82–83, 165
  cover stories used to protect, 89, 90
  euphemisms used in, 94
  guilt engendered by, 88, 154
  justification of, 78, 79, 81, 98
  opposition to, 77
  See also Factory farming; Meat eating; Slaughter of animals
animalization of women, 176–78
animal liberation, 77–100
  caring as basis of, 81–82
  defined, 77
  rights (justice) as basis of, 77–81, 84–86, 100
Animal Liberation (Singer), 13, 23, 34, 38, 130, 173
"Animal Liberation and Environmental Ethics" (Callicott), 155
animal liberation movement, 19–21, 24, 32n.9, 77–100
  sentimental approach to, 34, 137
animal rights
  arguments against, 62

animal rights *(cont'd)*
  early feminist advocates of, 40–41, 46
  and ecology, conflict between, 124–25n.22
  and feminist theory, 34–52, 60–64
  opposition to, 103
animal rights movement, 12, 13, 60
  caring as foundation of, 130–34, 141, 144
  history of, 23–24, 32n.22, 53n.7
  men as leaders of, 128, 186
  polarization of, 144
  trivialization of, 34, 127
  women in, 11, 23, 32n.22, 34–52, 128, 132, 134, 186
animal rights theory, 11, 12, 52n.1
  criticism of, 147
  difficulties in concept of, 14–15
  emotions denied in, 15, 45, 79, 174, 191
  and feminist theory, 59n.86
  natural rights approach to, 36–38, 44, 64–65, 147
  utilitarian approach to, 36, 38–40, 147
  See also Rights theory
animals
  biblical mandate to dominate, 87, 88–90
  feminization of, 175–76, 194n.10
  intelligence of, 14
  "language" of, 150–51
  personhood of, 14, 37
  reasons for caring about, 115–16
  and the right to life, 113–15
  as symbols, 127, 128, 136
  value of, 116, 118
  as willing victims, 96–97
  See also Animal companions; Cats; Dogs; Domestic animals; Horses; Rare and endangered species; Wild animals
Animals' Agenda, 132
animals and humans
  assumption of similarity between, 14–15
  as moral equals, 89
  relationship between, 15, 30, 107–16, 117, 151, 171
  See also Animal companions; Human–animal bond
animals and women
  derogation of, 41, 46
  linking of, 37, 41–42, 46, 56n.43, 57–58n.78, 60–61, 128, 132, 134
  oppression of, 60–61, 70–71, 73, 134, 171–73, 183, 191, 196n.56
  powerlessness of, 42, 171
animal subjectivity: denial of, 95–97, 134–37
animism, 48, 133
anorexia nervosa, 69–70, 73n.4, 76n.32
anti-Semitism, 166n.9
antivivisection movement (19th century), 35, 127
  and temperance movement, 55n.29
  women in, 46, 132
antivivisection movement (20th century), 58n.78
Aristotle, 110, 165
Arluke, Arnold, 98–99
attentive love, 51, 163–65, 169n.43
autonomous rights-holder: male ideal of, 171–72

Bacon, Francis, 43, 51
Baier, Annette, 160
Baker, Steve, 182
Balbus, Isaac D., 54n.27
Bambi (motion picture), 97
  hunters' objections to, 192n.64
Barnes, Don, 131
Bartlett, Kim, 135
Bauman, Batya, 11
Bearing the Word (Homans), 58n.78
Beauvoir, Simone de, 47
Benhabib, Seyla, 162
Bentham, Jeremy, 38–39, 195n.20
Bergh, Henry, 132
Bernard, Claude, 93
Bernstein, Manny, 126, 134
bestiality, 176
Between the Species, 128
Beyond Power (French), 48
Birke, Lynda, 179
Birnbacher, Dieter, 24
Blackwell, Elizabeth, 41, 46
Body in Pain, The (Scarry), 178

Bordo, Susan, 44, 69
bowhunting, 92, 93–94
    See also Hunting
Broida, John, 132
Browning, Elizabeth Barrett, 58n.78
Buber, Martin, 148, 168n.41
bullfighting, 135, 183

Callicott, J. Baird, 19–22; 32nn.9, 10, 16; 155
    on the relative value of living creatures, 19–20, 25, 118, 119–20
Capitalism and the Family (Zaretsky), 42
Capra, Fritjof, 18, 33n.33
Caring (Noddings), 13, 59n.86
caring activities of women: invisibility of, 172
caring attitude, 130–34, 167n.24
    and anger, 141
    and oppression, 171–73
    suppression of, 141, 143
caring ethic, 11, 68, 74n.16, 84–85, 120, 157, 159
    alternative to, 61, 75n.22
    appropriateness of, as applied to animals, 15–16
    caring versus rights (justice) in, 77–100
    compromise and accommodation in, 107, 109
    emotions valued in, 15, 52, 147–65, 173–74
    politicized, 65–68, 74n.16
    relationships valued in, 105, 107–16, 117–18, 122, 124n.16
    and rights theory, 11, 14–16, 52, 59n.86, 61, 74n.16, 103–23, 124n.16
    and the right to life, 113–15
    sympathy as basis of, 81–84, 147–65
    and vegetarianism, 69–73
    women's association with, 13, 75n.22, 128, 132, 134, 159, 162
caring theory. See Caring ethic
carnivorism. See Meat eating
Carrighar, Sally, 51
Carter, Janis, 51, 59n.84
"Cartesian Masculinization of Thought, The" (Bordo), 44
Cartesian view of animals as machines, 41–45, 96
    alternative to, 150
    criticism of, 38–39, 43–45
Case for Animal Rights, The (Regan), 13, 35, 36, 43–44, 173
    Kant criticized in, 148–49
cats, 131, 168n.41
    feral, 119–20, 121
    used in therapy, 86–87
    and women, bond between, 58n.78
Cavalieri, Paola, 143
Cavendish, Margaret, Duchess of Newcastle, 45, 57n.58
Cheney, Jim, 159–60
Chernin, Kim, 69
Child, Lydia Maria, 41, 55n.29
child rearing, 54n.27, 132
Chipko movement, 75n.24
Chodorow, Nancy, 57n.61
Chrystos, 41
circuses: opposition to, 52, 54n.23
Cobbe, Frances Power, 41, 132
    on emotion versus rationality, 35, 53n.7
Coleman, Sydney, 32n.22
Colette, 58n.78
Collard, Andrée, 86
Collins, Patricia Hill, 176–77
community, good of, 19–20
    and individual worth, 25
Comninou, Maria, 196n.57
companion animals. See Animal companions
compassion. See Sympathy
competition, 29
cover stories used to protect animal abuse, 89, 90–92, 97, 98–99
Crenshaw, Kimberlé, 194n.13
crime, 29
cross-species identity, 62–64, 74n.16
cultural feminism, 38–40, 48
    as basis for caring ethic, 36, 40, 52, 59n.86
    history of, 40, 54n.27
Curtin, Deane, 60–73, 158, 160

Darwin, Charles, 155, 179
Davis, Karen, 55n.30
Death of Nature: Women, Ecology,

Death of Nature (cont'd)
  and the Scientific Revolution
  (Merchant), 41
Decartes, René, 43–45
deep ecology theory, 159; 167nn.21, 24
deforestation, 66–67
Descent of Man, The (Darwin), 155
Dialectic of Enlightenment
  (Horkheimer and Adorno), 41
Dickinson, Emily, 58n.78
Dinnerstein, Dorothy, 57n.61
  on cultural feminism, 54n.27
Discourse on the Origin of Inequality (Rousseau), 38
dissection. *See* Vivisection "Diversity of Goods, The" (Taylor), 74n.16
"Dog in the Lifeboat, The" (Regan), 53n.10
dogs, 46, 53n.10, 131, 143
  attempts to understand, 150, 151
  as companions, 103–7, 126
  owners' obligation to, 106–7, 120, 123–24n.5
  relationships of, 105–6, 123–24n.5
  used in therapy, 86
  wild, 120–21
  and women, bond between, 34fn, 58n.78
dolphins, captive, 139
domestic animals, 103, 118–19, 167n.21
  dependency of, 15, 119–20
  priority of, 19
  value of, 119
domination of nature, women, and animals, 41–43, 46–48, 60–61, 65, 122, 175–76, 181
  biblical justification of, 87, 88–90
  roots of, 46–47, 54n.27, 57n.68
  See also under Hunting
Donovan, Josephine, 58n.78, 59n.85
drug corporations, 165
dualism, 21n.8, 29, 122
  divisiveness of, 175
  feminist critiques of, 17–18, 22–23, 47
  roots of, 18–21, 47

earth
  exploitation of, 122–23
  sacredness of, 122–23
Eastern religions, 33n.33
eating disorders and Cartesian thinking, 69–70
  See also Anorexia nervosa
Ebenreck, Sara, 28
ecofeminism, 60–73, 74n.16, 175, 177, 188
  defined, 60
  and morality, 73n.4
"Eco-Feminism and Deep Ecology" (Cheney), 159–60
ecology, 41, 48, 60–73
ecology movement: feminist critique of, 55n.30
"embedded self" versus abstract individualism, 105
emotion
  denigration of, 173–74
  and holism, 22–23
  men's perception of, 191
  and reason, 23–29, 42–43, 53n.7, 64, 79, 147–49
  rejection of, 15, 22–23, 45, 147, 157, 173, 188–89
  respect for, in caring ethic, 15–16, 52, 147
  training in, 153
  See also Sympathy
empathy
  and objectification, 133–34
  and reason, 54n.27, 74n.16
  and sympathy, 149, 152, 155
  of women, 42, 132–34
endangered species, priority of, 19
Enlightenment rationalism, 42
  and natural rights, 36, 44
  rejection of, 45, 172
Enquiry Concerning Human Understanding (Hume), 41
environmental ethics, 17–31, 31n.2
  emotion and reason in, 23–29, 64
  hierarchical thought in, 18–23
  roots of, 23
environmental movement, 23
  See also Ecofeminism
ethical humanists, 20–21
"Ethical Importance of Sympathy, The" (Acton), 149
ethic of care. *See* Caring ethic
ethics
  feminist approach to, 61, 63–64

and reason, 24
euphemisms for animal abuse, 92–95
exchange-value identity, 62–64
Expanding Circle, The (Singer), 85

factory farming, 27, 72, 86, 139, 158, 184
  justification of, 53n.9
  opposition to, 52, 54n.23, 143
  suffering caused by, 94, 136
  See also Animal farming; Slaughter of animals
Feinberg, Joel, 29, 64
fellow-feeling, 150, 153, 157
Female Novel of Adolescence, The (White), 57n.68
females:sexualization of, 175–76
feminine ethic. *See* Caring ethic
feminism
  and animal rights, 34–52, 61, 147
  and ecology, 41, 60–73
  emotion valued in, 26, 42–43, 52
  personal experience valued in, 27, 64, 73n.4
feminist care theory. *See* Caring ethic
Feminists for Animal Rights, 11
Finch, Anne, Lady Conway, 45
Fisher, John, 152, 156
Flanagan, Owen, 75n.22
Flax, Jane, 57n.61
Fossey, Diane, 51
Foucault, Michel, 45–46
Fox, Michael, 131, 132, 140
Francis of Assisi, Saint, 151
free speech
  and animal suffering, 182–83, 192–93
  and pornography, 192–93
French, Marilyn, 41, 48, 51
Frey, R. G., 80, 123n.1
Friedman, Marilyn, 160
friendship, 110–11
  between animals, 109–12
  severing of, 108–11; 113; 124nn.8, 11
"From Healing Herbs to Deadly Drugs" (Kheel), 161
Fuller, Buckminster, 29
Fuller, Margaret, 40–41

Fundamental Principles of the Metaphysics of Morals (Kant), 148
fur
  euphemisms used in production and marketing of, 93
  opposition to, 52, 54n.23, 141, 192–93
  suffering caused by, 135, 136
  women's use of, 35–36, 53n.9

Gaard, Greta, 167n.24
"Gender and Science" (Keller), 47
gestalt shift, 75n.22
Gilligan, Carol, 15, 162
  on caring and morality, 13, 28, 65, 159
  ethic of care developed by, 51, 64, 75n.22, 158–60
  on gender training, 132
  on rights (justice) and caring, distinction between, 13, 77
Gilman, Charlotte Perkins, 40–41
  on women's use of furs, 36, 53n.9
  writings of, 55n.29
Glasgow, Ellen, 58n.78
Go For Wand (racehorse), death of, 113–14
Goldman, Emma, 40
Goodall, Jane, 51, 59n.84, 120
Gorgias (Plato), 69
Grant, Douglas, 45
Gray, Elizabeth Dodson
  on environmental ethics, 30
  on moral decisions, 27
Griffin, Susan, 41, 50
Grimké sisters, 41
  vegetarianism of, 55n.29
Gruen, Lori, 196
guilt engendered by harming animals, 97, 98–99, 141
  expiation of, 87–88, 154
Gunn, Alistair S., 24

Habermas, Jürgen, 162
Harding, Sandra, 56nn.37, 43
Hartsock, Nancy, 159, 162
Hefferman, James D., 25
Hegel, G. W. F., 54n.27
Heinz hypothetical, 160–61
Held, Virginia, 158, 160
Heller, Agnes, 161

Herland (Gilman), 41
Herman, Judith, 185–86
Herzog, Harold, 127
hierarchical view of reality, 18–23
   and dualistic thinking, 21n.8, 22
   rejection of, 50
Hills, Adelman M., 132
Hoagland, Sarah, 190
holistic medicine, 91
holistic vision of nature, 18–23
Homans, Margaret, 58n.78
homophobia, 180
Horkheimer, Max, 41–43
horses, 104–5, 107–16
   friendship between, 109–12
   and humans, relationships between, 107–16, 117, 168n.41
   injuries to, 113–14, 124n.14
   suffering of, 137–38
   See also Ponies; Racehorses
human–animal bond, 11, 35, 118, 124n.13, 154
   as basis for animal therapy, 86–87
   as basis for feminist theory, 35
   examples of, 86–88, 105, 107–16
   love as basis of, 15, 30, 105
   obligations following from, 106–7, 114–15, 120, 122, 123n.5, 124n.13
humane moralists, 32nn.9, 16
humane societies, 11, 53n.7, 126, 130, 132, 154, 192
   and the temperance movement, connection between, 55n.29
   See also names of specific organizations
Humanitarian League, 53n.7
human rights, 60
humans and animals. See Animals and humans
human suffering, 178–82
   agential, 181, 188
   coping with, 184–91
   failure to care about, 188–91
   invisibility of, 190, 192
   responses to, 184–88
human supremacy, doctrine of, 89
Hume, David, 148, 154, 155
hunger. See World hunger
Hunt, Mary E., 195
hunting, 28, 86
   with bow, 92, 93–94
   cover stories used to protect, 91, 97
   guilt engendered by, 87, 88, 97,
   justification of, 78, 81, 91–92, 96–97, 98, 161, 167n.24
   language of, 92, 93–94, 97
   as male bonding ritual, 92
   and male domination, 57n.68
   opposition to, 45, 52, 54n.23, 58n.78, 77, 98, 102n.64
   protective devices of, 89
   as status symbol, 92
   See also Trapping
Husserl, Edmund, 41, 148, 152
   on empathy, 149–50
Hutchinson, Francis, 154

In a Different Voice (Gilligan):
   caring and morality discussed in, 13, 28, 65, 159
In Defense of Hunting (Swan), 97
individual rights and natural law, 29
individuals, relative value of, 19–20, 21–23, 25, 116, 118, 119–20
International Society for Animal Rights, 130
Introduction to the Principles of Morals and Legislation (Bentham), 38
intuition, 24–25
   See also Emotion

Jackson, Kathryn, 75n.22
Jagger, Alison, 162
Jasper, James M., 127
Jones, Helen, 130
justice, 148
   and sympathy, 153, 156, 157
justice theory. See Rights theory

Kant, Immanuel
   animals viewed as things by, 148–49
   criticism of, 36–37, 78–79, 100n.3, 148–49, 155, 158, 160
   emotion rejected by, 148–49, 152
   on morality, 24, 78
Kappeler, Susanne, 194n.3
Kaschak, Ellyn, 171–72, 175, 178, 185
Kaufman, Gus, Jr., 196n.45

Keller, Evelyn Fox, 47, 51
Kheel, Marti, 124n.12, 158, 161
Kimball, Robert, 127, 132
kin altruism, 85, 155
King, Ynestra, 41
Kingsford, Anna, 41
Kohlberg, Lawrence, 28, 33n.41
Koop, C. Everett, M.D., 90–91
Kovel, Joel, 190
Krannich, R. S., 127
Kultgen, John, 28

laboratory experimentation. *See* Vivisection
land ethic, 167n.21
  and moral worth, 20, 118, 120
language
  of animal exploitation, 92–95, 97
  of caring, 188
  of hunting, 92, 93–94, 97
  of nature, 150–51
  nonagential, 195n.30
  racist and speciesist, 181
  See also Euphemisms for animal abuse
language of rights, 62, 124n.16, 171, 174
  alternative to, 11, 61
  and ecofeminism, 60–61, 64, 74n.12
Lansbury, Coral, 46, 57n.71
Lauter, Estella, 49–50, 51
Leopold, Aldo, 19, 29, 118, 167n.21
lifeboat hypothetical, 53n.10
Locke, John: natural rights doctrine of, 36
logging industry, 165
Lovell, Mary F., 55n.29
Luke, Brian, 153, 158, 161

Machiavelli, Niccolò, 46–47
MacKinnon, Catharine A., 44–45, 177, 180, 189, 190
Magel, Charles, 128
magic, ethics of, 116–17, 122, 125n.25
male maturation process and the need to dominate, the, 46–48, 57n.68
Man and the Natural World (Thomas), 45
Manning, Rita, 161

Marchiano, Linda, 189
marginal human beings, 37, 162
  sexualization and animalization of, 176–77
  treatment of, 25, 62, 79–80
  vivisection of, 80–81
Marxism, 161
  as philosophy of domination, 42, 54n.27
Maternal Thinking (Ruddick), 13, 50–51
McCarthy, Colman, 76n.38
McClintock, Barbara, 51
McCrea, Roswell C., 53n.7
McMillan, Carol, 26
McNall, Scott, 177
meat eating, 34, 59n.86, 118–19
  as animal abuse, 36, 71–72
  and hunting, 91, 92
  justifications of, 62, 161, 187–88
  morality of, 27, 30, 71, 158
  unhealthfulness of, 90
  and world hunger, 30, 33n.51, 72
  See also Vegetarianism
mechanistic worldview, 18, 31–32n.3, 41–45, 96, 117
  critiques of, 43–44
medicine, male- versus female-centered, 91
men
  justice ethic of, 132
  and objectification, 133–34
  reliance on universals by, 28, 171
  respect for needs of, 193
  suffering of, 179–80, 184
  and violence, 28–29, 180–81
Mercer, Philip, 149, 150, 153, 155, 156
Merchant, Carolyn, 31n.3, 41
Metaphysics as a Guide to Morals (Murdoch), 148
Midgley, Mary, 26
  on the human–animal bond, 35, 118, 124n.13
Midnight Farm, The, 95
Miele, Joseph, 132
Moers, Ellen, 58n.78
moral agent, 37
  body as, 64, 69
moral decisions
  direct involvement in, 27, 30–31
  emotion in, 30–31, 52, 79

moral decisions *(cont'd)*
  physical removal from, 27
moral imagination, 153
morality
  and ecofeminism, 60–61, 63
  feminine conceptions of, 13, 60
  masculine conceptions of, 13
  and sympathy, 153–56, 158
moral patients, 37
"Moral Understandings" (M. U. Walker), 162–63
Morgan, Robin, 26
mothers, 47, 50
Murdoch, Iris, 50, 148, 163–64, 169n.43

Nagel, Thomas, 122
Narveson, Jan, 62
National Pork Producers Council, 94
National Rifle Association, 161
Native American thought, 49, 116–17, 125n.25
natural habitats
  destruction of, 52, 66–67
  need for preservation of, 65
natural law and individual rights, 29, 60
natural rights theory. *See* Rights theory
nature, 167n.24
  direct involvement with, 27, 30
  domination of, 41–43, 46–48, 60–61, 65, 122
  hierarchical view of, 18–23, 29
  holistic vision of, 18–23
  humans' relationship with, 151
  inherent value of, 22
  language of, 150–51
  as living organism, 31n.2, 49
  mechanistic view of, 18, 31–32n.3, 41–45, 117
  and women, 47, 49, 58n.78, 60–61, 65
nature ethics. *See* Environmental ethics
Nature of Sympathy (Scheler), 150
needs theory, 161–62
Neither Man nor Beast (Adams), 174
Nelkin, Dorothy, 127

Newcastle, Margaret Cavendish, Duchess of, 45, 57n.58
Newkirk, Ingrid, 126–27, 143
Nicholson, Linda, 159
Nichomachean Ethics (Aristotle), 37
Noddings, Nel, 13
  on caring as aim of education, 153
  caring ethic of, 59n.86, 67–68, 166n.15
nonhuman inferiority, doctrine of, 89
Nugent, Ted, 92

objectification
  and empathy, 133–34
  and exploitation, 134
  of women of color, 176–77
Obsession, The (Chernin), 69
O'Connor, Flannery, 58n.78
Okin, Susan Moller, 74n.16
Old Brown Dog (Lansbury), 46
Ortega y Gasset, José, 97

pain, 195n.20
  See also Suffering
patriarchal religion: feminist critique of, 29
patriarchy
  and the environment, 60
  and the notion of male superiority, 48, 60
  and oppression of animals, 60, 73, 170, 173–74
  and racism, 174–76
  and speciesism, 176
Patterson, Francine, 51
pecking order, 108–9
People for the Ethical Treatment of Animals, 126, 192
personal experience, 73n.4
  and moral decisions, 27–28, 64
personhood
  of animals, 14, 105
  and rights theory, 14, 36–37, 64
  of women, 37, 73n.4
pets. *See* Animal companions
phenomenological psychology, 128–29, 149, 150
Piaget, Jean, 133
Pitkin, Hanna Fenichel, 46–47

plant life, 57n.58
Plath, Sylvia, 58n.78
Plato, 20, 69
"Plea for the Chimps, A" (Goodall), 59n.84
Plous, Scott, 127
ponies, 171
pornography, 176, 182, 187–88, 194n.12
  and animal defense, 191–92, 196n.56
  and free speech, 192–93
  oppression of women in, 70–71, 176–77, 189–92
  racism and sexism in, 176
  and sadomasochism, 57n.71
Prince, The (Machiavelli), 46–47
prostitution, 190

quantum physics:holistic vision of, 18, 22–23

racehorses, 113–14, 124n.14
Rachels, James, 62–63, 179
racism, 37
  as cause of suffering, 180
  and patriarchy, 174–76
  rejection of, 79, 81
  and speciesism, 79, 81, 174, 176
rare and endangered species: priority of, 19
rationality. *See* Reason
reason, 24–26
  as basis of rights theory, 14, 35, 173
  and caring, 16, 54n.27, 77–100
  defined, 147
  and emotion, 23–29, 31, 35, 42–43, 64, 79, 147–49
  and justification of animal abuse, 80
  limits of, 24–26
  male bias toward, 147
  misuse of, 31
  as substitute for sensibility, 29
  and sympathy, 85–86, 150–51
"Reason and Feeling in Thinking about Justice" (Okin), 74n.16
Regan, Tom, 11, 54n.23, 131, 172
  animal rights theory of, 21–22, 51, 63, 75n.28, 195n.20
  on the Cartesian worldview, 43–44

  critiques of works by, 53n.10
  emotion rejected by, 35, 38, 45, 79, 147, 149, 157, 173
  ethic-of-care feminism criticized by, 157
  hierarchical view of animals of, 53n.10
  on Kant, 36–37, 78–79, 100n.3
  natural rights approach of, 36–38, 39–40, 147
  rights-based approach of, 36–38, 39–40, 77–80, 81, 84–86
relationships
  of animals, 65, 86, 88, 105–6, 123–24n.5
  and caring, 105, 117, 124n.16, 171
  obligations imposed by, 106, 114–15, 120, 122–23, 123n.5, 124n.13
  severing of, 108–11, 113, 124n.8, 11
religions
  anthropocentric versus vegetarian, 88
  Eastern, 33n.33
  patriarchal, 29
rescue of animals, 87, 88
research on animals. *See* Vivisection
Respect for Nature (P. Taylor), 169n.43
Reweaving the Web of Life (McAllister, ed.), 41
Richards, R. T., 127
Ricoeur, Paul, 151
rights
  defined, 62
  dualism of concept of, 29
  and values, 61
rights-based ethics, 61–64, 74n.16
  See also Animal rights
rights language. *See* Language of rights
rights theory, 11, 12, 36–40, 52, 75n.22
  and caring theory, 11, 14–16, 52, 59n.86, 61, 65, 74n.16, 124n.16, 147
  denial of emotions in, 15, 45, 52, 79, 174

rights theory (cont'd)
   difficulties in applying to animals, 14–15
   history of, 36, 38
   mechanistic worldview of, 44–45
   men's association with, 13, 75n.22
   rooted in market economy, 159–60
   See also Animal rights theory
rodeos: opposition to, 52, 54n.23
Rollin, Bernard, 21, 178–79, 183
Rooney, James, 124n.14
Rose, Hillary, 159
Rousseau, Jean-Jacques, 38–39
Ruddick, Sara, 13, 26, 50–51, 160
Ruether, Rosemary Radford, 41, 47, 48–49, 51
Rutledge, Archibald, 96
Ryan, Agnes, 41, 55n.29

Sacred Hoop: Recovering the Feminine in American Indian Tradition (Allen), 49
Salamone, Constantia, 35, 41
Salt, Henry, 53n.7
Sandel, Michael, 105
Sapontzis, Steve, 103, 123n.3
Scarry, Elaine, 178–79, 183, 193
Scheler, Max, 42, 148, 149, 150–53, 155, 156, 166n.9
Scholtmeijer, Marian, 58n.78
Schopenhauer, Arthur, 148, 153, 166n.9
   Kant refuted by, 149, 155–56
science
   feminist critiques of, 35, 41–47, 51
   preoccupation with methods of, 28
   rationalist ideology of, 53n.9
Second Sex, The (Beauvoir), 47
sensibility, 39
   See also Suffering
sensual empathy, 152
sentimentalism
   and animal rights, 54n.26, 137
   rationalists' contempt for, 23, 34–35, 38, 53n.7, 148
Serpell, James, 87, 89
sexism, 37, 102n.65
   rejection of, 79, 81
   roots of, 47
   and speciesism, 79, 81, 174
   and suffering, 180
Sexism and God-Talk (Ruether), 48
sexist stereotypes, 98
   vivisectors' use of, 97
sexologists (19th century), 46, 57n.59
sex-species system, 174–78, 180, 186–87, 196n.56
   as context for animal suffering, 174, 191, 193
   men's status in, 178, 182
sexual abuse of children, 186
sexual oppression, racialization of, 176–77, 194n.13
Sexual Politics of Meat, The (Adams), 70–71, 161, 170–71, 174, 176, 183, 191
Shaftesbury, Anthony Ashley Cooper, Third Earl of, 154
Shapiro, Kenneth, 151, 152
silence, women's experience of, 56n.43
Singer, Peter, 11, 54n.23, 59n.86, 123n.2, 130
   emotion rejected by, 34–35, 45, 79, 147, 173
   on ethics and univeral law, 23–24
   rights-based approach of, 77, 79–81, 85–86
   utilitarian approach of, 38–40, 147
   on women's use of fur, 53n.9
slaughter of animals, 27, 82–83, 158, 165, 184
   euphemisms used in, 93
   guilt engendered by, 87, 154
   opposition to, 52, 54n.23, 71, 89
   See also Animal farming
Smith, Adam, 154
snuff films, 70
Sovereignty of Good, The (Murdoch), 163
SPCA, 55n.29
speciesism, 59n.86, 66
   defined, 37, 53n.15
   and denial of suffering, 136
   and patriarchy, 176
   and racism and sexism, 79, 81, 174, 176

Sperling, Susan, 98, 127, 128
Spinoza, Baruch, 52n.2
Stanton, Elizabeth Cady, 41
   vegetarianism of, 55n.29
Starhawk, 30, 116–17
Stark, W., 153
starvation: meat eating as cause of, 30, 33n.51, 72
Stein, Edith, 148, 152
Steinbock, Bonnie, 80
steroids, 72
Stevenson, Gloria, 52n.1
Stoltenberg, John, 194n.7
Stone, Lucy, 41
   vegetarianism of, 55n.29
Stowe, Harriet Beecher, 41
"Study in Ethics, A" (Gilman), 36, 53n.9
suffering of animals, 127, 173–74, 182–84
   appropriation of, 183–84
   awareness of, 134–42, 147–65
   denial of, 45, 134–37, 182
   elimination of, 73
   and free speech, 182–83, 192–93
   invisibility of, 138–41, 154, 161, 182–83
   justification of, 182
   and language, resistance to, 178–79
   quantification of, 40
   and rights, 38–40, 78, 147–65
   sex-species system as context for, 191, 193
   and sympathy, 155, 157
   See also Human suffering
suffragists, 46
"Survival Training for Chimps" (Carter), 59n.84
survivors, 185–87
Swan, James, 97
sympathy, 82–86
   attempts to suppress, 87–88, 89–90, 97–99, 154
   education in, 153
   and empathy, 149, 152, 155
   as a form of knowledge, 150–51, 158
   as foundation of animal rights theory, 147–65, 167n.24
   as innate characteristic, 154–55
   and justice, 153, 156, 157
   and morality, 153–56, 158
   and reason, 85–86, 150–51
   rejection of, 147–49, 152, 157
   roots of, 153–54
   universalizability of, 158
Sympathy and Ethics (Mercer), 149

"Taking Sympathy Seriously" (Fisher), 152
Tao of Physics, The (Capra), 33n.33
Taylor, Charles, 74n.16
Taylor, Paul W., 24, 152, 164–65, 169n.43
temperance movement and humane movement, connection between, 55n.29
Thee Generation, The (Regan), 157, 172
Theory of Need in Marx (Heller), 161
therapy, animals used in, 86–87, 88
Thomas, Keith, 37, 45, 154
Three Guineas (Woolf), 35
Tiger, Lionel, 29
Tingley, Leanne, 132
Tong, Rosemarie, 153, 165
Tractatus (Wittgenstein), 41
trapping, 29, 36
   opposition to, 54n.23, 143
   See also Fur; Hunting
Turner, James, 23

"Understanding Dogs" (Shapiro), 151
unified sensibility, 26–27, 30, 33n.33
universalizability, 28, 74n.16, 157–58
use-value production, 159
utilitarian theory, 15, 20, 32n.9
   and animal rights theory, 36, 38–40, 52
   history of, 54n.26
   weaknesses of, 40

values and rights, 61
veal calves, treatment of, 95
vegan, 89
   defined, 72

vegetarianism, 41; 54–55n.29; 70; 76nn. 32, 37; 96; 189; 190
  and anorexia, 76n.32
  arguments for, 31
  early advocates of, 41, 55n.29
  and ecofeminism, 69–73
  and environmental ethic, 124–25n.22
  moral, 69–73, 75n.26
  as threat to animal farmers, 94
  women's commitment to, 55n.29, 73
  See also Meat eating
victims, 185–87
  perceived as willing, 96–97
  trivialization of, 189
violence, 185
  against women, 180–81, 195n.28
  men's propensity toward, 28–29, 181
  sexual, 181
  slaughter of animals as, 40, 72
vivisection, 86, 102n.63
  alternatives to, 126
  cover stories used to protect, 89, 90–91, 98–99
  euphemisms used in practice of, 93, 97
  guilt engendered by, 98–99, 154
  justification of, 39–40, 78, 79–81, 96–97
  of marginal humans, 80
  opposition to, 42–44, 51–52, 54n.23, 77, 80, 143
  as sadomasochism, 57n.71
  suffering caused by, 136, 138
  and sympathy for animals, 88–89, 98

Walker, Alice, 176
  on animal rights, 55n.30
Walker, Margaret Urban, 162–63
war, 29
Ward, Elizabeth Stuart Phelps, 41, 58n.78
Warren, Karen, 60–61, 65, 167n.24
Watson, Lyall, 29
WCTU, 55n.29
Weil, Simone, 50, 148, 163, 169n.43
Wertz, Fred J., 129
West, Robin, 16, 181
whales, rescue of, 87, 88

Wharton, Edith, 57n.78
White, Alan, 62
White, Barbara A., 57n.68
White, Caroline Earle, 41, 55n.29
wild animals, 103, 119–21, 138, 167n.21
  humans' obligations to, 120–21, 122
  interference with, 121
  in zoos, 126, 130, 131
Willard, Frances, 41
  vegetarianism of, 55n.29
witches, 47, 58n.78, 117
  eradication of, 43
Wollstonecraft, Mary, 41
Woman and Nature (Griffin), 50
Woman in the Nineteenth Century (Fuller), 40
women
  animalization of, 176–78
  in animal rights movement, 23, 32n.22, 54n.26, 55–56nn. 29–43 passim, 128, 132, 134
  and the caring ethic, 13, 75n.22, 128, 132, 134, 159, 162
  empathy of, 42, 132–33, 153
  and the environment, 66–67, 73
  men's need to control, 43, 46–47
  objectification of, 176–77
  oppression of, 46, 60–61, 65, 66, 68, 70–71, 73, 134, 171, 191, 196n.56
  and power, 47, 171
  suffering of, 178–79, 180–82, 184
women and animals. See Animals and women
Women as Mythmakers (Lauter), 49–50
women's rights movement (19th century), 37, 40–41
Woodhull, Victoria, 41
  vegetarianism of, 55n.29
Woolf, Virginia, on the killing of animals, 35
world hunger: meat eating as contributor to, 30, 33n.51, 72
Wuthering Heights (Emily Bronte), 58n.78

Zaretsky, Eli, 42, 159
zoos, 126, 130, 131
  redesigning of, 52